Teaching Struggling and At-Risk Readers

A Direct Instruction Approach

Douglas W. Carnine
University of Oregon

Jerry Silbert
University of Oregon

Edward J. Kame'enui
University of Oregon

Sara G. Tarver
University of Wisconsin, Madison

Kathleen Jungjohann
University of Oregon

PEARSON

Merrill
Prentice Hall

D1305288

Upper Saddle River, New Jersey
Columbus, Ohio

Library of Congress Cataloging-in-Publication Data

Teaching struggling and at-risk readers : direct instruction approach / Douglas W. Carnine
. . . [et al.].
    p. cm.
  Includes bibliographical references and index.
  ISBN 0-13-170732-9
  1. Reading--Remedial teaching. 2. Reading--Direct instruction approach. I. Carnine, Douglas.
  LB1050.5.T433 2006
  372.43--dc22

                                                              2006015975

Vice President and Executive Publisher: Jeffery W. Johnston
Senior Acquisitions Editor: Allyson P. Sharp
Editorial Assistant: Kathleen S. Burk
Senior Production Editor: Linda Hillis Bayma
Production Coordination: Lea Baranowski, Carlisle Publishers Services
Design Coordinator: Diane C. Lorenzo
Cover Designer: Jeff Vanik
Cover Image: Susan Jerde
Production Manager: Laura Messerly
Director of Marketing: Ann Castel Davis
Marketing Manager: Autumn Purdy
Marketing Coordinator: Brian Mounts

This book was set in Korinna by Carlisle Communications, Ltd. It was printed and bound by
R.R. Donnelley & Sons Company. The cover was printed by R.R. Donnelley & Sons Company.

Chapters 2 to 23 and Appendices A to D have been adapted for use in this book from materials that originally
appeared in *Direct Instruction Reading,* Fourth Edition, by Douglas W. Carnine, Jerry Silbert, Edward J.
Kame'enui, and Sara G. Tarver, copyright © 2004 by Pearson Education, Inc.

Pearson Education Ltd.
Pearson Education Singapore Pte. Ltd.
Pearson Education Canada, Ltd.
Pearson Education—Japan

Pearson Education Australia Pty. Limited
Pearson Education North Asia Ltd.
Pearson Educación de Mexico, S.A. de C.V.
Pearson Education Malaysia Pte. Ltd.

10 9 8 7 6 5 4 3 2 1
ISBN: 0-13-170732-9

To Zig Engelmann and Wes Becker
for their noble efforts in bringing
academic success to thousands of
struggling readers and
at-risk children.

Preface

Today's teachers find themselves faced with increasing numbers of students entering school at risk for reading failure.

Growing knowledge exists of how to bring reading success to all students, including those most at risk. In April of 2000, the National Reading Panel (NRP), a panel of scientists charged by the U.S. Congress with the responsibility of reviewing research in reading instruction and identifying methods that consistently relate to reading success, issued its long awaited report.

The NRP found that programs that provided systematic and explicit instruction in phonemic awareness, phonics, guided repeated readings to improve reading fluency, and direct instruction in vocabulary and comprehension were significantly more effective than approaches that were less explicit and less focused on the reading skills to be taught (e.g., approaches that emphasized incidental learning of basic reading skills).

Since the release of the NRP report, publishers of reading materials have begun to incorporate the research findings into their new editions. Whereas during the 1980s and 1990s most widely distributed reading programs did not provide instruction that was aligned with the research findings, most programs published since 2000 have incorporated them.

Just incorporating the teaching of research-based elements into an instructional program, however, does not guarantee that the program will be an effective instructional tool for the teacher of struggling readers and at-risk students. Even though publishers have begun to incorporate more research findings into their programs, teachers will find great differences among programs in how they incorporate instructional design principles. Teachers must be prepared to make needed modifications and adjustments to ensure a successful learning experience for all students, particularly the struggling reader and at-risk learner.

Teaching Struggling and At-Risk Readers: A Direct Instruction Approach is designed to provide teachers with specific information that can help them to be effective with all their students. The text provides information on incorporating instructional design and delivery principles into daily instruction, including

- structuring initial teaching procedures so that the teacher presentation is clear;

- using language and demonstrations that can be understood by all children;

- sequencing the instruction of content to be sure that all essential skills and knowledge are taught in an aligned and coherent manner;

- using teacher presentation techniques that foster a high degree of interaction between teacher and student; and

- providing adequate practice and review to develop high levels of fluency and accuracy.

The text is divided into three parts. Part 1 presents a general overview of the elements that contribute to an effective reading program for struggling readers and at-risk students. Separate chapters deal with instructional design principles and instructional delivery features. Part 2 presents information on the teaching of specific skills, and is divided into five sections: phonemic awareness, phonics, fluency, vocabulary, and comprehension. Each section includes chapters that deal specifically with the beginning stage of instruction (kindergarten through beginning first grade) and the primary stage (mid-first through third grade). Part 3 presents suggestions for organizing the school and classroom for reading instruction, with separate chapters for kindergarten, first grade, and second grade and third grade. Each of these chapters discusses the use of assessment in that grade level and how to establish programs for students reading at grade level and learners reading below grade level.

This text is not intended to be a definitive handbook. As we work with students, we continue to learn, and this learning enables us to improve our strategies and procedures. The main purpose of the text is to empower teachers by providing them with specific suggestions for problems they will encounter in the classroom. It is our hope, however, that the systematic procedures recommended here will stimulate the development of even better techniques. Furthermore, we encourage teachers to view learning to read as an outcome of instruction, rather than a function of inalterable learner attributes. We also encourage commercial publishers to design better programs for students. Overall, we hope that this book contributes to better teaching methods for all students, particularly the hard-to-teach struggling readers and at-risk students.

Acknowledgments

We are grateful to many people. In particular, we are grateful to Zig Engelmann, who over 40 years ago developed what is now referred to as Direct Instruction and showed how its use could prevent failure for our most struggling readers and at-risk students. Many of the procedures in this book were derived from the *Reading Mastery* series, *Language for Learning, Horizons, Reasoning and Writing,* and *The Corrective Reading Series,* authored by Engelmann and his colleagues. Englemann, much earlier than others, incorporated the systematic and explicit teaching of phonics, phonemic awareness, vocabulary, fluency, and comprehension into his programs. He recognized the importance of explicitly teaching foundational language and reasoning skills while students were learning how to read so that the door to higher-order comprehension could be opened to all students. His programs still remain in a class by themselves as models of how to create success for all students, particularly the most vulnerable learners.

In addition to ideas gained from these programs, many ideas were contributed by colleagues and students, including Gary Davis, Mary Gleason, Linda Carnine, Sarah McDonagh, Carrie Beck, David Howe, Vicky Vachon,

Nancy Woolfson, Billie Overholser, Anita Archer, Scott Baker, Elaine C. Bruner, Vonnie Dicecco, Robert Dixon, Phil Dommes, Jane Dougall, Frank Falco, Ruth Falco, Mickey Garrison, Alex Granzin, Tracey Hall, Cheri Hansen, Lisa Howard, Sheri Irwin, Joleen Johnson, Jean Osborn, Barak Rosenshine, Sandra Schofield, Marcy Stein, Marilyn Stepnoski, Candy Stevens, and Joan Thormann. Other colleagues provided important support and encouragement, namely Barbara Bateman, Wes Becker, Mark Gall, Joe Jenkins, Marty Kaufman, Deb Simmons, and Ruth Waugh.

Discover the Merrill Education Resources for Special Education Website

Technology is a constantly growing and changing aspect of our field that is creating a need for new content and resources. To address this emerging need, Merrill Education has developed an online learning environment for students, teachers, and professors alike to complement our products—the *Merrill Education Resources for Special Education* Website. This content-rich website provides additional resources specific to this book's topic and will help you—professors, classroom teachers, and students—augment your teaching, learning, and professional development.

Our goal is to build on and enhance what our products already offer. For this reason, the content for our user-friendly website is organized by topic and provides teachers, professors, and students with a variety of meaningful resources all in one location. With this website, we bring together the best of what Merrill has to offer: text resources, video clips, web links, tutorials, and a wide variety of information on topics of interest to general and special educators alike.

Rich content, applications, and competencies further enhance the learning process.

The *Merrill Education Resources for Special Education* Website includes:

Resources for the Professor—

- The **Syllabus Manager™**, an online syllabus creation and management tool, enables instructors to create and revise their syllabus with an easy, step-by-step process. Students can access your syllabus and any changes you make during the course of your class from any computer with Internet access. To access this tailored syllabus, students will just need the URL of the website and the password assigned to the syllabus. By clicking on the date, the student can see a list of activities, assignments, and readings due for that particular class.
- In addition to the **Syllabus Manager™** and its previously listed benefits, professors also have access to all of the wonderful resources that students have access to on the site.

Resources for the Student—

- Video clips specific to each topic, with questions to help you evaluate the content and make crucial theory-to-practice connections.
- Thought-provoking critical analysis questions that students can answer and turn in for evaluation or that can serve as a basis for class discussions and lectures.
- Access to a wide variety of resources related to classroom strategies and methods, including lesson planning and classroom management.
- Information on all the most current relevant topics related to special and general education, including CEC and Praxis standards, IEPs, portfolios, and professional development.
- Extensive web resources and overviews on each topic addressed on the website.
- A message board with discussion starters where students can respond to class discussion topics, post questions and responses, or ask questions about assignments.
- A search feature to help access specific information quickly.

To take advantage of these and other resources, please visit the *Merrill Education Resources for Special Education* Website at

http://www.prenhall.com/carnine

Educator Learning Center: An Invaluable Online Resource

Merrill Education and the Association for Supervision and Curriculum Development (ASCD) invite you to take advantage of a new online resource, one that provides access to the top research and proven strategies associated with ASCD and Merrill—the Educator Learning Center. At **www.educatorlearningcenter.com**, you will find resources that will enhance your students' understanding of course topics and of current educational issues, in addition to being invaluable for further research.

How the Educator Learning Center Will Help Your Students Become Better Teachers

With the combined resources of Merrill Education and ASCD, you and your students will find a wealth of tools and materials to better prepare them for the classroom.

Research

- More than 600 articles from the ASCD journal *Educational Leadership* discuss everyday issues faced by practicing teachers.
- A direct link on the site to Research Navigator™ gives students access to many of the leading education journals, as well as extensive content detailing the research process.
- Excerpts from Merrill Education texts give your students insights on important topics of instructional method, diverse populations, assessment, classroom management, technology, and refining classroom practice.

Classroom Practice

- Hundreds of lesson plans and teaching strategies are categorized by content area and age range.
- Case studies and classroom video footage provide virtual field experience for student reflection.
- Computer simulations and other electronic tools keep your students abreast of today's classrooms and current technologies.

Look into the Value of Educator Learning Center Yourself

A 4-month subscription to the Educator Learning Center is $25 but is **FREE** when packaged with any Merrill Education text. In order for your students to have access to this site, you must use this special value-pack ISBN number **WHEN** placing your textbook order with the bookstore: 0-13-195845-3. Your students will then receive a copy of the text packaged with a free ASCD pincode. To preview the value of this website to you and your students, please go to **www.educatorlearningcenter.com** and click on "Demo."

Brief Contents

Contents

NOTE: Every effort has been made to provide accurate and current Internet information in this book. However, the Internet and information posted on it are constantly changing, so it is inevitable that some of the Internet addresses listed in this textbook will change.

PART 1

Foundations

CHAPTER 1

Overview of Struggling Readers and At-Risk Students

This book attempts to provide teachers with information that relates directly to what happens in their classroom. Our goal is to provide information that will empower teachers to provide instruction that maximizes student reading performance while improving the children's self-concept. The book is focused on techniques that will be effective with all children, but are of particular importance to struggling readers and at-risk students.

Who Are the Struggling Readers and At-Risk Students?

Researchers have recently identified two broad classes of emergent literacy skills that children bring with them to school, and that have a substantial impact on how easily they learn to read. One group of skills, which can be called *literacy-related skills,* includes experiences with the sounds of English and letter knowledge. The other skills, which can be called *language skills,* include vocabulary and conceptual knowledge. Knowledge of literacy-related skills is a particularly important predictor of the ease with which children acquire word reading accuracy and fluency, while broad oral language facility (vocabulary in particular) becomes critically important to the growth of reading comprehension skills once children learn to read words efficiently.

Struggling Readers. The great majority of children who enter school at risk for difficulties in learning to read fall into one of two broad groups. The struggling reader enters school with *adequate general language ability* but cognitive weaknesses limited to the literacy-related domain. Their primary problem in learning to read involves learning to translate between printed and oral language. They have difficulties learning to accurately and fluently read printed words.

At-Risk Students. On the other hand, at-risk children, coming largely from families of lower socioeconomic status, enter school with less-developed broad oral language knowledge and less-developed literacy-related knowledge. These children enter school without knowledge of the language of instruction and almost immediately start to fall behind in their academic career because the instruction provided to them assumes knowledge of many concepts and skills the students do not possess. Throughout the book, the term "instructionally naive student" will often be used to refer to the young at-risk child.

How Urgent Is the Need for Improvement?

Dr. G. Reid Lyon, Chief of the Child Development and Behavior Branch of the National Institute of Child Health and Human Development (NICHD), in testimony before the Subcommittee on Education Reform of the U.S. House of Representatives in March of 2001, spoke of the large numbers of children not succeeding in reading and the effects:

> According to the National Center for Educational Statistics (1998), 38 percent of fourth graders nationally cannot read at a basic level—that is, they cannot read and understand a short paragraph of the type one would find in a simple children's book. Unfortunately, reading failure is disproportionately prevalent among children living in poverty. Indeed, in many low-income urban school districts the percentage of students in the fourth grade who cannot read at basic level approaches 70 percent. The educational and public health consequences of this level of reading failure are dire. Of the ten to 15 percent of children who will eventually drop out of school, over 75 percent will report difficulties learning to read. Likewise, only two percent of students receiving special or compensatory education for difficulties learning to read will complete a four-year college program. Surveys of adolescents and young adults with criminal records indicate that at least half have reading difficulties, and in some states the size of prisons a decade in the future is predicted by fourth grade reading failure rates. Approximately half of children and adolescents with a history of substance abuse have reading problems. It goes without saying that failure to learn to read places children's futures and lives at risk for highly deleterious outcomes. It is for this reason that the NICHD considers reading failure to reflect a national public health problem. . . . It is clear from our NICHD research that this type of failure affects children negatively earlier than we thought. By the end of first grade, children having difficulty learning to read begin to feel less positive about themselves than when they started school. As we follow children through elementary and middle school years, self-esteem and the motivation to learn to read decline even further. In the majority of cases, the students are deprived of the ability to learn about literature, science, mathematics, history, and social studies because they cannot read grade-level textbooks. Consider that by middle school, children who read well read at least 10,000,000 words during the school year. On the other hand, children with reading difficulties read less than 100,000 words during the same period. Poor readers lag far behind in vocabulary development and in the acquisition of strategies for understanding what they read, and they frequently avoid reading and other assignments that require reading. By high school, the potential of these students to enter college has decreased substantially. Students who have stayed in school long enough to reach high school tell us they hate to read because it is so difficult and it makes them feel "dumb." As a high school junior in one of our studies remarked, "I would rather have a root canal than read."

Can We Provide Success for the Struggling Reader and At-Risk Child?

In continuing testimony in front of Congress, Dr. G. Reid Lyon testified:

> The majority of children who enter kindergarten and elementary school at-risk for reading failure can learn to read at average or above levels, but only if they are identified early and provided with systematic, explicit, and intensive instruction in phonemic awareness, phonics, reading fluency, vocabulary, and reading comprehension strategies. . . early identification of children at-risk for reading failure coupled with the provision of comprehensive early reading interventions can reduce the percentage of children reading below the basic level in the fourth grade (e.g., 38 percent) to six percent or less.

Research on Reading Instruction

The largest, most comprehensive evidence-based review ever conducted of research on how children learn to read began in 1997. Congress had asked the Director of the NICHD in consultation with then U.S. Secretary of Education Richard W. Riley, to convene a national panel to review the scientific literature and determine, based on that evidence, the most effective ways to teach children to read. The Panel was composed of 14 individuals and included leading scientists in reading research, representatives of colleges of education, reading teachers, educational administrators, and parents. For its review, the Panel selected research from the approximately 100,000 reading research studies that have been published since 1966, and another 15,000 that had been published before that time. Because of the large volume of studies, the Panel selected only experimental and quasi-experimental studies, and among those considered only studies meeting rigorous scientific standards in reaching its conclusions.

The report focused on five areas of reading instruction: phonemic awareness, phonics, fluency, text comprehension, and vocabulary.

The major findings of the National Reading Panel report are:

- *Phonemic awareness.* The Panel found explicitly and systematically teaching children to orally manipulate phonemes (tiny segments of sound) significantly improves children's reading and spelling abilities.
- *Phonics.* The Panel found that phonics instruction produces significant benefits for all children. Phonics instruction is a way of teaching reading that stresses the acquisition of letter-sound correspondences and their use in reading and spelling. The greatest improvements in reading were seen from systematic phonics instruction. Systematic synthetic phonics, in which students are explicitly taught to convert letters into sounds and then blend the sounds to form recognizable words, was found to benefit both students with learning disabilities and low-achieving students without disabilities. Moreover, systematic synthetic

phonics instruction was significantly more effective in improving low socioeconomic status (SES) children's alphabetic knowledge and word reading skills than instructional approaches that were less focused on these initial reading skills.

- *Fluency.* The Panel found that fluency instruction has a significant and positive effect on word recognition, fluency, and comprehension. Fluency is one of several critical factors necessary for reading comprehension. Fluent readers are able to read orally with speed, accuracy, and proper expression. Despite its importance as a component of skilled reading, fluency is often neglected in the classroom. The Panel found no evidence that encouraging students to engage in independent silent reading improved fluency.

- *Text comprehension.* The Panel found that text comprehension could be improved by instruction that helps readers use specific comprehension strategies. These strategies can help students understand what they read, remember what they read, and communicate with others about what they read. Effective comprehension instruction is explicit and direct.

- *Vocabulary.* The Panel found that while most vocabulary is learned indirectly, explicit vocabulary instruction does lead to gains in comprehension. However, methods must be appropriate to the age and ability of the readers. Repetitions and multiple exposures to vocabulary items are important. Vocabulary is very important to reading comprehension, since readers cannot understand what they are reading without knowing what most words mean.

The National Reading Panel report is available at the Panel's website, **www.nationalreadingpanel.org.** The findings have been summarized for teachers and other professionals in a document published by the National Institute for Literacy called *Put Reading First: The Research Building Blocks for Teaching Children to Read* (2001). This document, as well as a number of other recent research reports, can be found on the National Institute for Literacy's Partnership for Reading website, **http://www.nifl.gov/partnershipforreading/publications/k-3.html.**

Is There a Difference in the Instruction for Children Struggling or At Risk for Different Reasons?

An important point about the language and literacy-related abilities required in learning to read is that delay in both these areas can be the result of either neurobiological factors that are genetically transmitted and constitutionally based, or they can be caused by a lack of adequate instruction and language experience in the child's preschool or home environment. Thus far, no conclusive evidence exists that the particular cause (genetics or environment) of a child's delay in either of these domains is relevant to the type of instruction he or she will require in learning to read. Children whose lack of preparation for learning to read is the result of genetic factors, as well as those who have been denied adequate learning opportunities in their preschool environment, will require interventions in reading that are more *explicit and comprehensive, more intensive,* and *more supportive* than children currently receive in many classrooms (Torgesen, 2004).

Children with general oral language delays plus literacy-related delays will require special instruction in a broader range of knowledge and skills than those who come to school lacking only in literacy-related ability. However, since both groups have weaknesses in the literacy-related domain, *both kinds of children* will require special support in the growth of early word reading skills if they are to make adequate progress in learning to read.

What Are the Characteristics of School Programs That Provide Success for the Struggling Reader and At-Risk Child?

Early intervention. The first years of instruction (pre-kindergarten through first grade) are particularly important for children who have literacy- and/or language-related deficits. An intensive program during these years can make a great impact in closing the academic gap between the struggling reader or at-risk child and his or her more academically prepared peers.

Schools that produce success for the struggling reader and at-risk child will administer screening assessments when children begin their school career in order to identify children who are behind in prerequisite literacy- and language-related skills. A systematic plan is initiated immediately to provide the intensive instruction needed to close the academic gap.

Systematic reading program. A comprehensive reading program that contains aligned activities from all the essential components of reading instruction (phonemic awareness, phonics, fluency, vocabulary, and comprehension) is used. The introduction of all this content is carefully sequenced within a grade level and across grade levels. The reading program is sequenced so that when a student moves from grade to grade each year the reading instruction presented is part of an aligned sequence.

Plans are made to meet the needs of children at, below, or above grade-level performance standards. Instructional materials are selected primarily based on proven effectiveness with the student population. The overall program is very systematic, with new information introduced at a realistic rate and adequate practice provided to enable children to develop accuracy and fluency in applying what they have learned.

Explicit lesson delivery. Instruction is highly explicit. Reading lessons are very interactive and children are highly engaged and successful. Teachers present tasks to facilitate student mastery. Children respond frequently and teachers provide immediate feedback to their students' responses. Student performance is carefully monitored and corrections are immediately provided to prevent children from developing serious error patterns or misconceptions.

Data-driven instruction. Assessments are used to place students at their instructional level and to monitor their performance during the school year. Progress-monitoring assessments are frequently given to ensure that students are learning what is being taught. Adjustments are made immediately upon determining that a child is not learning at a desired rate.

Prioritization of available time and resources to support reading achievement. In deciding how to use time, the prime consideration is how much instruction children will need in order to reach grade-level performance standards. In deciding how to use staffing resources, the prime consideration is to provide children with the instructional group settings in which the child is most likely to achieve at an accelerated rate.

Beginning and Primary Stages of Reading

Because the first months of reading instruction are immensely important, we devote a substantial amount of this book to the beginning reading stage. The beginning reading stage refers to the period when students are learning to read the first several hundred words presented in the classroom reading program. Some students may come to school able to read many words. For these students, little instruction may be needed for them to complete the beginning stage. Other students will enter school with very little ability to read words. These students may require anywhere from 6 months to 1 year of instruction before completing the beginning stage.

The primary stage refers to the time after the beginning stage (roughly midway through the first grade) through the third grade. The relationship between decoding and comprehension instruction changes as students progress through the grades. In the beginning stages of reading instruction a large proportion of time is devoted to teaching decoding skills as students learn generalizable skills and strategies that will enable them to decode many words. By the end of the primary grades, most specific decoding skills and strategies have been taught. The proportion of the lesson devoted to teaching comprehension strategies grows as the time spent on decoding decreases.

How to Use This Book

This book is divided into three major parts. Part 1 provides an overview of the major elements to be considered when developing a reading program for the struggling reader and at-risk child. Part 2 provides specific information for providing explicit and systematic research-based instruction in each of the five areas of reading. Part 3 provides tools for assessing, placing, and grouping students for instruction as well as specific grade-level suggestions on how to implement reading instruction to meet the needs of all learners.

Part 1 includes three additional chapters, each of which deals with an aspect of providing explicit and systematic reading instruction. Chapter 2 focuses on instructional materials. The more carefully thought out and constructed the instructional materials, the more energy the teacher can devote to teaching interactions with students. Chapter 3 addresses instructional design principles that underlie explicit and systematic instruction and how to use these principles in analyzing program material and making needed modifications. Chapter 4 discusses presentation techniques (how a teacher presents the content of lessons).

Part 2 is organized around the five areas of reading instruction: phonemic awareness, phonics, fluency, vocabulary, and text comprehension. Part 2 includes specific information for providing explicit and systematic instruction in each of these areas. Separate chapters will address the skills taught during the beginning reading stage and skills taught during the primary reading stage. An exception is the chapter on phonemic awareness as the skills related to phonemic awareness are taught just during the beginning stage.

Each chapter in Part 2 will include the following:

- ■ *Teaching formats.* Teaching formats are provided for presenting important skills and strategies, including directions on what the teacher and the students are to say and do. We have found that providing detailed formats is helpful because teaching involves very specific behaviors. Teachers do not teach students to read words in some abstract fashion. They point to particular words, give information, ask questions, and so forth. The detailed formats in this book will hopefully be useful in teaching particular content. In addition, they serve as models for teachers to use in designing formats for teaching content not covered in-depth in the text. Detailed formats planned prior to teaching allow the teacher to focus his or her full attention on the students' performance when teaching.

- ■ *Correction procedures.* For each format, in-depth correction procedures for errors that students are likely to make will be provided.

- ■ *Critical teaching behaviors.* Suggestions on how to present the format in a manner that will keep instruction highly interactive and how to monitor children's performance are presented for each format.

- ■ *Sequencing suggestions.* Guidance is provided on when a particular skill can be introduced and how introduction of the skill is coordinated with the introduction of other skills.

- ■ *Example selection.* Criteria are specified for constructing sets of examples that will be presented in teaching formats during a lesson. For example, when teaching the students to read words with the suffix -*ed,* the criteria calls for a mix of words that is designed to introduce the students to the full range of sounds represented by that suffix. The mix includes words that end with the /t/ sound (*hopped*), words that end with the /d/ sound (*hummed*), and words in which the suffix forms an extra syllable (*handed*).

Part 3 begins with a chapter that provides guidelines on organizing the classroom and school for reading instruction. Information on how to assess, schedule, group, and place students for reading instruction and select appropriate instructional materials are provided as well as guidelines for meeting the needs of children who are behind in grade-level reading. Additional chapters provide specific information and guidelines for reading instruction in kindergarten, first grade, and second and third grade.

CHAPTER 2

Instructional Materials: Essential Features of Effective Reading Programs

Using a well-constructed reading program is critical for teachers working with struggling readers and at-risk students. Carefully thought-out and well-constructed materials allow the teacher to concentrate his or her full attention on the students. A teacher with poorly constructed instructional materials will have a much more difficult job as constant modifications in materials will be needed.

An overall classroom and school reading program may include one or more of the following types of materials.

Comprehensive Core Reading Programs

A comprehensive core reading program is a set of sequentially aligned teacher and student instructional materials that is designed to systematically teach reading and language arts content for students in kindergarten through sixth grade. The programs, which are produced by major publishing houses, are designed so that they will cover virtually all the state-specified content standards. At the time of this writing, five major publishers account for the bulk of these programs' sales.

The advantage of these core programs is their inclusion of a wide range of content. However, this advantage can also be a disadvantage. Most of these programs contain so many topics that priority content often does not receive the depth and breadth of instruction needed to ensure the success of every student. These comprehensive core programs are referred to by many educators as *basal reading programs*.

Beginning in the late 1990s, California, Texas, and Florida required that basal programs, in order to be adopted in their respective states, must be aligned with scientifically based reading research. These requirements, along with the publication of the National Reading Panel report, and the passage of the No Child Left Behind legislation, have had a major effect on the design of core comprehensive programs. Since 2002, all the major publishers of comprehensive core reading programs have published new programs that are significantly more aligned with the research findings. Even so, significant differences still exist among the programs in their potential effectiveness as instructional tools, particularly for teachers responsible for the education of struggling readers and at-risk children.

A serious problem detracts from the potential effectiveness of these programs. Because of the need of publishers to make new editions in a relatively short time, adequate time does not exist to thoroughly field test the programs, determine what tasks students have difficulty with, and rewrite lessons to buttress against these problems. Field testing and revisions based on field testing are important elements of instructional design for programs for struggling readers and at-risk students. The lack of field testing and the lack of in-depth teaching of critical content result in most basals failing to meet the needs of struggling readers and at-risk students.

Focused Core Reading Programs

Focused core reading programs address the essential skills students need to be accomplished readers. However, these programs are not designed to cover all the aspects of language arts instruction as the comprehensive core reading programs. Because of the more focused aspect of these programs, many have been particularly effective with struggling readers and at-risk students because they provide more in-depth treatment of the core content. Many schools have adopted these programs and supplemented them with teacher-made materials to create a reading program that meets all content standards. These reading programs have also been used successfully with nonreaders and very poor readers in second and third grade in order to provide an accelerated catch-up program.

Supplementary Materials

Supplementary materials provide instruction or practice on just one or two areas of reading instruction. An increasing number of publishers are producing programs that focus on phonemic awareness and/or phonics, including exercises to teach letter-sound correspondences and word reading. Some publishers are producing programs focused on fluency development, and many publishers produce text materials designed for extra reading practice. A great difference exists in the quality with which these programs are constructed. Use of these programs can be problematic when the instructional sequences and strategies are different from the core program being used in the classroom.

Intervention Materials

Intervention materials are designed for children who are performing below grade level. Publishers of comprehensive core reading programs will have components that are designated as intervention materials, but as of the writing of this book unfortunately none of these intervention materials provide for systematic instruction for children who are significantly below grade level. The core publisher's intervention materials provide some extra practice in a slightly simpler manner than the regular core lessons. For children who are significantly behind, these materials are not sufficient. A number of schools rely on the use of focused core reading programs to serve as intervention programs for their struggling readers and at-risk children.

Computer-Based Instruction

A variety of computer-based programs are available. Most are marketed as supplemental or intervention programs.

Many computer-based programs teach or provide practice to younger children on phonics and phonemic awareness. There are also programs designed to help teachers motivate children to read more books. These programs determine a child's reading level, indicate books at the child's reading level, provide comprehension questions for the books, and include motivational-type record-keeping features. A few programs are more comprehensive, providing aligned instruction in all critical areas of reading instruction.

A limitation of computers, particularly during the early stages of reading instruction, is that computers cannot yet reliably interpret children's oral responses and thus cannot give children reliable feedback on their verbal responses. Computer programs, though, can serve as useful supplementary tools that can provide practice for some skills and instruction in others. For example, a computer program might present comprehension strategies and then provide a series of application items to which the computer will provide immediate feedback to correct a wrong response. Some computer programs are becoming "intelligent," in that the amount of practice and what is practiced depends on student performance.

Constructing a School Reading Program

The core reading program in a school should be selected to meet the needs of the majority of the school's children. If the majority of a school's children are at risk, the core reading program should be highly systematic and explicit, containing adequate practice, carefully controlled rates of introducing new skills, and clear teaching demonstrations. In contrast, if the majority of a school's children are more instructionally sophisticated, the reading program should still be grounded on scientifically based reading research, but may be less explicit. However, for children who are at risk, a more explicit and systematic program should be used. Struggling readers and at-risk children should have all their instruction in the highly explicit and systematic program so they are able to make the accelerated progress needed to reach grade-level standards.

In second grade and above, comprehensive materials should be available for children who are significantly below grade level. These programs should include systematic and explicit teaching, and be designed to accelerate students' progress in all areas of reading.

More specific information of instructional materials by grade appears in Part 3.

Focus on What Works

School personnel must act as very diligent consumers when selecting reading programs. The words *research-based* in a brochure cannot be relied on to indicate that a program is, in fact, research based. Even among programs that are aligned with the findings of scientifically based reading research, significant differences exist in regard to how well the programs can meet the needs of at-risk children. Putting in exercises that are aligned with the research will not by itself make a program effective with the struggling reader or at-risk child. The construction of the entire program determines its effectiveness.

The most powerful evidence of a reading program's potential effectiveness is data on the student reading achievement from schools with a similar student and teacher population that used the particular program. Teachers, particularly those serving populations with high numbers of struggling readers and at-risk children, should select programs that have produced high levels of student performance in comparable schools. Again, teachers must be very careful in examining publishers' claims.

Effectiveness rather than inclusiveness should be the major factor in selecting a core reading program. In the past, schools often used checklists with multiple factors to evaluate programs. The problem with these checklists was that the extent to which the programs covered all content in state standards became the main criteria in program selection. Thus, reading programs that provided only superficial coverage of critical content received higher ratings than programs that had in-depth coverage of critical content because the former covered a wider range of content, though most of it was covered superficially.

Sometimes schools may locate a reading program that has produced high levels of student performance in schools serving similar student populations, but the program may not include coverage of every topic included in the state standards. We suggest that in such instances the school seriously consider adopting the program that has produced good results, and then obtain or construct supplementary materials to teach the content for the other standards.

Modifying Reading Materials

Most comprehensive core reading programs will require modifications in order to meet the needs of struggling readers and at-risk students. Descriptions of five common problems requiring modifications for these students follow.

1. *Too many lesson activities.* Many core programs include a large number of activities in each lesson. There are more activities than there is time to teach all the activities. The teacher's guides unfortunately do not provide clear guidance regarding which tasks are the most essential. The teacher must be able to identify the most important tasks and schedule instruction so that priority topics are included in daily lessons.

2. *Vague directions for the teacher.* Most core programs do not provide clear directions to teachers on how to explicitly teach specific skills. The teacher must be prepared to structure the teaching of tasks so demonstrations are clear and instruction is interactive.

3. *Lack of assessment for placement and ongoing progress monitoring.* Most programs lack systematic assessments to help teachers in placing students in the program at the beginning of the school year and monitoring the extent to which the students are learning the content during the year. During the school year, frequent ongoing assessment on critical skills such as fluency is needed to ensure that children are learning the critical reading skills.

4. *Too much too fast.* Most core comprehensive reading programs introduce new information and skills at too fast a rate for the struggling reader and at-risk student. Too much is introduced at one time with too little practice provided in order to enable students to develop mastery before proceeding to more advanced topics. Teachers need to be prepared to analyze teaching strategies, identify component skills, create teaching demonstrations for each of these components, and then provide adequate practice to facilitate student mastery of the entire strategy

5. *Language of instruction doesn't match student needs.* Most core reading programs do not carefully control the vocabulary or syntax the teacher uses when presenting information to children. Words and sentence structures that are not commonly understood by the children will appear in teacher demonstrations. For example, some kindergarten programs will use the terms *same* and *different* in early lessons. The problem is that many at-risk kindergartners will not understand these terms; thus, frustration is likely for both the student and teacher. Teachers will need to modify the wording in teacher presentations to ensure that the children understand all the terms used.

Part 2 of this text will present examples of teaching that will show teachers how to deal with the major problems just described and other problem areas. Our goal is to provide the reader with specific examples of how to make success possible for all children.

CHAPTER 3

Explicit and Systematic Instructional Design

Teachers must be able to evaluate reading programs so they can select ones that provide systematic and explicit instruction. They must also be able to, when necessary, modify programs to make them sufficiently explicit and systematic to meet the needs of the struggling reader and at-risk student. This chapter presents instructional design principles that teachers can utilize in both these tasks. The following aspects of program design are discussed: devising instructional strategies, developing explicit teaching procedures, selecting examples, sequencing skills, introducing new information at a realistic rate, and providing adequate practice and review.

Devising Instructional Strategies

Whenever possible, instructional programs should teach students to rely on strategies rather than require them to memorize information. Teaching children strategies makes instruction more efficient. For example, teaching the students the letter-sound correspondences and a sounding-out strategy enables children to read any word that contains these letter-sound relationships. Once children have mastered sounding out, each time a new letter-sound correspondence is taught the child will be empowered to read a number of new words. Let's say that the students already know the sounds for the letters *m, s, t, f, d, r, n, h,* and *a*. The introduction of the letter *i* results in the student being able to read these new words: *sit, it, fit, hit, mid, hid, tin, fin, miss, rim, dim, him, if,* and *in*.

Developing Explicit Teaching Procedures

Instruction is explicit when the teacher clearly, overtly, and thoroughly communicates to students how to do something.

Use Explicit Teaching Demonstrations

The procedures for teaching explicitly are different for the younger child who has little experience with formal instruction and the child who has already had some formal instruction. A good deal of the early information, skills, and strategies that children need to learn can be taught using a simple *model, lead, test* teaching procedure. A *model* is simply a demonstration by the teacher. For example: the teacher segments a word slowly (mmmaaannn), then blends by saying it fast (man); the teacher points to the letter *s* and says its sound (ssss); or the teacher points to the letters in a word and sounds out the word without pausing between sounds (sssuuunnn), then says the word at a normal rate (sun).

In a *lead* step, the teacher helps the student make the desired response. The most common method of leading in teaching beginning reading has the teacher make the response with the students as they try to apply what the teacher has just demonstrated. For example, when students are first learning to sound out a word, the teacher provides a model, then leads, responding with the students ("Say it with me, sssuuunnn"). Young children may need a number of lead trials before they can make the desired response. The teacher continues leading, responding with the students, until they can make the correct response several times in a row. Note that leading is not required on all responses, just those that the child is not able to correctly imitate after a demonstration.

The *test* step consists of the teacher having the students make the response without assistance. For example, after the teacher models and leads sounding out, the children are then directed to respond on their own, "By yourselves, sound it out."

Use of the model-lead-test presentation procedure can enable teachers in prekindergarten through first grade to significantly accelerate the progress of their at-risk students. Rather than waiting for the students to learn the myriad of language concepts that a child would need to know to benefit from language-ladened teaching demonstrations, the teacher can present important word-reading skills from day one. The *Reading Mastery* Series authored by Siegfried Engelmann presents an excellent example of how the model, lead, test procedures can be used to accelerate beginning reading instruction for the at-risk student.

As students progress into the primary stage. The model-lead-test procedure is not used as often because students now have sufficiently developed language to understand explanations.

Control the Language Used in Teaching Skills and Strategies

During the beginning reading stage, the teacher, working with children at risk because of language-related delays, should structure teacher demonstrations to avoid language-ladened presentations. The problem with highly language-ladened explanations is that the child is unlikely to understand the teacher's explanations.

Teacher explanations must be carefully constructed so that they can be easily understood by the students. This need for language control is important at all stages of learning, but particularly when children are first beginning formal instruction in prekindergarten through first grade. Many at-risk children enter school with very little knowledge of the language of instruction. They do not know colors, shapes, preposition or comparison concepts such as same and different, or sequential concepts such as first, next, and last.

Vocabulary and sentence structures that students do not understand should be avoided. This point is simple but often overlooked. Suggested explanations in the kindergarten teachers' guides of core reading programs often contain words that average and above-average students may understand, but these same words often confuse at-risk students. Student failure in day-to-day lessons is often caused by teachers failing to preteach critical vocabulary. If teachers are going to use words like *above, below, first,* or *next,* they should assess students to be sure they understand those words, and if not, provide for teaching of these concepts *before* using them in teacher explanations. The chapter on beginning vocabulary (Chapter 15) in Part 2 includes directions for teaching this vocabulary.

Introduce One New Skill at a Time

When teaching struggling readers and at-risk students, it is especially important to control the amount of new learning presented. Construct teaching presentations so that each presentation includes only one new skill. Teaching presentations that attempt to teach more than one new skill cause two problems. First, when students have to learn two new skills at the same time, they are more likely to fail because the learning load is twice as great as when one new skill is introduced. Second, when students fail, the teacher cannot readily tell which skill caused the failure. This makes diagnosis and remediation difficult. For example, in teaching students to decode consonant-vowel-consonant-final e (CVCe) words, such as *like* or *made,* a teacher presents this rule: *When a word ends in* e, *say the name for the first vowel.* Students who do not know what a vowel is, or were not taught vowel names before encountering this rule, would have to learn several new skills at once: what a vowel is, vowel names, and the rule. Students who say "lick" for *like* may not know the vowel name for *i* or may not know how to apply the rule. Consequently, a teacher would not know whether to help the students with vowel names or with applying the rule.

Provide Guided Practice in Applying Strategies

Throughout this text, a number of teaching formats will appear that specify exactly how the teacher can present specific strategies. The formats include directions on what the teacher and the students are to say and do. Formats will gradually decrease in structure. In introductory formats, the teacher models or demonstrates the steps in a strategy and provides structured practice in applying the strategy. For example, during the latter part of the first year of phonics instruction, letter combinations such as *ar, ee,* and *ai* will be taught. The sounds of these letter combinations cannot be simply presented in isolation with the hope that students will be able to use this knowledge to read words containing these combinations. The program should include specific teaching of how to read words with these combinations. In the introductory format, the teacher provides examples of words with the new combination underlined (f<u>ar</u>m), and has the students read the underlined new sound first, then read the word.

The teacher gradually reduces help and prompting. Eventually the students apply the steps in the strategy by independently reading these words without underlined letters. Teacher guidance from modeling, to prompted application, to independent application of a strategy is referred to as *scaffolding instruction.*

Selecting Examples

Present Appropriate Introductory Examples

When presenting a format that introduces a new skill or strategy, the teacher presents a set of examples. The examples in the set are appropriate only if the student can use the new strategy and information that was taught previously to come up with the correct answer. For example, when teaching students to sound out simple phonetically regular words, the examples would be limited to words that contain only the letters for which students have been taught the letter-sound correspondences. If the students know the letter-sound correspondences for only the letters *m, s, a, d, f, r, t,* and *i,* the teacher should not present the word *met* since it contains an unknown letter (*e*).

Constructing sets of examples is particularly important when teaching vocabulary. A set of examples is appropriate only if it demonstrates the teacher's intended meaning. A set of examples may be inappropriate if the student can learn an interpretation other than the intended one. For example, when teaching the vocabulary word *thick* to a young child, a teacher may utilize a thick pen and a thick pencil as examples of thick. Since both of these objects are writing tools, a child might interpret thick as having something to do with writing rather than with size. More on selecting examples will be presented in the vocabulary chapter.

Provide Discrimination Practice

After a new strategy is introduced, students need practice in determining when and when not to use that new strategy. Selecting appropriate examples for discrimination exercises involves creating the right mix of examples. In addition to examples applicable to the new strategy, other examples must also be included. These other examples review similar previously taught strategies. A range of examples is necessary so that students are required to differentiate when to use the new strategy and when to use previously taught strategies. For example, when students learn to read CVCe words, the teacher would include examples of the new word type (*cane* and *robe*), as well as the words that do not follow the rule (*can* and *rob*) in the discrimination format. Including these similar words provides important discrimination practice.

Sequencing Skills

Sequencing involves determining an optimal order for introducing new information and strategies. Sequencing significantly affects the difficulty or ease students have when learning new skills. Four sequencing guidelines tend to reduce student error rates.

Teach Preskills of a Strategy Before the Strategy Is Presented

The most critical sequencing guideline is teaching components of a strategy before the strategy is introduced. Since the components must be taught before the strategy itself, the components can be referred to as *preskills*. In the strategy for decoding CVCe words, knowing the names of the vowels is a preskill, which is introduced before the strategy is presented. Another illustration of preskills involves dictionary skills. To prepare older students to locate words in a dictionary, teachers should provide preskill instruction on (a) saying the alphabet; (b) comparing target words to guide words by looking at the first, second, or third letter; and (c) knowing whether to turn toward the front or back of a dictionary after opening it to a particular page. Another example is sounding out. The preskills of the sounding-out strategy include (a) identifying the sound for each letter, (b) knowing that words are read from left to right, (c) blending the sounds, and (d) saying the blended sounds as a word. Teaching preskills and enabling children to gain proficiency with these skills before a new strategy is introduced facilitates student success.

Introduce High-Utility Skills Before Less Useful Ones

The guideline of sequencing high-utility skills before less useful ones can be illustrated with irregular words. Very common irregular words, which students encounter many times in primary readers (e.g., *was, said, have*), are introduced before less common and, therefore, less useful words (e.g., *tomb, heir, neon*). Another example involves letter-sound correspondences: the letters *a, m, s,* and *i* are introduced earlier than the letters *v, x,* and *j* because they appear more often in words in primary readers. Introducing the more common letters first enables students to read more words.

Introduce Easy Skills Before More Difficult Ones

The guideline of introducing easy skills before more difficult skills can be illustrated with letter-sound correspondences and word types. Easier-to-say sounds (*a* and *m*) should appear before more difficult-to-pronounce sounds (*l* and *e*). Similarly, shorter phonetically regular words (*sun, cat*) are easier to sound out than longer regular words (*stand, plant*) and should be introduced first.

Separate Strategies and Information Likely to Be Confused

The guideline of separating information and strategies that are likely to be confused can be illustrated with the letters *b* and *d,* which are similar in shape and sound. If *b* and *d* are introduced in a close time span, students are more likely to develop confusion between them than if they were separated by a longer time span. If *b* is introduced during the third week of a program, *d* might be introduced in the eighth week, after eight or nine other less similar letters have been introduced. Another illustration involves the similar irregular words *were* and *where*. Since they are similar in sound and appearance, they would be introduced several weeks apart.

Sequencing guidelines sometimes conflict with each other. For example, exceptions to a strategy often need to be introduced early because they are useful. For example, the letters *ai* represent the long-a sound in virtually all the words in which *ai* appear together. Students are taught a strategy of saying the long-a sound when they see *ai*. The word *said* is an exception to this strategy. However, *said* would be introduced early in a reading program as an irregular word because it is a very useful and frequently appearing word. Similar conflicts arise when a skill is difficult, which suggests a late introduction, yet is very useful, which suggests an earlier introduction. Obviously, compromises are necessary to resolve these conflicts. The way a compromise is made usually depends on the relative importance of the guidelines in conflict. It may also depend on how your reading program is designed.

Introducing New Information at a Realistic Rate

The rate at which new information is introduced should be carefully planned out. An instructional program may introduce new content at a rate that may be appropriate for a highly prepared child, but this rate may be inappropriate for a struggling reader or at-risk child. For example, if a child enters school with an extensive knowledge of letter names and knows about half of the letter sounds, an instructional program that introduces a new letter-sound correspondence in each lesson might be appropriate. However, if a child entered school with little or no knowledge of letter names and letter sounds, a rate of one new letter-sound correspondence per lesson would not be realistic. The rate at which new content is introduced in an instructional program should be based on extensive field testing. An instructional program that introduces information at too fast a rate will likely result in frustration and failure for the student.

Providing Adequate Practice and Review

An instructional program should provide adequate practice for the development of both accuracy and fluency. Sufficient practice must be provided within each lesson and across lessons. When a new strategy is introduced, within-lesson practice includes a concentrated or massed presentation of examples to provide the student the practice necessary to master applying the strategy. The massed practice continues over several consecutive lessons. Review, which is sufficient practice across a number of lessons, is needed to ensure that students retain the strategies and information taught and develop fluency in using these strategies. A pattern of massed practice in the first several lessons and systematic review in subsequent lessons is critical for retention. Teachers must often supplement reading programs that do not supply sufficient practice.

CHAPTER 4

Explicit and Systematic Lesson Presentation Techniques

The manner in which a teacher presents lessons is as important as the instructional design underlying the content being presented. This section includes a discussion of lesson presentation techniques that have been shown to elicit high degrees of student engagement, contribute to efficiency in instruction, and help provide a successful learning environment for students.

Different teacher presentation techniques are appropriate for different stages of reading instruction. For example, when children are first learning to read, instruction is in small groups and is highly interactive, with children primarily making oral responses and the teacher providing immediate feedback on their responses. Once children have learned to read accurately and with fluency, reading instruction techniques will be more varied. The instruction in an upper-grade classroom in which all children are performing at grade level will include a variety of instructional activities. Sometimes the teacher may present lessons to the entire class. Other times, children may work collaboratively by providing feedback to each other. If some children have difficulty with a particular concept or strategy, the teacher may provide small-group instruction to the struggling students.

Another example of how a specific technique is used differently at different times involves the teacher monitoring student performance. During early reading instruction, the teacher listens to oral responses and watches children's mouths to see how they are pronouncing words. Monitoring in the later grades focuses more on the teacher reviewing student written work and providing a combination of oral and written feedback. In general, teachers teaching beginning reading skills must be proficient in the presentation techniques needed to maintain student participation in highly interactive verbal exchanges between teacher and students. Intermediate-grade teachers must be more skilled in managing students across a number of instructional settings.

The remainder of this chapter explains teaching techniques effective for working with groups of students: small-group instruction, including unison oral responding, signaling, pacing, monitoring (including giving individual turns), correcting errors, teaching to mastery, diagnosing, and developing student motivation; and whole-class instruction. Although most of the examples used involve situations in which younger students are being taught, teachers of older students who have not yet mastered primary-grade content should find much of the discussion relevant.

Small-Group Instruction

The instructional techniques described here are designed for small groups composed of children who are at the same instructional level. During small-group beginning reading instruction, students are more likely to be attentive if seated close to the teacher. For beginning reading instruction, we recommend seating the students in chairs, without desks or tables, in a semicircle or in two rows directly in front of the teacher. The teacher sits facing the group, looking out over the classroom so that he or she can monitor the entire class. The students in the group should be facing toward the teacher and away from the other students so they will not be distracted.

Easily distracted students should be seated closest to the teacher to make it easier for the teacher to monitor their performance and give encouraging pats or handshakes. It is interesting to note that just the opposite pattern often occurs with less-proficient students seated farthest from the teacher. Teacher monitoring of distractible and instructionally naive students is easier when they are seated in the middle of the group rather than on the sides (see Figure 4.1). For written exercises, lapboards or clipboards can be provided.

Unison Oral Responding

During the beginning reading and early primary stage, the teacher maximizes students' active responding by structuring tasks to incorporate unison responses. Unison responding, in which all the students respond at the same time, facilitates a high degree of active student involvement. Much of the instruction in the beginning and early primary stage is suitable for unison responding since

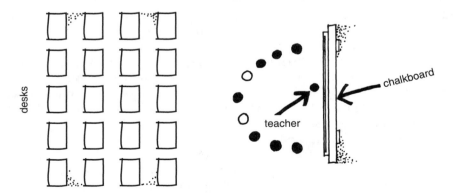

Figure 4.1

Suggested Seating Arrangement. An open circle (O) indicates naive or easily distractable students. Note that these students are not placed next to each other

the tasks are of a nature where there is just one correct answer (e.g., when shown the letter *m* and asked, "What sound?", the students answer, "mmm"). The advantage of frequent unison responses is that all students actively practice each skill throughout an instructional period. Unison responses also provide the teacher with frequent information about each student's performance.

Teachers can structure tasks to be highly interactive by keeping explanations short and giving students frequent opportunities to respond. Unison responding can significantly accelerate student progress, particularly for children who are more instructionally naive. If the teacher presented tasks only to individuals instead of the group, some students may answer only a few times during a period. Such infrequent responding often results in inattentiveness on some students' part, less practice on important reading skills, and restricted information about student performance on the teacher's part.

Signaling

For the advantages of unison responding to be fully realized, teachers have to utilize a number of techniques. The first technique involves making it clear when students are to respond. Unison responding is most effective when all the children in a group create their own response and none rely on mimicking other children's responses. Some children are initially less confident than others and will have a tendency to rely on others to come up with the answer. A technique referred to as *signaling* is used to facilitate active self-initiated responding.

A signal is a cue given by the teacher that tells students when to make a unison response. The effective use of signals allows participation by all students, not just the higher performers who, if allowed, tend to dominate the lower-performing students. For example, if a teacher neglects to use a signal when presenting a complex comprehension question, higher-performing students are likely to respond long before lower performers have had a chance to organize and produce their responses. As a result, the lower-performing students may learn to copy responses from the other students, or they may just give up. Either result leads to a reduction in the amount of practice these lower-performing students receive. A signaling procedure can avoid this problem.

To signal a unison response, the teacher (a) gives directions, (b) provides a pause for think time, and (c) signals for the response. In giving directions, the teacher tells the students the type of response they are to make and asks the question. For example, if presenting a word-list reading exercise on the board, the teacher might instruct the children, "Say each word when I touch it."

After the directions comes the pause for think time. The duration of think time is determined by the length of time the lowest-performing student needs to figure out the answer. (If one student needs significantly longer to answer than the other students in the group, the teacher should not slow the group for this child. The teacher should consider providing extra individual practice for that student or placing the child in a lower-performing group.) For easier questions (simple tasks involving review of previously taught skills), the think time may be just a second, while for more complex questions, the think time may last several seconds. Carefully controlling the duration of think time is a very important factor in maintaining student attentiveness and providing students with a successful learning experience.

The final step in the signaling procedure is the actual cue to respond. A cue or signal to respond may be a clap, finger snap, hand drop, tap on the board, or any similar type of action. In some tasks, the teacher would say "Get ready" a second before signaling. The consistent use of "Get ready" a second before the actual signal can help in ensuring a clear signal. The "Get ready" cue is particularly useful when students are looking at a reading passage or during teacher-directed written tasks, since students are looking down and cannot see a hand signal from the teacher.

The essential characteristic of any good signal is its clarity. The signal must be given so that students know exactly when they are expected to respond. If a signal is not clear, students will not be able to respond together. The teacher should use the students' behavior to evaluate the clarity of his or her signals. A repeated failure by children to respond together usually indicates that the signals are unclear or that the teacher has not provided adequate think time. Demonstrations of signaling procedures can be found on the Associations for Direct Instruction website (**www.ADIhome.org**). The signaling video is in a section labeled "movie clips—countdown to lesson one."

Pacing

Anyone who has observed young children watching TV shows such as "Sesame Street" can attest to the value of lively pacing in keeping students attentive. Teachers need not put on an elaborate show to foster attention but should be familiar enough with their material to present it in a lively, animated manner and without hesitation. Teachers who are well-versed with their materials will not only be able to teach at a more lively pace, but will also be able to focus their attention more fully on the students' performance.

However, providing a briskly paced presentation does not mean that a teacher rushes students, requiring them to answer before they have had time to figure out the answer. The key to providing an effectively paced presentation is to not have "down time" after the students make a response. When the students respond, the teacher immediately either begins the directions for the next question or the correction to the current task. A teacher working with younger students on oral tasks in which children identify the most common sound of letters would pace his or her presentation so that children are responding about 10 to 15 times a minute. The teacher works on a set of questions for a period of time without interruption, then transitions to a new task with some kind of quick change-up between the tasks. For example, during an early reading lesson, the teacher might work intensively for a period of 3 to 5 minutes on a letter-sound task and then spend 15 seconds acknowledging students' efforts with verbal praise and physical contact in the form of handshakes, high fives, pats, and so forth, then proceed to a phonemic awareness task. As students become more mature, the time they work without a change-up increases.

Monitoring Group Responses

When a group of students respond orally at the same time, it will generally be very difficult for the teacher to hear mistakes made by only one or two of the students, especially when an incorrect response sounds similar to the correct response. For example, if one student in a group of eight students says the word *sit* instead of *sick* or says the sound /m/ instead of /n/, the error will be difficult to hear. Besides listening to student responses, teachers can monitor student performance by watching the children's eyes and mouths. By watching the mouth, the teacher can determine if children have positioned their lips and tongue in the position necessary to produce the desired response. For example, suppose a teacher points to the letter *m,* and a child who is responding has her mouth open when responding. Since producing the sound /m/ requires closed lips, the student's pronunciation is most probably incorrect. The teacher also watches the eyes of the children to determine if they are attending. If a student is not looking at the appropriate instructional materials, the child may be mimicking other students' responses rather than initiating his or her own answer.

However, a teacher cannot be looking at the faces of all children each time the group responds. Consequently, a teacher must systematically switch from student to student during the lesson, while focusing primarily on lower-performing students. For example, in a group of eight students, five children seldom have difficulty while the other three sometimes make errors. In this scenario, the teacher arranges the students' seats so that the three who are more likely to have difficulty are seated in or near the center of the group. The teacher watches them for two or three responses and then shifts his or her attention to the students on the left side of the group for a response or two. The teacher then shifts his or her attention back to the students in the middle for several responses before watching the students on the right side. By always returning to the students in the middle and watching them respond, the teacher monitors their responses about twice as often as responses of the higher-performing students seated on either side.

Monitoring with Individual Turns

Individual turns are a very important monitoring tool. Children may appear to be answering correctly and initiating their own responses during unison responding instruction, but they may in fact be mimicking other children. The teacher gives individual turns after he or she feels that the group has mastered all the steps in a format during unison responding. By providing adequate group practice before calling on individuals, the teacher avoids needlessly embarrassing a student. Because individual turns can be time-consuming if a group is large, turns need not be given to every child. The teacher can test a sample of children on a sample of the questions presented. The teacher presents individual turns to the more instructionally naive students and some of the higher performers. The teacher presents steps that were troublesome for children during the unison responding exercise or that were troublesome on past lessons. If a number of children make errors when individual turns are given, the teacher knows that he or she did not provide enough practice to the group during the unison responding part. Likewise, if a particular student makes errors on individual turns, the teacher knows that more attention must be paid to monitoring that student's responses during unison responding in future lessons.

The importance of careful monitoring cannot be overemphasized. The sooner a teacher detects an error the easier it will be to remedy that error. Each day a student's error goes undetected the student is, in essence, receiving practice doing something the wrong way. For each day a student responds incorrectly, a teacher may have to spend several days reteaching that skill. Thus, careful monitoring is a prerequisite for efficient instruction.

Correcting Errors

Detecting and immediately correcting student errors is essential in accelerating students' learning. The correction procedure for incorrect responses during small-group instruction is directed toward the whole group and consists of as many as five steps: model, lead, test, firm up, and delayed test. For example, in presenting a letter-sound correspondence task, the teacher points to o and asks, "What sound?" A student responds, "/ŭ/." First, the teacher models the correct answer, saying, "ŏŏŏ." Second, the teacher may lead (respond with the children, "Say ŏŏŏ with me. Get ready, ŏŏŏ"). The teacher responding with the students (leading) ensures they hear a correct response as they practice producing the response. Leading is needed only when students have difficulty making the response (saying the sound). Third, the teacher tests, asking the students to answer on their own.

The fourth step is the firm up. Instead of presenting the next task or new material, the teacher repeats the series of items that just preceded the missed item and then the missed item itself. For example, during second grade, a word-reading exercise might include several lists, each containing five words. If a student misses a word in a list, the teacher corrects the word, then returns to the beginning of that list and repeats the list before moving to the next list. The purpose of the firm-up step is to provide students with repeated extra practice on the missed item.

The last step is a delayed test in which the teacher tests the group or individual on the missed item at a later time in the lesson. With instructionally naive students, several delayed tests may be given during a lesson so that they will receive repeated practice within a lesson. If the students make errors on the delayed test, the teacher corrects the mistake again and firms up the response. A teacher should keep track of student errors so that missed items or skills can be retaught and practiced in the next day's lesson.

Note that all these steps are directed to the entire group. When an individual makes an error, the teacher does not single out the child, but directs the correction to the group and has the entire group respond.

The goal of this correction procedure is to enable all children to master all the content as they progress from task to task and lesson to lesson.

The correction procedure for more complex higher-order tasks is somewhat different than lower-order tasks that can be corrected by modeling the answer. The teacher would guide the students through a series of thinking steps to determine the answer. For example, let's say the students have read an expository passage containing the following statement, "When objects are heated, they expand." The students then read about a metal ball left outside at 40° in the morning. In the afternoon, the temperature rises to 95°. The students are asked, "What do you know about the size of the metal ball in the afternoon?" A student answered incorrectly, "It got smaller." The teacher corrects by asking a series of questions: "What do we know about objects that are heated? What was the temperature of the ball in the morning? What was the temperature of the ball in the afternoon? Did the temperature get hotter or colder? So did the ball expand? What does expand mean?" This procedure helps students apply the strategy for coming up with the answer and also provides the teacher with information about where specific problems may lie.

Teaching to Mastery

Teaching to mastery requires a great deal of teacher skill and awareness. Obviously, the teacher working with more instructionally naive learners will have to provide more practice and correction than the teacher working with more sophisticated learners. Teachers have to be able to keep children motivated as they present this practice. Teachers should be positive and encouraging throughout the lesson. Teachers should respond with a great deal of enthusiasm when children respond correctly.

Not teaching to mastery can lead to later problems for students. For example, during beginning reading, if the students do not receive adequate practice to learn the letter-sound correspondences, they are likely to have difficulty later in the program when sounding out words is presented. Teaching to mastery can be a very efficient procedure in the long run. If teachers bring children to mastery on each task in each lesson, they will note that children need fewer repetitions each day to reach mastery. Bringing children to mastery, however, is dependent on the instructional design of the reading program. If important skills are not practiced daily or if new information is introduced too quickly, bringing children to mastery is much harder.

Diagnosing

As children progress in an instructional program, their errors on current tasks may be the result of not being firm on earlier prerequisite skills. For example, when sounding out a word, the prerequisites are (a) knowing the letter-sound correspondence for each letter in the word, (b) being able to blend the sounds to create a word, and (c) being able to translate the blended sounds into a word said at a normal rate. Diagnosis is sometimes very obvious. If, for example, a student says "sit" for the word *sat* and "mit" for *mat,* the teacher would diagnose the student's problem as a confusion of the letter-sound correspondence for *a* and *i,* since the student said the wrong sound for the letter *a* in both words. During a lesson, the teacher provides an immediate correction to the group using the model, lead, test, firm up, delayed test procedure. If the error is persistent, the teacher would also design future lessons to include more teaching and review of previously taught letter-sound correspondences that were missed. Several assessments are included in Part 3 of this text to help with diagnosing word-reading problems.

Diagnosis becomes more challenging as the children engage in more complex activities. For example, a student may have missed a complex comprehension question because of not knowing a particular word (*expand*), not having enough background information about a particular topic, or not applying a series of steps to infer the answer. Teachers may need to work individually with students having trouble to determine the specific cause of the errors, and then structure lessons to provide more instruction on particular areas of need.

Motivation

Some students come to school eager to learn and eager to please the teacher. They are intrinsically motivated, work hard, and have pride in their work. With such students, motivation is not a concern and praise and recognition will be sufficient for these students. Other students have less interest in learning, will give up easily, and are not as eager to please the teacher. The teacher must take particular care to use techniques that foster student success and develop a positive interest in learning when working with less-motivated students. A first step in motivating these students is demonstrating to them that they can succeed in reading. This is done by carefully designing and effectively presenting lessons. Second, the teacher should provide high levels of reinforcement for being attentive and participating in instruction. At first, with younger students the teacher may use extrinsic rewards such as physical contact, pats, and handshakes or tokens such as earning points on the board or marbles in a jar that can be exchanged for tangible rewards. The teacher should utilize effective management techniques for off-task behavior, such as praising other children specifically for producing the desired behavior instead of directing attention to, or nagging, off-task students. As the students engage in lessons with high degrees of positive reinforcement and experience success in daily lessons, they will develop positive attitudes toward learning to read. As they recognize their own success they will be well on the road toward developing intrinsic motivation.

Whole-Class Instruction

Large-group or whole-class instruction becomes more common as children progress from the "learning to read" stage to the "reading to learn" stage. Whole-class instruction utilizes some of the same techniques used in teaching a small group, particularly on tasks that call for responses in which there is only one correct answer, such as reading words in a list, and saying the most common sound of letter combinations. Whole-class and small-group instruction are the same in that the teacher has the students sit in an arrangement where the teacher can readily monitor the performance of the students most likely to have difficulty. If the classroom is arranged in rows, the teacher would have lower-performing students sitting in the front rows in the middle so that the teacher can more readily monitor their performance. Signaling and pacing would be the same as in small groups. Corrections would, as in small-group instruction, be directed to the group rather than individuals.

One difference between whole-class and small-group instruction is in regard to teaching to mastery. During whole-class instruction, if there are children who are performing significantly below the majority of the class, the teacher would not spend inordinate amounts of time during whole-class instruction repeating tasks until these children are firm. This repetition could result in other children becoming inattentive and embarrass the children having difficulty. Instead, the teacher would work with the struggling students during a small-group session at another time. Ideally, the work with these children during the small group should prepare them for successfully participating in whole-class instruction.

Instruction

CHAPTER 5

Phonemic and Phonological Awareness

What Is Phonemic and Phonological Awareness?

Both phonological awareness and phonemic awareness involve the identification and manipulation of parts of *spoken* language. *Phonological awareness,* the broader category, includes awareness of the larger parts of spoken language as well as awareness of the smaller parts. Included among the larger units of spoken language are words, syllables, onsets, and rimes; thus, phonological awareness refers to oral activities such as rhyming. *Phonemic awareness,* in contrast, refers only to awareness of phonemes, the smallest units of spoken language. In most reading programs, phonemes are often referred to as "sounds" or "isolated sounds" (i.e., /s/, /m/, /a/, etc.). Linguists do not agree on the number of distinct sounds in English; however, most report the number of sounds as between 42 and 44 distinct sounds.

Phonemic awareness is a subcategory of phonological awareness that is focused more narrowly on identifying and manipulating individual sounds within words. Phonemic awareness includes both awareness that spoken words are composed of individual sounds and the ability to manipulate those sounds in a variety of ways.

A number of activities to build phonemic awareness are found in reading programs. These activities include:

- *Phoneme isolation.* Children recognize individual sounds in a word (i.e., the first sound in *fit* is /f/).
- *Phoneme identity.* Children recognize the same sound in different words (i.e., the first sound /r/ is the same in *rat, rim,* and *rice*).
- *Phoneme categorization.* Children recognize the "odd" word in a set of words (i.e., in the set of words, *top, tin,* and *hen,* the word *hen* does not belong since it doesn't begin with /t/).
- *Phoneme blending.* Children listen to a sequence of phonemes and combine them to form a word (i.e., the sounds /s/ /u/ /n/ make the word *sun*).
- *Phoneme segmentation.* Children break a word into its separate sounds, saying each individual phoneme (i.e., the word *grab* is composed of the sounds /g/ /r/ /a/ /b/).

■ *Phoneme deletion.* Children recognize the word that remains when a phoneme is removed from a word (i.e., the word *spark* without the /s/ is *park*).

■ *Phoneme addition.* Children make a new word by adding a phoneme to an existing word (i.e., if you add the phoneme /s/ to the word *pot,* you have the word *spot*).

■ *Phoneme substitution.* Children replace one phoneme for another to make a new word (i.e., Start with the word *rug.* Change /g/ to /n/. The new word is *run*).

Two of these phonemic awareness skills, blending and segmenting, have been identified as most critical. The reason most probably stems from the fact that blending and segmenting are directly related to sounding out words. Blending has the students translate a series of sounds into a word said at a normal rate ("rrrraaammm" becomes *ram*). Blending explicitly demonstrates that words are composed of strings of smaller units of speech or phonemes. In the blending task, the students are provided with an extended opportunity to "hear" those smaller units of speech (i.e., phonemes) and then translate what they have heard into familiar spoken words.

Segmenting has the students identify the sounds that make up a word. Segmenting is easiest when the students simply produce a series of sounds without a pause (as in saying a word very slowly, "mmmmaaaannnn"). Segmenting is more difficult when students hear a word and say each phoneme separately in sequence (m-a-n). We recommend that in the beginning stage of reading instruction teachers model and teach segmenting without stopping between sounds. With a little initial practice, students can learn to segment without pausing between sounds and then utilize this important skill in subsequent sounding-out activities.

The tasks of blending and segmenting words do the following:

1. Show the students that words are composed of discrete sounds (i.e., teaches phonemic awareness skills).

2. Provide practice in saying sounds before the letter-sound correspondences are introduced. This practice is particularly important for difficult-to-say sounds such as "th."

3. Prepare students for later sounding-out exercises that require blending (saying sounds without pausing between them).

Rhyming, a phonological awareness skill, was identified by the National Reading Panel as an important skill that helps students focus on parts of spoken language that are smaller than syllables but larger than phonemes. A rime is the part of a syllable that contains the vowel and all that follows it (the rime of *man* is -an; of *shop*, -op). Teaching rhyming prepares students to put word parts together.

Why Phonemic and Phonological Awareness Is Important—The Research Connection

Research of the late 1980s and early 1990s showed clearly that students who enter first grade with a wealth of phonological and phonemic awareness are more successful readers than those who do not (Kame'enui, 1996; Smith, Simmons, & Kame'enui, 1995).

Figure 5.1 summarizes the conclusions of the National Reading Panel in regard to phonemic awareness. The research clearly indicates that phonemic awareness skills can be taught explicitly to students who lack these skills when they enter kindergarten or first grade. The National Reading Panel concluded that phonemic awareness instruction is most effective when it:

- Uses letters of the alphabet as students are taught to manipulate phonemes
- Focuses on only one or two rather than several types of phoneme manipulation
- Includes blending and segmenting of phonemes in words
- Makes explicit how phonemic awareness skills are applied in reading and writing tasks

---

- Phonemic awareness can be taught explicitly.
- Phonemic awareness instruction helps children learn to read and spell.
- Phonemic awareness instruction is most effective when students use letters of the alphabet as they are taught to manipulate phonemes.
- Phonemic awareness instruction is most effective when it focuses on only one or two rather than several types of phoneme manipulation.
- Phonemic awareness instruction produces greater benefits in reading when it includes blending and segmenting of phonemes in words.
- Phonemic awareness instruction is most effective when it makes explicit how children are to apply phonemic awareness skills in reading and writing tasks.
- Phonemic awareness instruction helps all types of children improve their reading, including normally developing readers, children at risk for future reading problems, readers with disabilities, preschoolers, kindergartners, first graders, children in second through sixth grades with reading disabilities, and children across various socioeconomic levels.
- Phonemic awareness instruction should consume no more than 20 hours of instructional time over the school year.
- Phonemic awareness instruction is more effective when delivered to small groups of students than when delivered to individual students or to the whole class.

Figure 5.1

National Reading Panel Conclusions from Scientifically Based Research on Phonemic Awareness Instruction

Adapted from the NRP Report of the Subgroups, Chapter 2, Part 1, Phonemic Awareness Instruction, pp. 5–7.

How It Fits into the Reading Program

An important question not answered by research is whether all phonemic awareness and phonological awareness skills need to be explicitly taught. No definitive research-based answer exists to this question. Some very effective reading programs such as *Reading Mastery* include just the essential phonemic awareness skills directly related to reading words: blending, segmenting, and rhyming. Other reading programs that have been successful include a wider range of tasks.

Teachers will probably be best served by following the sequence of the core reading program that they are using. Teachers need to be careful though not to unduly delay beginning reading instruction while spending excessive time working on complex phonemic awareness skills such as substitution and deletion. Word reading can begin when children know several letter-sound correspondences and can do oral blending and segmenting tasks.

The teaching of oral blending and segmenting should begin about 2 to 3 weeks before students begin to sound out words. Because oral blending and segmenting do not require knowledge of letter-sound correspondence and do not require students to look at written letters (graphemes) or words, instruction on these phonemic awareness skills can begin before any letter-sound correspondences have been introduced. Ideally, blending and segmenting will be taught beginning early in the kindergarten school year.

Blending a series of continually-said sounds (mmmaaannn) to form a word (man) is the easier skill and should be introduced first. Segmenting a word into sounds can be introduced when students are able to blend a group of words with no errors, which usually occurs within several days. These auditory tasks should be continued for the first few months of instruction during the beginning stage.

Rhyming with the use of letters can be introduced after students can do blending and segmenting exercises with 3-letter words and have learned at least 10 letter-sound correspondences.

How to Teach Phonemic and Phonological Awareness Through Explicit Instruction

Blending

Blending requires the student to translate a series of blended sounds into a word said at a normal rate. When sounding out a written word, students should hold each continuous sound for 1 to 2 seconds, thus producing a series of sounds, "mmmaaannn." Then they will have to blend this series of sounds into a word pronounced at a normal rate, "man." The oral phonemic awareness blending task directly prepares students for translating the blended sounds into a word said at a normal rate when sounding out words.

Table 5.1

Format for Blending Sounds

Teacher	Students
1. (Teacher gives instructions.) "Listen, we're going to play a say-the-word game. I'll say a word slowly, then you say the word fast."	
2. (Teacher says the word slowly, then students say it fast.) "Listen. (Pause.) iiiiffffff. What word?" (Signal.)	"If."
3. Teacher repeats step 2 with three more words: *sad, fun, am.*	
4. Teacher repeats the set of words until students can respond correctly to all the words, making no errors.	
5. Teacher gives individual turns to several students.	
CORRECTING ERRORS	
1. Teacher says correct answer, "Sad."	
2. Teacher models the entire task: "My turn. (Pause.). Ssssaaad. What word? Sad."	
3. Teacher leads, "Do it with me. Sssaaad. What word? (Signal)." Teacher and students respond together: "Sad."	"Sad."
4. Teacher tests (students do it by themselves). "Your turn (pause). Ssssaaad. What word?" Signal.	"Sad."
5. Return to the first word in the exercise.	

Table 5.1 presents a format for teaching oral blending. The teacher presents a set of four to five words. For each word, the teacher says the word slowly, holding each sound for a second or two and not pausing between sounds. After saying the word slowly, the teacher pauses an instant, and then says, "What word?" The students are to reply by saying the word at a normal rate. After the teacher firms the group on all words in the set, (firming means the teacher has the group respond in unison until the group responds without an error on all words in a row), the teacher gives individual turns to several children.

Correcting Errors. Students may make three types of mistakes when blending sounds to form a word: (a) leaving out a sound (the teacher says "sssaaad," but the child leaves off the final consonant saying "sa"), (b) mispronouncing a sound (the teacher says "ssseeelll," but the student says "sil"), or (c) saying the word slowly (imitating the teacher). The correction procedure, which is the same for all types of mistakes, consists of the teacher (a) modeling the correct response, (b) leading the students by responding with them, (c) testing the students on the missed word by having them answer by themselves, and (d) returning to the first word in the format.

Here is a typical correction sequence: The teacher is presenting the following set of words: *if, rat, sad, am, fit.*

- Teacher says, "Ssssaaaad." Student says "Sid" instead of "Sad."
- Teacher says correct answer, "Sad."
- Teacher models entire task: "My turn. (Pause.) Ssssaaaad. What word?" "Sad."
- Teacher leads—teacher and student respond together: "Do it with me. Ssssaaaad. What word?" (Signal.) "Sad." (Teacher says "Sad" with the students.)
- Teacher tests—only students respond. "Your turn. (Pause.) Ssssaaaad. What word?" (Signal.) "Sad."
- Teacher returns to first word in format: "Let's see if we can do all the words without making any errors."

Usually one or two students in a group will make an error while the rest of the students respond correctly. Teachers should occasionally begin the correction procedure by praising a student who responded correctly (e.g., "Good answer, Tia"). This praise will demonstrate to students that the teacher places importance on correct responding. Teachers should not be negative with students who make errors. Praise a student who got the answer right, as the praise keeps the lesson positive and motivates other students. The teacher does not generally single out the student who made the error, but presents correction to the entire group, having all the students respond. When presenting individual turns at the end of the format, the teacher tests a student on any word the student missed during the exercise.

Segmenting a Word

The segmenting a word format (see Table 5.2) teaches students to say a word slowly, holding each continuous sound for about 1 1/2 seconds, and switching from sound to sound without pausing. The teacher presents a set of four words. For each word, the teacher first models saying the word slowly, sound by sound, without pausing. The students then say the word slowly, switching from sound to sound without pausing as the teacher signals. The teacher repeats each word in the exercise until the students can say the word slowly without pausing or stopping two times in a row.

Correcting Errors.   Students can make three types of mistakes in segmenting a word: (a) not saying a sound correctly, (b) pausing between sounds, or (c) not switching sounds when the teacher signals for the students to say the next sound. The correction procedure for any of these errors includes these steps:

1. Stop the students as soon as you hear the wrong response and say the correct sound (or tell the student the problem if he or she paused or did not follow the signal).
2. Model the correct response.

Table 5.2

Format for Segmenting

Teacher	Students
1. "We're going to say words slowly. We'll say a new sound each time I signal."	
2. First word: *sad*. "I'll say it slowly. Listen. (Pause.) Ssssaaaddd. You say it slowly. Get ready." (Teacher signals each time students are to switch to the next sound.) "Again. Get ready." (Signal.)	"Ssssaaaddd." "Ssssaaaddd."
3. Teacher repeats procedure in step 2 with three more words. Next word. *me*. "I'll say it slowly. Listen. (Pause.) Mmmmeee. You say it slowly. Get ready." (Signal.) "Again. Get ready." (Signal.) Next word: *mom*. "I'll say it slowly. Listen (Pause.) Mmmmooommm. You say it slowly. Get ready." (Signal.) "Again. Get ready." (Signal.) Next word: fit. "I'll say it slowly. Listen (Pause.) Ffiit. You say it slowly. Get ready." (Signal.) "Again. Get ready." (Signal.)	"Mmmmeee." "Mmmmeee." "Mmmmooommm." "Mmmmooommm." "Ffiit" "Flit"
4. Teacher repeats the set of words until students can say every word slowly, making no errors.	
5. Teacher gives individual turns to several students.	

CORRECTING ERRORS

1. Stop students as soon as you hear an error.	
2. Model the correct response. "Listen, I'll say it slowly, mmmmeee."	
3. Lead the students. "Say it slowly with me. Get ready, mmmmeee." "Again. Get ready." (Signal.) mmmmeee	"Mmmmeee." "Mmmmeee."
4. Test the students. "Your turn. Listen. (Pause.) Mmmmeee." "Say it slowly. Get ready."	"Mmmmeee."

3. Lead the students in making the response.

4. Test the students.

5. Return to the beginning of the exercise.

Here is a typical correction sequence:
The teacher is presenting the following set of words: *am, not, rug, sad.*

■ Error when segmenting "Nnnooot," a student says "Nnnuuu."

■ Teacher stops the students as soon as she hears "uuu."

■ Teacher says correct sound, "Ooooo."

■ Teacher models (emphasizing the sound the student said incorrectly): "My turn. Nnnooot."

■ Teacher leads: "Listen. "Nnnnooot. Say it with me. Get ready. (Signal.) Nnnooot." (Teacher says "Nnnooot" with students "Again. Get ready." (Signal.) Nnoot.

■ Teacher tests: "Your turn Listen. Nnnnooot. Say it slowly. Get ready." (Signal.) Nnnooot.

■ Teacher returns to first word in task (*am*).

The correction procedure for students pausing between sounds is basically the same as for mispronounced words except that the teacher does not have to say a missed sound. The teacher tells the students not to stop between sounds. The teacher then models, leads, tests, and returns to the first word of the exercise. The teacher leads the students until it appears that the students have responded twice in a row correctly, then goes on to the test step.

The correction procedure for students failing to switch sounds when the teacher signals would begin with the teacher praising students who followed the signal, then modeling, leading, and testing as previously shown.

Segmenting and Blending

The two auditory skills, blending and segmenting, are combined in a single format in Table 5.3. This format can be introduced when students are able on the first trial to respond correctly to all the words in a blending format and in the segmenting format. In this new format the teacher says the word slowly, then the students say the word slowly (rrrrammm), then say it at a normal rate (ram).

Critical Behaviors

Modeling Saying the Word Slowly.   When saying a word slowly in the blending or segmenting format, the teacher (a) says each continuous sound for about 1 1/2 seconds, (b) does not pause between sounds, and (c) is careful not to distort any sound. For example, when saying the final consonant of a word, the teacher must be careful not to add an "uh" sound, but to say the word *sad* as

Table 5.3

Segmenting and Blending—Combined Format

Teacher	Students
1. First you'll say a word slowly, then you'll say it fast.	
2. "Listen. (Pause.) Rrrraaannn. Say it slowly. Get ready." (Teacher signals each time students are to switch to the next sound.) "What word?" (Signal.)	"Rrraannn." "Ran."
3. "Listen. (Pause.) Sssiiiccck. Say it slowly. Get ready." (Signal.) "What word?" (Signal.)	"Ssssiiiick." "Sick."
4. "Listen. (Pause.) Mmmmaaad. Say it slowly. Get ready." (Signal.) "What word?" (Signal.)	"Mmmaaaad." "Mad."
5. "Listen. (Pause.) iiiffff. Say it slowly. Get ready." (Signal.) "What word?" (Signal.)	"iiiffff." "if."
6. Teacher repeats steps 2 through 5 until students are able to respond correctly to all words.	
7. Teacher gives individual turns to several students.	

"sssaaad," not "sssaaduh." Similarly, teachers must be careful not to add an "uh" sound to words that begin or end with stop sounds (*b, c, d, g, h, j, k, p, q, t*). In modeling a word that begins with a stop sound, the teacher pronounces a word such as *pin* by combining the /p/ and /ĭ/ sound and then elongating the /ĭ/ sound, pronouncing *pin* as "piiiiiiinnnnn" not as "puhiiiiinnnn."

Signaling. The blending and segmenting tasks are among the first tasks presented to students at the beginning of the school year. When presenting the first blending and segmenting exercises to the students, the teacher is not only teaching the blending and segmenting skills, but is also teaching the students how to respond in unison as members of a group. The teacher must present the signal to respond in a manner that makes it clear to the students exactly when they are to respond and when to listen.

In the blending exercises, the teacher begins with her hand held up in front of her (as someone indicating another person to stop). The teacher signals the students to say the word at a normal rate by moving his or her hand up and down in a quick drumbeat motion. The up-down motion should be done crisply and without hesitation. The students respond on the down motion, just as the teacher's hand hits an imaginary drum. The up-down motion should be done the same way every time. Any hesitation or inconsistency makes a unison responding difficult because the students don't know when to respond.

The signal for segmenting a word begins with the teacher holding up her hand in a fist with the palm facing the teacher. After the teacher says "Get ready," the teacher pauses an instant, then signals the students to respond by holding up his or her index finger for approximately 1 1/2 seconds, then extending a second finger for the second sound, then 1 1/2 seconds later extending a third finger for the third sound. Students should switch from sound to sound each time the teacher extends a finger. When holding up a finger, the teacher's movement is quick so that students know when to start saying the new sound. This signaling procedure is illustrated below. A demonstration of the procedure appears on the Association for Direct Instruction website (**www.Adihome.org**). The video appears in the movie-clips section.

A slight modification of the signaling procedure is necessary when words begin with stop sounds (*b, c, d, g, h, j, k, p, q, t*). When the teacher models these words, the teacher says the first two sounds of the word as one unit. For example, when segmenting the word *hat* the teacher begins by saying "haaa." The teacher says the initial-consonant sound for an instant and then begins the next sound without any pause or distortion.

The signal for words that begin with stop sounds begins with the teacher extending two fingers in quick succession, almost simultaneously, while saying the first two sounds of the word. The teacher holds the vowel slightly longer than usual (about 2 seconds), then extends a third finger to signal students to say the third sound.

Monitoring Students' Responses.   When students respond orally in unison, hearing an incorrect response can be difficult; therefore, the teacher should look at the students' mouths as they make the responses. The position of the students' lips and tongues helps to tell the sounds the students are making. For example, if a student's mouth is open when the student is supposed to be making the /m/ sound, the teacher knows the student is not making a correct response.

The teacher should also watch the students' eyes. The students' eyes should be directed toward the teacher's face. Young children unconsciously watch an adult's mouth movements to learn how to say sounds and words. Students should watch the teacher's mouth as the teacher models. Watching the students' eyes also lets the teacher know if the students are attending to the teacher's signals.

Note that in all three formats the teacher is directed to pause before saying a word slowly. The purpose of the pause is to ensure that the students hear the word as a distinct unit. The pause should be just for an instant.

Pacing.   When presenting a format the teacher presents several words in a row, pausing no longer than several seconds to make a quick one- or two-word praise comment (e.g., good, great) between the student response and the teacher instructions for the next word. After a set of several words, the teacher can spend 5 to 15 seconds praising students.

The concept of presenting a set of words with little extraneous language between each word is an important one. Presenting a set of tasks with no interruption is a very powerful method for keeping students attentive.

The number of words in a set and the relative intensity of teacher praise depend on the difficulty the students have with the formats. The less difficulty students have, the more words should be included in a set and the less effusive the praise.

Individual Turns.   As a general rule, when a blending or segmenting format is presented, the teacher has the students respond in unison until the teacher is fairly certain all students can respond correctly to all the words. Individual turns are then given.

The main purpose of individual turns is to make a final check to see whether students are able to respond correctly. During the first week of instruction an individual turn may be given to most students. Later, fewer individual turns are needed. The teacher may give an individual turn to each weaker student, but just to one or two stronger students. The purpose of giving individual turns to higher performers is not only to monitor their performance, but also to ensure that the teacher does not inadvertently stigmatize some students as lower performers by always calling on just them for individual turns.

If a student makes an error on an individual turn, the teacher should direct the correction to the whole group, present the individual turn again to the student who made the error, and again present it as a delayed test at the end of individual turns. If the student makes an error on the delayed test, the teacher should assume that the child needs reteaching on the entire set of words prior to the next lesson. If several children in a group make an error on an individual turn, the teacher should assume that the entire group needs reteaching on the entire set of words. The teacher should present the entire exercise again later in the lesson.

Selecting Examples.   Blending and segmenting exercises are done with a set of four to five words. Initial blending and segmenting should only include words made up of two and three sounds and begin with continuous sounds. More difficult types of words are presented in auditory tasks a week or so before that type is introduced in word-reading exercises.

The teacher must make certain the set of words is not too predictable because a predictable set may cause the students to anticipate words and not attend carefully to what the teacher says. For example, if the same vowel appears in all words, the words form a predictable order; the students may then respond according to the pattern rather than to what the teacher says. If the teacher presented the following set: *Sam, lap, rat, man,* the students might start anticipating that all words have the /a/ sound.

To avoid a predictable list, the teacher constructs a list in which the same letter does not appear in the same position in more than two consecutive words.

Rhyming

Rhyming is an important phonological awareness skill because it (a) prepares students to see the relationship between letter clusters that represent the same sounds in different words, such as *fan, pan, tan,* and *man;* and (b) prepares students for sounding out words that begin with stop sounds. Rhyming can be introduced when the students have mastered the combined segmenting and blending format with two and three sound words that begin with continuous sounds and know about ten letter-sound correspondences.

In the rhyming format (see Table 5.4), the students start with an initial sound (an onset), and then blend on a syllable that begins with a vowel (the rime). For example, the onset sound *m* is blended with the rime *at* to form the word *mat.* In presenting the format, the teacher writes several letters on the board (e.g., *m, r, s*). On the first days of presenting the format the teacher models rhyming by saying a series of rhyming words, beginning with those letters (e.g., *mat, rat, sat*). After modeling, the teacher then has the students rhyme while responding in unison. Over the first weeks that rhyming is presented, the letters written on the board should have continuous sounds. After the students can correctly do the rhyming tasks with continuous sounds, words that begin with stop sounds can be included. For example, a set might include these words: *fill, hill, pill, mill.*

The correction procedure follows these steps:

The teacher is presenting a task in which the students rhyme the rime *at* with the letters *r, m,* and *s.* On the task in which the teacher signals the students to begin with "m" and rhyme with "at," a student says "mit"

- Teacher says the correct answer, "Mat."
- Teacher models: "My turn. Rhymes with at. (Signal.) Mat."
- Teacher leads: "Let's do it together. Rhymes with at. (Signal.) Mat." (Teacher responds with the students.)
- Teacher tests: "Your turn. Rhymes with at. (Signal.) Mat."
- Teacher returns to first letter in the list.

Commercial Programs

Many commercial reading programs teach phonemic awareness skills in a manner that is likely to be problematic for the struggling reader or at-risk child who enters kindergarten or first grade with little literacy-related knowledge. The following are common problems:

1. There is not sufficient emphasis on blending and segmenting. Blending and segmenting are not taught in consecutive lessons. Therefore, there is not adequate practice for students to develop mastery.

2. There will be a wide variety of phonemic awareness tasks taught within a short lesson span. The introduction of too many different kinds of tasks over a short period can be overwhelming.

Table 5.4

Rhyming Format

Teacher	Students
(Teacher writes on board:)	

Teacher	Students
1. "Listen. I'm going to rhyme with (Pause.) *at*. What am I going to rhyme with?" (Signal.)	"At."
2. (Teacher models:) (Teacher puts finger on ball of first arrow and says:) "My turn: Rhymes with *at*. (After a 1-second pause, teacher moves finger rapidly across arrow and says:) *Mat*."	
3. (Teacher repeats step 2 with remaining arrows.)	
4. (Teacher tests:) (Teacher puts finger on ball of first arrow and says:) "You're going to rhyme with *at*. What are you going to rhyme with? (Signal.)	"At."
Rhymes with *at*." (After a 1-second pause, teacher moves finger quickly across arrow.)	"Mat."
5. (Teacher repeats step 4 with remaining arrows.)	
6. (Teacher gives individual turns to several students.)	

CORRECTING ERRORS

1. Teacher says correct answer, "Mat."	
2. Teacher models: "My turn. Rhymes with at. (Signal.) Mat."	
3. Teacher leads the students: "Do it with me. Rhymes with *at*." (Signal) (Teacher responds with the students.)	"Mat"
4. Test the students: "Your turn. Rhymes with *at*." (Signal.)	"Mat."
5. Return to the first letter in the exercise.	

3. The teaching demonstrations for phonemic awareness tasks tend to be wordy and potentially confusing for the instructionally naive student. For example, a typical task taken from a popular reading program directs the teacher to tell the students that the teacher will describe a turkey. The teacher then tells the students that if the word that describes the turkey begins with the same sound as the word *turkey,* they should lift the letter *t* and trace the letter in the air. The teacher's guide presents the sentence, "Is it a tall turkey?" emphasizing the words *tall* and *turkey*. Then, using the same sentence form, the teacher substitutes the following words for *tall: tired, muddy, terrible, tough, little,*

and *tiny*. The activity concludes with the teacher writing on the board all the words that begin with *t*. The teacher reads each word, then asks a student to circle the *t* at the beginning of the word. This activity is potentially confusing for the instructionally naive child because of all the extraneous language. The task could be simplified by just saying two words and asking if the words begin with the same sound.

4. The tasks are not highly interactive with frequent student responses. Some tasks instruct the teacher to just call on individual students to respond. There is not clear direction to teachers to ensure that all children have mastered the task.

Solution

The problems of inadequate emphasis on blending and segmenting and teaching demonstrations for those skills that are not clear can be dealt with by incorporating the blending and segmenting formats in this chapter into daily lessons. Blending and segmenting should be taught daily until the students can do these tasks with no errors, and then be systematically reviewed. Early tasks should be done with short two- and three-sound words. Words with more sounds should be introduced gradually.

Teachers should be prepared to modify complex tasks by eliminating complex language that students may not know and by teaching component skills. For example, a worksheet task might have pictures of a frog, a hat, and a rug and instructions for the teacher to say "Circle the words that have the same last sound as the word *dog*." Teachers should not assume that students understand what is meant by the term *last* (or *first* or *middle*). Nor should they assume that students understand the meaning of the word *same* or that students can extract a sound from a word. The teacher should be prepared to present exercises designed to teach the prerequisite skills and knowledge. A good deal of teaching may be necessary for students to be able to successfully circle words that end with the same sound as a given word. The teacher might first have to teach the students to identify the individual sounds in a word that was said at a normal rate (the more difficult type of segmenting), then teach the students to identify the last sound in a word and also teach the concept of same.

Wording for teaching segmenting

Teacher	*Students*
■ My turn. I'll say the sounds in *mud*.	
■ The first sound in *mud* is /mm/.	
■ The middle sound is /ŭŭ/.	
■ The last sound is /d/.	
■ Your turn. Say *mud*.	
■ Get ready. (Signal.)	"mud."

■ What's the first sound? (Signal.)	"Mm."
■ What's the middle sound? (Signal.)	"uu."
■ What's the last sound? (Signal.)	"d."

The teacher models and tests students on several words, then presents several words without modeling the answers first. The exercise is continued daily until the students can respond correctly to four words presented without a teacher model.

Wording for identifying the last sound in a word

Teacher   *Students*

- ■ My turn. I'll say the last sounds in some words.
- ■ Listen, *rat*. The last sound in *rat* is /t/.
- ■ Listen, *Sam*. The last sound in *Sam* is /m/.
- ■ Listen, *fill*. The last sound in *fill* is /1/.
- ■ Your turn. *Rat*. What's the last sound in *rat*? (Signal.)   "t"
- ■ Your turn. *Sam*. What's the last sound in *Sam*? (Signal.)   "m"
- ■ Your turn. *Fill*. What's the last sound in *fill*? (Signal.)   "1"

The teacher models and tests students on several words, then presents several words without modeling the answers first. The exercise is continued daily until the students can respond correctly to four words presented without a teacher model.

Wording for determining if sounds are the same

- ■ I'll say sounds and tell you if they are the same or not the same.
- ■ Listen, mmm mmmm. Those sounds are the same.
- ■ Listen, rrrrrr rrrrrrrr. Those sounds are the same.
- ■ Listen, mmm rrrr. Those sounds are not the same.
- ■ Listen, ffff mmmm. Those sounds are not the same.
- ■ I'll say sounds. You tell me same or not same.
- ■ Listen, ffff mmmm. Tell me about those sounds.
- ■ Listen, ffff ffff. Tell me about those sounds.
- ■ Listen, rrrr rrrr. Tell me about those sounds.
- ■ Listen, rrrr mmmm. Tell me about those sounds.

The teacher models and tests students on sets of sounds, then presents several sets without modeling the answers first. The exercise is continued daily until the students can respond correctly to four words presented without a teacher model.

These preskill exercises give the teacher a means to make a correction if a student makes an error on a workbook exercise in which he or she is to circle words that end with the same sound.

Again, we caution teachers on not spending excessive time on complex phonemic awareness exercises. Once the students have mastered oral blending and segmenting, we recommend a focus on teaching students to sound out words rather than spending excessive time on phonemic awareness tasks. This focus on word reading is particularly important for students who enter first grade unable to sound out words.

Application to Your Curriculum

Evaluate Phonemic Awareness in Your Core Reading Program (Level K and 1 only)

1. When are the following skills introduced? (lesson day or number)

   Segmenting:

   Blending:

   Rhyming:

2. What strategies are specified for introducing the skills? How explicit are these strategies? Do they show students what to do?
3. How clear are the teaching demonstrations? Is the wording carefully controlled for clarity?
4. How much teacher modeling and leading is provided to students? Do students eventually respond without the teacher first modeling?
5. What corrections are specified for student errors?
6. What examples are provided? Are there problems with these examples?
7. What opportunities are the students given to practice the skills over time? Is there daily practice in the days after a skill is first introduced? Are these opportunities sequenced from easy to more difficult?
8. What modifications would you make based on your answers to the previous questions?

At a Glance   Teaching Blending and Segmenting

Rationale

- Shows students that words are composed of discrete sounds (phonemic awareness)
- Provides practice in saying sounds before the letter-sound correspondences are introduced
- Provides practice in linking blended sounds into words
- Prepares students for sounding-out word exercises that require blending

Materials	List of words selected by the teacher. Students shouldn't see the words—this is an auditory skill!
Blending; What to Do	You say a word slowly, holding continuous sounds for approximately 1 to 2 seconds and not pausing between the sounds. Then ask students to say the word. Students say the word at a normal rate.
Blending; Correcting Mistakes	Immediately tell students the correct word—don't let them guess. Then say the blended sounds of the word again so students can hear the phonemes again, and then ask students to tell you the correct word.
Segmenting; What to Do	Model saying words slowly by saying each phoneme without stopping between the sounds. Then have students say the words slowly without stopping between the sounds. Signal movement from sound to sound by holding up successive fingers for each sound when you model saying the sounds and when the students say the sounds. This signaling procedure will keep the students answering together and not answering ahead of others.
Segmenting; Correcting Mistakes	• Model correct segmenting. Lead the students by having them segment the word with you. Test the students by having them segment by themselves. • If students stop between the sounds, tell them to keep their "motors running" and model how you say the word slowly without stopping between the sounds. Have the students say the word slowly with you several times until firm. Then provide the model again and have them do it by themselves.

continued

Selecting Examples	Practice with four to six words daily. For the first weeks include two- and three-sound words that begin with continuous sounds, then move to words that begin with stop sounds, then longer words.
	• Make the list of words "unpredictable." Do not have the same letter in the same position in more than two consecutive words.
When to Do It	• Introduce blending and segmenting a week or two before beginning sounding-out word reading.
	• These short exercises can be done several times during your reading instruction *and* at other times during the day.
	• Introduce combined blending and segmenting exercises when students can do blending formats and segmenting formats without error.
	• Instruction should begin in kindergarten and continue until students can successfully sound out a word type in word-reading exercises.
Strategic Integration	• As students master blending and segmenting with different types of words (CVC, CCVC, etc.), these words can then be included in word-reading exercises in which students sound out the words.
	• Integrate segmenting activities into spelling practice. Teach students to segment a word said at a normal rate into component sounds.

At a Glance   Teaching Rhyming

Rationale

- Prepares students to see the relationship between common letter combinations that represent the same sounds in different words (word families)
- Prepares students for sounding out words that begin with stop sounds

| **Materials** | Write two to three letters on the board (initially, use continuous sounds). |
| | Draw an arrow under each letter. |

continued

What to Do	• Tell the students what to rhyme with (am, op, it, en, ump) and have them say this rime.
	• Place finger on ball of arrow. When you move finger along the arrow, students say the sound and add the rime, making a word.
	• Initially, the teacher should model this task, then have students do the task.
Correcting Mistakes	• If students say the wrong word, say the correct word, then model the task again, starting with telling them what you will rhyme with. Have the students do the task with you, then by themselves.
Selecting Examples	• Practice daily with up to three sounds and three rimes until students can respond correctly without making mistakes.
	• Begin with continuous initial sounds and VC rimes (mat). When students can do these tasks without error, introduce sets of words in which at least one word begins with a stop sound letter.
When to Do It	• Introduce rhyming with initial continuous sounds after students can successfully blend and segment and after they can identify seven continuous sounds.
	• Instruction should begin in kindergarten and continue until students can successfully rhyme words and sound out words with initial stop sounds.
Strategic Integration	• Use words that the students will be sounding out in upcoming word-reading exercises.

CHAPTER 6

Overview of Phonics Instruction

What Is Phonics Instruction?

Phonics instruction teaches the relationships between the letters of written language (graphemes) and the individual sounds of spoken language (phonemes) and how these relationships are used to read and write words.

The goal of phonics instruction is to help children learn and use the alphabetic principle—the understanding that written letters correspond to spoken sounds and that the correspondences are systematic and predictable. Knowledge of the alphabetic principle helps children to (a) recognize familiar words accurately and automatically, and (b) decode new words independently.

In teaching phonics, a teacher must be aware of the power and the limitations of phonics. The limitations of phonics stem from the fact that English is not a truly phonetic language in which each letter always represents only one sound. Although about half the letters in the English language are highly regular in that they nearly always represent the same sound, the other half of the letters are not as consistent in regard to the sound represented by the letter. The sounds these less-consistent letters represent varies, depending on the context in which they appear. To determine what sound a particular letter represents, the reader must take into account the letters that precede or follow it in a word. For example, if the letter *o* is followed by another *o,* the letter *o* may make the /oo/ sound as in *moon,* or the /oo/ sound as in *good.* Similarly, when *o* is followed by the letter *u,* the *ou* combination may make the /ou/ sound as in the word *shout* or the /oo/ sound as in the word *would.* The letter *o* can also represent or combine with other letters to make the /ŏ/ sound as in the word *mom,* the /ō/ sound as in the word *hope,* and the /ŭ/ sound as in the word *done.* Obviously, the sound the letter *o* makes is determined by the letters that follow. The consonant *t* is also not consistent. If *t* is followed by the letter *h,* the *t* and *h* join to represent either the voiced /th/ sound as in *that,* or the unvoiced /th/ sound as in *think.* But if *t* is followed by *ion,* the *t* represents the /sh/ sound as in *action.* Again, the sound the *t* represents is determined by the letters that follow it.

The power of phonics stems from the fact that knowing the sound usually represented by individual letters and frequently appearing combinations of letters will enable a child to read many words. Despite the variations, there is a good deal of consistency in letter-sound relationships in the English language.

For example, the letter combination *ai* represents the same sound in over 95% of the words in which it appears. Likewise, the letters *sh* are very predictable, nearly always representing the /sh/ sound as in the word *wish.* By teaching aspiring readers the sound correspondences for single letters and common letter combinations, the teacher is able to teach decoding strategies through a generalization process rather than through a memorization process.

Key Terms

Throughout this book, we will use several key terms related to phonics. The definition of these terms and an explanation of their importance follow.

Most Common Sounds

The most common sound of a letter is the sound that the letter usually represents when it appears in a short, one-syllable word, such as *man* or *stop.* Table 6.1 lists the most common sound of each of the 26 letters. The word next to each letter illustrates the most common sound of that particular letter.

Table 6.1

Most Common Sounds of Single Letters

Continuous Sounds		Stop Sounds	
a	(fat)	b	(big)
e	(bet)	c	(can)
f	(fill)	d	(did)
i	(sit)	g	(got)
l	(let)	h	(his)
m	(mad)	j	(jet)
n	(nut)	k	(kiss)
o	(not)	p	(pet)
r	(rat)	q	(quit)
s	(sell)	t	(top)
u	(cut)	x	(fox)
v	(vet)		
w	(wet)		
y	(yes)		
z	(zoo)		

Stop Sounds vs. Continuous Sounds

A continuous sound is a sound that can be said for several seconds without any distortion. A stop sound can be said for only an instant. Words beginning with a stop sound, such as *pad,* are more difficult for students to sound out than words beginning with a continuous sound, such as *sad.* Because of the difference, a slightly different procedure is used when the teacher presents stop sounds than is used to teach continuous sounds. The list in Table 6.1 designates which letters correspond to stop sounds and which letters correspond to continuous sounds.

Regular Words

A regular word is any word in which each letter represents its respective, most common sound. For example, the words *am, cat, mud, best,* and *flag* are regular words because each letter in each word represents its most common sound.

Irregular Words

Irregular words are words that a student cannot read by applying the letter-sound correspondence knowledge that the student has learned in the reading program. For example, the word *was* is irregular because neither the letter *a* nor *s* represents the sound typically associated with that particular letter.

In designing a reading program, the teacher needs to be aware that words that are irregular at one point in a reading program may not be irregular at a later point in the reading program. For example, the word *park* would be irregular early in a reading program when the students have only been taught to associate the letter *a* with the short-a sound. Later in the program, students will be taught the letter correspondence for the letter combination *ar.* The letter combination *ar* is highly consistent in representing the *r*-controlled vowel sound heard in words like *park, hard,* and *start.* Once students learn the *ar* sound, the word *park* would no longer be considered an irregular word.

Some words will always be considered irregular because they contain letter-sound correspondences unique to that word or a few words. Examples of this type of irregular word include *was, they, said,* and *break.* In these words, one or more letters represent a sound that is not common for that particular letter. The term *sight words* is sometimes used to refer to irregular words.

Consonant Blends

A consonant blend occurs when two or three consonants appear consecutively in a word and each consonant represents its most common sound. Consonant blends may appear at the beginning or end of words. Table 6.2 illustrates common initial- and final-consonant blends. Words that begin with consonant blends are more difficult to decode than words that begin with single consonants. An initial-consonant blend that contains a stop sound will make a word more difficult to decode than will a consonant blend with two continuous sounds.

Table 6.2

Consonant Blends

INITIAL-CONSONANT BLENDS									
Two-Letter Blends Continuous Sounds First				**Two-Letter Blends Stop Sound First**				**Three Letters**	
fl	(flag)	sc	(scat)	bl	(black)	pl	(plug)	scr	(scrap)
fr	(frog)	sk	(skip)	br	(brat)	pr	(press)	spl	(split)
sl	(slip)	sp	(spin)	cl	(clip)	tr	(truck)	spr	(spring)
sm	(smack)	sq	(square)	cr	(crust)	tw	(twin)	str	(strap)
sn	(snip)	st	(stop)	dr	(drip)				
sw	(swell)			gl	(glass)				
				gr	(grass)				

FINAL-CONSONANT BLENDS						
Two-Letter Blends Continuous Sounds First				**Two-Letter Blends Stop Sound First**		**Three Letters**
ft	(left)	nd	(bend)	ct	(fact)	Words formed by adding an *s* to two-letter blends (e.g., belts, facts)
ld	(held)	nk	(bank)	pt	(kept)	
lk	(milk)	nt	(bent)	xt	(text)	
lp	(help)	sk	(mask)	bs	(cabs)	
lt	(belt)	st	(west)	ds	(beds)	
mp	(lamp)	ls	(fills)	gs	(rags)	
ms	(hams)			ps	(hips)	
ns	(cans)			ts	(bets)	

Regular Word Types

Regular word types may be described by the patterns of vowels and consonants they contain. Table 6.3 lists word types in their relative order of difficulty. In the first column, the letters "V" for vowel and "C" for consonant are used to describe the various types. A CVC word begins with a consonant letter, followed by a vowel, and another consonant. The word *sat* is a CVC word since *s* is a consonant, *a* is a vowel, and *t* is a consonant. The second column indicates the relative ease or difficulty of that word type. The third column illustrates each word type. This table provides general guidelines, not hard and fast rules for the teaching of each word type. Some students may find words of an earlier type more difficult than words of a later type.

Table 6.3

Simple Regular Words—Listed According to Difficulty

Word Type	Reason for Relative Difficulty/Ease	Examples	Notes
VC and CVC words that begin with continuous sound	Words begin with a continuous sound.	it, fan	VC and CVC are grouped together because there are few VC words.
VCC and CVCC words that begin with a continuous sound	Words are longer and end with a consonant blend.	lamp, ask	VCC and CVCC are grouped together because there are few VCC words.
CVC words that begin with stop sound	Words begin with a stop sound.	cup, tin	
CVCC words that begin with stop sound	Words begin with stop sound and end with a consonant blend.	dust, hand	
CCVC	Words begin with a consonant blend.	crib, snap, flat	Words that begin with two continuous consonants are the easier of words that begin with blends. These words are grouped with the rest of blends since there are relatively few such words.
CCVCC, CCCVC, and CCCVCC	Words are longer.	blend, clamp, spent, scrap, scrimp	

Letter Combinations

A letter combination is a group of consecutive letters that represents a particular sound(s) in the majority of words in which it appears. Knowing the most common sounds of letter combinations greatly expands students' abilities to decode new words. For example, a student who can decode all types of regular words and has just learned the *ee* letter combination will be able to decode these new words: *bee, bleed, beet, breed, peel, see, teen, wee, creek, deer, flee, fleet, green, greet, jeep, keep, weep, canteen, indeed, upkeep,* and *fifteen.*

Table 6.4 lists the letter combinations that we suggest presenting. We recommend presenting the letter-sound relationship for a letter combination if the letter combination represents one sound in over half the words in which it appears

Table 6.4

Letter Combinations

Letter Combination	Sample Word	Percentage	Frequency	Type
ai[a]	maid	90%	254	vowel digraph
al[b]	halt	NA	NA	l-controlled
ar	car	75%	518	r-controlled
au	haul	94%	146	vowel digraph
aw	lawn	100%	75	vowel digraph
ay	stay	97%	131	vowel digraph
ch	chip	63%	313	consonant digraph
ea[a]	beat	60%	294	vowel digraph
ee[a]	need	98%	285	vowel digraph
er	fern	97%	313	r-controlled
igh	high	100%	88	vowel digraph
ir	first	100%	104	r-controlled
kn	know	100%	41	consonant digraph
oa	load	94%	126	vowel digraph
ol[b]	hold	NA	NA	l-controlled
oo	boot	59%	173	vowel digraph
or	short	55%	312	r-controlled

(continued)

Table 6.4 (Continued)

Letter Combination	Sample Word	Percentage	Frequency	Type
ou	cloud	84%	285	vowel diphthong
ow	own	50%	124	vowel digraph
oy	toy	98%	48	vowel diphthong
ph	phone	100%	242	consonant digraph
qu	quick	100%	191	none
sh	shop	100%	398	consonant digraph
th[c]	thank	74%	411	consonant digraph
ur	burn	100%	203	r-controlled
wh	whale	85%	89	consonant digraph
wr	wrap	100%	48	consonant digraph

[a]When computing percentages from the Hanna et al. study (1966), we combined some combinations that were followed by *r* (air, eer) with the respective combination without *r* (ee, ai). We found that even though there is a sound difference when *r* follows the combinations, students can decode words by pronouncing the most common sound of the letter combination and then saying the /r/ sound.

[b]The percentage and frequency of the l-controlled letter combination was not available.

[c]Although /th/ represents the unvoiced sound in most words (e.g., think), in many high-frequency words (*this, that, them, than, then, the, those, these*) the *th* is voiced. We recommend introducing this less-common, or minor sound of *th* first, because students use it in sounding out many high-frequency words.

and if it appears in five or more common words. The letter combinations are listed alphabetically in the left column of the table. The second column contains words that illustrate the most common sound of each letter combination. The third and fourth columns give data from a computer analysis of the most common 17,300 English words (Hanna et al., 1966). The third column lists the percentage of total words in which the letter combination represents its most common sound. (Note that these percentages vary from study to study, depending on the sample of words used.) The fourth column gives the number of words in which the particular letter combination represented its most common sound. In the fifth column, the letter combinations are classified as vowel digraph, consonant digraph, r-controlled vowel, or diphthong.

Letter combinations include consonant digraphs (*th, sh, kn*), vowel digraphs (*ai, ea, oo*), diphthongs (*oi, ou*), and *r*- and *l*-controlled vowels (*ar, ir, ol*). A digraph consists of two consecutive letters that represent one sound. An *r*- (or *l*-) controlled vowel is a vowel followed by the letter *r* (or *l*). A diphthong consists of two consecutive vowels, each contributing to the sound heard.

The distinction between types of letter combinations is more important to speech teachers than to reading teachers. Nonetheless, reading teachers should be aware of the terms since they often appear in teachers' guides and professional literature.

VCe Pattern Words

In a VCe pattern word, a single vowel is followed by a consonant, which, in turn, is followed by a final *e* as in the words *lake, stripe,* and *smile.*

In approximately two-thirds of the one-syllable words containing VCe patterns, the initial vowel represents the long sound (the letter name). In the other one-third of the words in which there is a VCe pattern, the vowel sound is sometimes the most common sound of the initial vowel (*give*) and sometimes a sound that is neither the most common sound nor the long sound (*done*).

Since the initial vowel represents its long sound in many one-syllable VCe pattern words, we recommend teaching the rule that when a word ends in *e,* the initial vowel says its name. The one-syllable, VCe pattern words in which the initial vowel makes a sound other than its long sound should be treated as irregular words.

Affixes—Prefixes and Suffixes

Structural analysis involves teaching students to decode words formed by adding prefixes, suffixes, or another word to a base word. The word *repainting* is formed by adding the prefix *re* and the ending *-ing* to the base word *paint* (re + paint + ing = repainting). Affixes sometimes will represent different sounds. For example, the suffix *-ed* will sometimes represent the /t/ sound as in *hopped,* the /d/ sound as in *hummed,* or a separate syllable as in *handed.* Spelling changes are often needed when suffixes are added to base words. For example, note what happens when the ending *-ed* is added to *hope* and *hop* (hope + ed = hoped, hop + ed = hopped). *Hoped* is formed by dropping the *e* in *hope.* *Hopped* is formed by doubling the final *p* in *hop.* These spelling changes require the students to learn skills to discriminate similar words such as *hoped* and *hopped.* Exercises that show students how word parts are combined will help students decode words with spelling changes.

Why Phonics Instruction Is Important— The Research Connection

Few areas of education and pedagogy have been debated as exhaustively, continuously, and perhaps as rancorously as those on how to teach beginning reading. This debate is age old—perhaps more than 100 years old—and according to Stanovich reaches back to the "beginning of pedagogy" (Bower, 1992, p. 138).

The National Reading Panel (NRP) report finally has changed the nature of this debate. The NRP concluded that their examination of numerous studies provided solid support for the conclusion that systematic and explicit phonics instruction makes a bigger contribution to children's growth in reading than alternative programs providing unsystematic or no phonics instruction. In addition, the evidence indicated that systematic phonics instruction was successful with children from all SES backgrounds (2000). See Figure 6.1 for a summary of the findings on phonics by the National Reading Panel.

The National Reading Panel (2000) concluded that synthetic phonics programs were especially effective for younger, at-risk readers and for readers with disabilities. The Panel's conclusions regarding the synthetic-analytic contrast were:

> For children with learning disabilities and children who are low achievers, systematic phonics instruction, combined with synthetic phonics instruction produced the greatest gains. Synthetic phonics instruction consists of teaching students to explicitly convert letters into phonemes and then blend the phonemes to form words.
>
> Moreover, systematic synthetic phonics instruction was significantly more effective in improving the reading skills of children from low socioeconomic levels. Across all grade levels, systematic synthetic phonics instruction improved the ability of good readers to spell. (p. 5)

How Phonics Instruction Fits into the Reading Program

Phonics is an integral part of the entire beginning stage (Kindergarten to mid-first grade) and the first year and a half of the primary stage (mid-first grade through second grade).

Systematic and explicit phonics instruction is more effective than nonsystematic or no phonics instruction.	Systematic and explicit phonics instruction is particularly beneficial for children who are having difficulty learning to read and who are at risk for developing future reading problems.
Systematic and explicit phonics instruction significantly improves kindergarten and first-grade children's word recognition, spelling, and reading comprehension.	Systematic phonics instruction helped children at all socioeconomic levels make significantly greater gains in reading than did non-phonics instruction.
Systematic and explicit phonics instruction is most effective when it begins in kindergarten or first grade; to be effective with young learners, it should begin with foundational knowledge involving letters and phonemic awareness.	Systematic phonics instruction is effective when delivered through tutoring, through small groups, and through teaching classes of students.
Systematic phonics instruction includes teaching children to use their knowledge of phonics to read and write words.	Approximately 2 years of systematic and explicit phonics instruction is sufficient for most students.

Figure 6.1

Scientifically Based Conclusions About Beginning Phonics Instruction

Adapted from the NRP Report of the Subgroups, Chapter 2, Part 2, "Phonics Instruction," pp. 93–96.

During the beginning stage, students learn letter-sound correspondences for single letters and a sounding-out strategy to read simple regular words. After students develop ease with sounding out, a gradual transition is made from sounding out words to reading them at sight. Initial word-reading exercises are done with regular VC and CVC words that begin with continuous sounds. More difficult regular word types are introduced only when students demonstrate mastery of easier types. Irregular words, in which one or more letters do not represent their most common sound, ideally are not introduced until students have developed ease in sounding out regular words.

The beginning stage may take from the first 3 months to the first year of instruction, depending on the literacy and language skills the students bring to school. Students who come to school with a good deal of knowledge of letter-sound correspondences and experience with phonemic awareness may complete this stage very quickly. Other students who enter school with very little literacy-related preparation may require anywhere from 6 months to 1 year of instruction to complete the beginning stage. Some reading programs begin teaching phonics skills in kindergarten while other programs begin teaching word-reading skills in first grade. We recommend that phonics instruction begin in kindergarten.

The reason for our recommendation for beginning phonics instruction in kindergarten lies in the importance of children reaching grade level proficiency in reading text by the end of first grade. Children who are at grade level proficiency by the end of first grade have a much higher probability of success in future grades. Beginning phonics instruction in kindergarten provides much more instructional time for students to reach the first grade goal. Since kindergarten children are less experienced, instruction needs to be very carefully planned and presented.

During the primary stage, the focus moves to teaching students the letter-sound correspondences for groups of letters. The first letter combinations can be introduced after students know the most common sounds of about 20 single letters and can decode passages made up of regular words at a speed of about 20 words per minute. This speed indicates that students are no longer laboriously sounding out but rather are beginning to perceive words as units, which makes decoding words that contain letter combinations much easier. Common affixes, such as *-ed, -er, -ing,* and *-y,* can also be introduced at this time.

The strategy to decode VCe pattern words should be introduced after students have been taught to identify six to eight letter combinations and can decode words containing those combinations. Reading words with letter combinations gives students practice in looking at units of letters. This skill will prepare students for VCe words in which the initial vowel sound is determined by a letter *e* at the end of a word.

Specific suggestions for teaching components of phonics appear in the next four chapters in this section. The first two chapters deal with teaching letter-sound correspondences. The next two chapters deal with applying the knowledge of letter-sound correspondences to word reading in isolation and in text.

CHAPTER 7

Letter-Sound Correspondence— Beginning Stage

This chapter presents procedures designed to provide the struggling reader and at-risk child with success in learning letter-sound correspondences during the first months of reading instruction. The procedures incorporate instructional design principles that are important for all children, but particularly the struggling reader and at-risk learner.

Sequence

Four guidelines can be used for determining an order for introducing letter-sound correspondences:

1. Separate visually or auditorily similar letters.
2. Introduce more useful letters first.
3. Introduce lowercase letters first.
4. Introduce only one sound initially for a new letter.

Separate Visually or Auditorily Similar Letters

The more similar two letters are, the more likely students will confuse them. Separating similar letters from each other in their order of introduction reduces the possibility of student confusion. The greater the similarity between two sounds or letters, the greater the number of letters that should separate them. Two factors determine the probability of confusion: auditory similarity (how alike the most common sounds of two letters are) and visual similarity (how alike the appearance of two letters is). The following sounds are auditorily similar: /f/ and /v/, /t/ and /d/, /b/ and /d/, /b/ and /p/, /k/ and /g/, /m/ and /n/, /ĭ/ and /ĕ/, and /ŏ/ and /ŭ/. The following letters are visually similar: *b* and *d*, *b* and *p*, *q* and *p*, *n* and *m*, *h* and *n*, *v* and *w*, and *n* and *r*.

Similar sounds should be separated by the introduction of at least three other dissimilar sounds. For example, if the sound /t/ is introduced on lesson 40, the sounds /r/, /l/, and /m/ might be introduced before /d/, which is auditorily similar. Students have the most difficulty with pairs of letters that are both visually and auditorily similar: (*b*, *d*), (*m*, *n*), (*b*, *p*). These letters (plus *e* and *i*) should be separated by at least six other letters.

Table 7.1

Upper- and Lowercase Letters Grouped According to Visual Similarity

Dissimilar				Same					Moderate Similarity			
aA	eE	qQ	bB	cC	kK	oO	pP	sS	fF	mM	jJ	nN
rR	dD	gG	hH	uU	vV	wW	xX	zZ	tT	yY	lL	iI

Introduce More Useful Letters First

More useful letters are those that appear most often in words. Learning such letters early enables students to decode more words than learning less useful letters. For example, knowing the sounds for the letters *s, a, t,* and *i* will allow students to decode more words than knowing the sounds for *j, q, z,* and *x.*

Introduce Lowercase Letters First

Lowercase letters should be taught before uppercase letters since words in reading material are mostly composed of lowercase letters. A student knowing all lowercase letters would be able to decode all the words in the following sentence: "Sam had on his best hat." A student knowing only uppercase letters could read none of the words. An exception to this guideline can be made for lowercase and uppercase letters that look exactly the same, except of course for size (e.g., sS, cC). These lower- and uppercase letters may be introduced at the same time. Upper- and lowercase letters are classified according to their visual similarity in Table 7.1. This guideline is important when working with children who enter school with little knowledge of letters.

Introduce One Sound for a Letter

Introduce just one sound for a letter when first introducing a letter. Some letters represent more than one sound. For example, the letter *c* usually represents the /k/ sound as in *cat,* and sometimes the /s/ sound as in *face.* The sequence that we will present introduces the most common sound of each single letter.

The chart presented in Table 6.1 illustrates the most common sound for each of the 26 letters. The letters are grouped as continuous sounds or stop sounds. Note that for the vowels, we list the short sound as the most common sound.

Some reading programs will initially introduce the long sound of some vowels (/ē/ as in *me*) as the most common sound for the letter rather than the short sound (/ĕ/ as in *met*). This is perfectly acceptable as long as the program eventually introduces the short sound for *e* and follows the overall guidelines for sequencing the introduction of letter-sound correspondences.

A Sample Sequence.   Table 7.2 contains one possible order for introducing letters. We are not suggesting that this is the only or even the best sequence for

Table 7.2

An Acceptable Sequence for Introducing Letters

a m t s i f d r o g l h u c b n k v e w j p y T L M F D I N A R E H G B x q z J Q

introducing letters. It is just one sequence that derives from the guidelines specified here. Note the following about Table 7.2:

1. The letters that are visually and/or auditorily similar—*e, i; b, d; m, n;* and *b, p*—are separated by 13, 7, 13, and 6 letters, respectively. Other potentially confusing pairs (*d, t; f, v; h, n; k, g; v, w; n, r*) are also separated.

2. Uppercase letters that are not the same in appearance as their respective lowercase letters are introduced after most lowercase letters have been introduced. Upper- and lowercase letters that are identical are introduced at the same time and, thus, these uppercase letters are not listed on the chart.

3. More useful letters are introduced before less useful letters. The lowercase letters *j, y, x, q,* and *z* are introduced toward the end of the sequence. The first two letters, *a* and *m*, were chosen not only because they are more useful letters, but also because they are easy to pronounce. Starting with easy-to-pronounce letters makes initial sound tasks easier for instructionally naive students.

Rate and Practice

The rate at which new letters are introduced should be contingent on student performance. Teachers working with students who enter school with little knowledge of letter-sound correspondence will find an optimal rate (one which introduces new letters quickly while minimizing errors) for introducing new letters is about one each second or third day. This rate assumes that the teacher presents daily practice on letter-sound correspondences. Without adequate daily practice, an optimal rate is not possible. However, the rate of introduction should always be dependent on the students' performance.

When the first five letters are being taught, a new letter should not be introduced if the students are unable to correctly produce the sound for each of the previously introduced letters. Rather than presenting a new letter, the teacher should review previously taught letters for several days, concentrating on the unknown letters. After the first five letters have been introduced, a new letter can be introduced if the students are having difficulty with just one letter-sound correspondence; however, that letter should not be similar to the letter being introduced. For example, a new vowel (*e*) can be introduced even though students are having difficulty with *b* and *d*. However, the vowel *e* should not be introduced if the students are having difficulty with any previously introduced vowel since all vowel sounds are similar.

Teaching Letter-Sound Correspondence Through Explicit Instruction

The basic procedure for teaching letter-sound correspondences includes an introductory format and a discrimination format. In the introductory format, the teacher models saying the new sound while pointing to the letter and tests the students on their ability to say the new sound. In the discrimination format, the teacher tests the new letter-sound correspondence along with previously introduced letter-sound correspondences. The introductory format is used for the first two or three lessons when a new letter-sound correspondence appears. The discrimination format appears daily throughout the school year once the second letter-sound correspondence has been taught.

Introductory Format

In the introductory format, the teacher models by saying the sound, then tests by having the group say the sound. The teacher first has the students respond in unison on signal. Then, when the teacher thinks that the group can respond correctly, he or she tests students individually (see Table 7.3).

Table 7.3
Introductory Format for Letter-Sound Correspondences

Teacher	Students
1. (Teacher writes on the board: m.) "When I touch under the letter, you say the sound. Keep saying the sound as long as I touch it."	
2. (Teacher *models* the sound. Teacher holds her finger under the letter and says:) "My turn." (Teacher moves finger out and in, touching under the letter for 2 seconds if it is a continuous sound and for an instant if it is a stop sound. Teacher says the sound while touching under the letter, then quickly moves her finger away from the letter and immediately stops saying the sound.)	
3. (Teacher *tests* by having the group say the sound several times by themselves, and finally gives individual tests to all students. The purpose of the individual test is to enable the teacher to correct mispronunciations early.)	
a. (Teacher points under the letter and says:) "What sound?" (Signal.) (Teacher touches under letter for about 2 seconds.)	"mmmmmmm"
b. (Teacher repeats step *a* several times, touching under the sound from 1 to 3 seconds.)	
4. (Teacher tests the students individually.)	

Discrimination Format

In the letter-sounds discrimination format, the new letter-sound correspondences and previously introduced letter-sound correspondences are reviewed. Students receive the practice they need to quickly and accurately say the sound for different letters, a skill necessary for sounding out words. A new letter-sound correspondence is taught in the introductory format. If the students have no difficulty saying the sound, the letter can appear in the discrimination format.

To prepare to present the discrimination format in a lesson, the teacher writes the new letter several times on the board intermingled with previously introduced letters. The new letter is written several times to prevent the students from cueing on where the letter is written rather than on the shape of the letter. When presenting the exercise, the teacher follows an alternating pattern in which he or she gradually increases the number of other letters pointed to between each occurrence of the new letter. The format shown in Table 7.4 illustrates the use of the discrimination format shortly after the letter-sound correspondence for the letter *f* has been taught.

During the first month of reading instruction, the letter-sound-discrimination exercises should be presented twice in each lesson: once early in the lesson and once later in the lesson. The reason is simply to provide extra practice. Later in the program when students begin reading words, the word reading itself will be a form of practice for letter-sound correspondences and only one discrimination letter-sound correspondence task needs to be presented in a lesson.

As with the introductory-sound format, the teacher has the group respond in unison until it appears all students are responding correctly to all sounds. The teacher then gives individual turns.

It is important to note that the discrimination format directs the teacher to pause 2 seconds after pointing to a letter before signaling the students to respond. This pause is to allow the students time to think of their response. After the students know about 12 letter-sound correspondences, the teacher can present the letters twice, first going through all the letters with a 2-second pause, then going through the letters again with just a 1-second pause.

Critical Behaviors

Signaling.   The focus of the first lessons is teaching students to respond on signal. To follow the signal, students begin saying a sound as soon as the teacher touches under the letter and continue to respond as long as he or she touches it. Teaching students to say a sound continuously for several seconds is a very important preskill for sounding out words. When students initially sound out a word, students will say each sound for 1 to 2 seconds. During the time they are saying one sound, they simultaneously look ahead to the next letter. For example, while the students say the /m/ sound in *mad,* they look ahead to figure out the sound for the letter *a*. Students who cannot hold a sound for several seconds are likely to have difficulty sounding out words.

Table 7.4
Discrimination Format for Letter-Sound Correspondences

Teacher	Students
(Teacher writes on board several letters that have been previously taught, along with the new letter. Note that the new letter appears several times in different positions:)	

i

a f m	
s n f	
r f o	

1. (Teacher gives instructions.)
   "When I touch under a letter, you say the sound. Keep saying the sound as long as I touch under it."

2. (Teacher tests new sound. She or he points to the first letter, pauses 2 seconds says "What sound," then moves her or his finger out and in, touching under the letter for about 2 seconds if it is a continuous sound, and for an instant if it is a stop sound.) (Teacher immediately either corrects or points to the next letter.) — Students say the sound.

3. (Teacher tests on all letters. She or he points to a letter, pauses 2 seconds, says "What sound," then moves her or his finger out and in, touching under the letter.) — Students say the sound.
   (The teacher follows an alternating pattern in which she or he gradually increases the retention interval for the newly introduced letter by pointing to more review letters before returning to the new letter. For example, if the new letter is *f,* the teacher points to the letters in this order:)
   f   a   f   r   m   f   s   i   o   f   n   i   r   o   f

4. (Teacher gives individual tests. Every day the teacher should test several students on all vowels introduced up to that time and test individual students on any sounds that have caused difficulty for them in the past week.)

The signaling procedure begins with the teacher pointing to a letter and giving students think time to remember its sound. The teacher points under the letter (not touching the board), making certain that the teacher's hand or body is not blocking the student's view of the sound. After providing about 2 seconds of think time, the teacher signals for the students to respond by moving his or her finger away from and back toward the letter. This out-and-in motion is done crisply with the finger moving away from the board (about 3 inches) and then immediately back to the board (see Figure 7.1). When the finger touches the board below the letter, the students are to respond. The out-and-in motion is

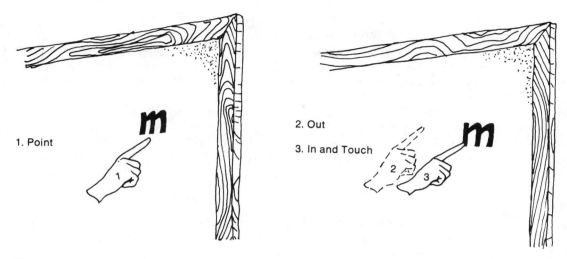

Figure 7.1
Point, Out-In, and Touch Signal

done the same way every time it is used. Any hesitation or inconsistency makes a unison response difficult because the students cannot tell when they are supposed to answer. The teacher signals the students to stop responding by moving his or her finger away from the board in a rapid, distinct movement.

A modified signaling procedure is used for the stop sounds (/b/, /c/, /d/, /g/, /h/, /j/, /k/, /p/, /q/, /t/, and /x/). Since these sounds can be pronounced for only an instant, the teacher signals by touching the board below the letter for only an instant.

Modeling.   Continuous consonant sounds should be said without any distortion. The letter *m* is said "mmmm," not "uummm" or "mmmmmuuu." Stop sounds should be pronounced without the "uh" sound being added. For example, the letter *d* should not be pronounced "duh." Vowel sounds must also be pronounced accurately. Some teachers have a tendency to distort vowel sounds. They start out with a distorted sound and then change it into the correct sound (e.g., pronouncing *i* as "uuiii") or start with the correct sound and then distort it (e.g., pronouncing *i* as "iiieee"). Care should be taken to avoid distorting sounds.

Pacing.   Brisk pacing is not only an important method for maintaining student attention, but it also affects academic performance. Pacing should be fast enough to keep the students attending, but not so fast they do not have time to recall the answer and therefore begin to guess and make errors. A basic pacing rule in presenting the letter-sound correspondence discrimination format is for the teacher to provide a "thinking pause" between pointing to a letter and before giving the signal for the students' response. Then, after the students respond, the teacher should quickly move to the next letter. The thinking pause gives all students enough time to come up with a response. A longer thinking pause may be given for sounds that have caused the students difficulty in previous lessons. However, the teacher should provide extra practice on the letter so that, by the end of the discrimination format, the students can respond with only a 2-second pause.

The extra think time for difficult letters is illustrated in the following text. Let's say that the teacher is presenting a letter-sound correspondence task with the letters *m, s,* and *d,* and the students had trouble with the letter *d* on the previous lesson. Note how the teacher gives more thinking time for the letter *d.*

- Teacher points to *m,* pauses 2 seconds, then signals.
- Immediately after students respond, teacher points to *s.*
- Teacher pauses 2 seconds, then signals.
- Immediately after students respond, teacher points to *d,* and says, "Remember this tough sound," then pauses 4 seconds before signaling.
- Teacher repeats above steps, but gives only a 2-second pause when presenting *d* again.

Another critical aspect of pacing is immediately moving to the next letter after the students make a correct response. Note from the previous scenario that immediately after the students make the response for the letter *m,* the teacher moves to the next letter *s,* then gives the students time to think. The rapid movement after students respond is a big help in keeping students attentive.

Developing Automaticity.   The goal of the letter-sound correspondence formats is not only to enable students to produce the sound associated with the letter, but also to enable them to make the response with relative ease.

In the discrimination format, we recommended that teachers use a 2-second thinking pause before signaling. Teachers working with instructionally naive students may find the students need a great deal of practice to be able to respond with this pause. To keep the students' frustration level low, the teacher can start the discrimination format with a 3-second thinking pause before each signal. When the students can respond correctly to all the letters with no more than a 3-second pause, the teacher challenges the students by saying, "You did a great job. I'll go faster this time."

As the school year progresses, the thinking pause should be gradually reduced; so by the end of the beginning stage, the students can respond with no more than a 1-second thinking pause before each letter.

Extra practice sessions of about 2–3 minutes each can be presented several times during the school day to provide needed extra practice.

Monitoring.   Monitoring student performance during group responding is done by listening to the students' responses and watching their mouths and eyes. Since the teacher cannot watch every student on every response, he or she watches only a few students at a time. He or she continually scans the group, focusing on one or two students for one response and then shifting attention to other students for the next response. The teacher looks at a student's eyes and mouth. If a student's eyes are not directed toward the letters, the student is probably not paying attention. Looking at the student's mouth can help the teacher determine whether the student is responding correctly. To produce a sound, a student's lips and tongue must be in a certain position. For example, when a student makes the /l/ sound, his or her mouth should be open with the front edge of the tongue touching the upper palate. If the student's mouth or tongue is not in this position, he or she is probably not pronouncing the sound correctly. For some sounds—(c, g), (d, t), (f, v), (p, b), (s, z), and all short vowel sounds—the teacher cannot rely on looking at the student's mouth because the lips and tongue are placed in similar positions for more than one sound. Consequently, the teacher must listen very closely to these sounds.

The basic teaching rule is to present an exercise with unison responding until the teacher feels that all students can produce the correct sounds. Even when the teacher listens and watches carefully to unison student responses, he or she cannot be certain that all students are responding correctly. Individual turns at the end of a format help the teacher be certain that students can respond correctly.

In the introductory format, teachers give individual turns to every student to ensure that the students are saying the new sound correctly. The faster the teacher spots a mispronunciation error, the easier it will be for the teacher to correct the error. In the discrimination format, teachers test several students each day individually on the new letter, all the vowels introduced up to that time, plus any troublesome consonants.

Teachers should individually test all students weekly or biweekly on all letters introduced to date in order to determine if students can produce the sounds for all letters with no more than a 2-second pause. During this test, which is not to be presented during group instruction, the teacher should let students respond at their own rates. Teachers should record not only the letters for which the students are unable to say the correct sound, but also the letters for which the students *can* say the correct sound, yet take more than 2 seconds to produce the sound. More practice on these letter-sound correspondences is needed. The teacher would test individually any student who makes errors during group teaching more often.

Correcting Mistakes.   Three types of student errors may occur: a confusion error (saying the sound for a different letter), a pronunciation error (saying a sound in a distorted manner), and a signal error (not beginning the response when the signal is given). The basic correction for all the errors includes these four steps:

1. Modeling the correct answer.
2. Leading, if necessary.

3. Testing the group on the missed letter, then alternating between the missed letter and other letters in the format.

4. Retesting, later in the lesson, individual students who made an error.

Confusion Errors.   In a confusion error, a student might say the sound *m* for the letter *n*. The teacher would do the following:

1. Model the correct sound "Listen: Mmm."

2. Test the students on the missed letter, then alternate between it and other previously identified letters that have been correctly identified. If the student said a sound represented by another letter, the teacher does not include this letter in the firm up. If the student said *n* for the letter *m*, the letter *n* would not appear in the firm up for *m*. The teacher gradually increases the number of review letters that are included. The teacher continues to alternate between the missed letter and familiar letters until the students identify the missed letter correctly after at least three other letters are tested just prior to the missed letter. The examples might look like this: first a test on *m*, then an alternating pattern of *a, m, s, i, m, r, f, g, m.*

3. Retest students later in the lesson who have made errors on *m*. The teacher retests by pointing to *m* and asking, "What sound?" If the student says the wrong sound, the teacher should follow the procedure in steps 1 and 2.

Keep in mind that the sooner confusion errors are spotted, the easier it will be to correct them. Older students who have been confused on a pair of letters for years will take much more time to remedy than younger students.

If a student is having chronic problems with a pair of letters (e.g., *b* and *d*), the teacher might work on one letter of the pair and exclude the other letter from the practice sets. When the students are able to correctly identify the letter being presented for three consecutive days, the teacher can reintroduce the other letter of the pair.

Pronunciation Errors.   Pronunciation errors can be as serious as confusion errors, especially if made on vowel sounds. The more distorted the pronunciation of a sound, the greater the students' difficulty will be in discriminating it from similar sounds appearing in later lessons. For example, if a student distorts the /ĭ/ sound so that it is very similar to the /ĕ/ sound, the student will have difficulty when the /ĕ/ sound is introduced and may confuse i and e in word reading, saying "led" for *lid.*

The correction for a mispronunciation error is similar to that for a confusion error. When a student mispronounces a sound, the teacher does the following:

1. Models, saying the correct response. "Listen: Mmmmm."

2. Leads, saying the correct response with the students, while leading the teacher checks to see whether the lips and tongue of the student

who made the mistake are positioned properly. If the position is incorrect, the teacher models again saying, "Watch my mouth when I say the sound." The teacher says the sound and watches the student's eyes to make certain the student is attending. Next, the teacher leads by having the students say the sound with him or her while watching the student's mouth. Leading is used most often when students mispronounce a sound. "Listen: Mmmm. Say it." "Mmmm." (Teacher responds with students.) "Listen again: Mmmm. Say it." "Mmmm." (Teacher responds with students. Teacher responds with student until student makes two consecutive correct responses.)

3. Tests, alternating between the missed letter and other letters, using the same pattern as for confusion errors. Teacher points to each letter and asks, "What sound?"

4. Retests later in the lesson.

The main difference in the correction procedure for pronunciation errors and the correction procedure for confusion errors is in the lead step. In the lead step, the teacher says the sound, then has the students say the sound with him or her. The teacher directs the students to watch his or her mouth as the teacher says the sound. Watching the teacher's lips and tongue as the teacher says the sound will help the students in placing their lips and tongues in the correct position to say the sound. The teacher may have to present 5 to 15 repetitions before the students make an acceptable response. As noted in the previous correction scenario, before each student response, the teacher models saying the sound, then has the students say the sound with him or her.

The teacher should set a reasonable goal for the lead step. If the student does not have any speech problems, the goal is to have the student say the sound perfectly. If the student has a lisp or other speech problem, the teacher should set a reasonable approximation of the sound as a goal. The teacher should continue the lead step until the student can make two consecutive acceptable responses. Quite often a student who has an initial difficulty saying a sound will make an acceptable response, but on the next trial will make an unacceptable response. Providing extra practice for students to make two consecutive acceptable responses will result in steady improvement over a period of days. A student may need 15 repetitions before he or she is able to make two consecutive acceptable responses the first day, then only 10 responses the next day, and fewer each following day. Providing practice to help students say sounds correctly is very challenging for the teacher. The teacher must decide what student response will be the goal for each session. The teacher must be careful not to set up unreasonable goals. The outcome of instruction is not only for students to produce the desired response but also to see themselves as capable persons. During instruction the teacher should be very encouraging. After several student responses, the teacher should encourage the students and praise them for their effort: "You kids are working hard. This is a tough sound." When a student finally makes two consecutive acceptable responses, the teacher should act very excited and praise the student profusely: "That's great! You did it. I knew you would be able to do it. You didn't give up and you got it right. Great, great, great!"

Teachers working with students who have poor enunciation should provide extra practice in imitating sounds. The teacher can do a daily exercise in which students simply imitate sounds the teacher says. In the exercise, the teacher says a sound for several seconds, then has the student say it for several seconds. "I'll say a sound, then you say it with me. Listen, aaaaaaaa. Get ready." (Signal.) The teacher introduces a sound in imitating exercises a week or so before it appears in the phonemic awareness blending and segmenting exercises and letter-sound correspondence exercises.

Signal Errors. In a signal error, students do not begin and/or end their responses when the teacher signals. The correction procedure is to praise a student who followed the signal, model, lead, and test. "Emily, good saying the sound when I touched the board. Everybody, watch me follow the signal. . . . Follow the signal with me. What sound?.. By yourselves. What sound?.."

Teachers should expect some students to need many signal corrections the first several days of isolated sounds instruction. To make learning to follow signals easier during the first few days of instruction, the teacher can exaggerate each part of the signal. After pointing to the letter, the teacher exaggerates the "out" portion of the signal by moving his or her hand 6 inches from the board, rather than just 3 inches. The teacher can also emphasize when to begin responding by hitting the board to create a "thud," which tells the students to respond. To exaggerate the end of the signal, the teacher moves his or her hand 6 inches in a quick motion away from the board.

A second prompt a teacher can use to train students to follow signals involves varying the interval for holding a sound. Each time the teacher signals the students to respond, the teacher touches under the letter for a different amount of time. For example, the teacher might touch under the letter for 3 seconds the first time, then 1 second, and finally 2 seconds. The purpose is to show the students that they should hold the sound as long as the teacher points to the letter and not for some fixed interval.

During the first few days of sounds instruction, teachers should be effusive with their praise for students learning to follow the signals. Nearly all students can learn to follow sound signals in one or two days if they are motivated. The teacher can make the exercise into a game. The teacher can challenge the students with a statement such as, "I'm going to try to trick you. It's really hard to watch my finger and say the sound just when I'm touching the letter." This game format is usually very motivating for students.

After the first week of instruction, the teacher should be careful in responding to signal errors. If a student is making frequent signal errors, the teacher should test that student individually and work with that child at a different time, so as not to take too much group time.

Selecting Examples.   The introductory sounds format includes just the letter being introduced. A new letter appears for two or three consecutive lessons. The discrimination format includes six to eight letters. For the first week or two, selecting examples is easy; all previously introduced sounds are included in the format. After the students know more than eight letters, the teacher must select which letters to include. Including all the letters introduced so far can make the format too time-consuming. The following guidelines can be used to select letters for the discrimination format:

1. a. As a general rule, include the new letter in the discrimination format on the second day the letter appears in the introductory format.

   b. If the new letter being introduced is visually and auditorily similar to a previously introduced letter, do not include the similar previously introduced letter in the discrimination format on the lessons in which the new letter appears in the introductory format. Thereafter include the similar letter every day for the next 2 weeks.

2. Once a new letter is introduced in the discrimination format, it should appear daily for about 2 weeks.

3. Put extra emphasis on vowels. Include all vowels introduced to date in almost every lesson.

The chart in Table 7.5 demonstrates the integration of example-selection criterion into daily lesson construction. The chart shows the examples that might be included in the introductory and discrimination formats during the time in which the letter *b* is introduced. Note that on days 1, 2, and 3, the letter *d* does not appear in the discrimination format since *b* is appearing in the introductory format. On day 4, the letter *d* appears along with the letter *b*. The teacher concentrates on providing discrimination practice on *b* and *d*, as well as reviewing other earlier-introduced letters. Note also the extra review on vowel letters, as well as the consonants *c, l,* and *h* that were recently introduced.

Table 7.5

Sample 4-Day Example-Selection Sequence for Letter-Sound Correspondence Tasks

Day	1	2	3	4
Introductory Format	b	b	b	
Discrimination Format	cuh	hoi	bui	ucb
	log	bul	hat	odi
	ia	cr	cl	tf

Using Commercial Materials

Many commercial reading programs will introduce letter-sound correspondences in a manner that is likely to be problematic for the struggling reader and at-risk child who enters kindergarten or first grade with little literacy-related knowledge. Below are common problems.

Too much information introduced at once. Some reading programs will introduce capital letters and lowercase letters simultaneously. Some reading programs will introduce letter names and letter sounds simultaneously. Some reading programs will introduce upper-and lowercase letters and letter names simultaneously with introducing the letter-sound correspondence. Some reading programs will introduce more than one sound for a letter. For a child who comes into school with a good deal of knowledge of letters and sounds, such situations might not be problematic because in fact the child already knows much of what is being presented. For the child who does not have any knowledge of letters and sounds, too much information at once generally leads to confusion as the child is overwhelmed with information.

Sequence that is potentially confusing. Some reading programs sequence the introduction of letters without consideration to the similarity of similar sounds or appearance. For example, one program introduced the letters in alphabetical order. This sequence resulted in the letters *b* and *d, m* and *n,* and *e* and *i* being introduced in close proximity.

Too rapid an introduction. Some reading programs introduce new letter-sound correspondences at a faster rate than is realistic for the child who enters school with little literacy-related information. In one program, a new letter-sound correspondence was introduced each day.

Potentially confusing teacher presentations. Some reading programs present letter-sound correspondences in a manner that incorporates language that at-risk students may not understand and/or that does not provide students with clear models of how to say the sound. For example, a reading program may refer the students to a card showing a picture that represents the sound for the particular letter. Equating the sound with an object can result in the students saying a sound that is distorted. Let's say that the card for the letter *r* shows a rooster. The child would likely distort the sound, saying "rrrooo" instead of "rrrr."

Too little practice. Some reading programs do not provide daily practice with letter-sound correspondences. A letter-sound correspondence may appear for several lessons and then not be reviewed for a number of days.

Solutions to Problems

The easiest problems to solve are problems of potentially confusing teacher presentations and too little review. The teacher can simply use the formats presented in this chapter and construct exercises to be presented daily. Preparing these exercises will take only several minutes a day.

The problems of too much information introduced at one time can be more difficult to solve. If letter names and capital letters are introduced simultaneously with lowercase letters, the teacher can simply focus on letter sounds and lowercase letters. If, however, uppercase letters and use of letter names are incorporated into other exercises, teachers will need to be sure to prompt students on information that has not been taught.

A program with a poor sequence for introducing letter-sound correspondences is most problematic. If letter-sound correspondences are introduced in a sequence that is potentially confusing, the teacher will have to make many changes throughout the program, delaying the introduction of some correspondences and making many adjustments in other exercises.

Application to Your Curriculum (Level K and 1 only)

Evaluate Teaching of Letter-Sound Correspondences in Your Core Reading Program

1. List the letter-sound correspondences in the order of introduction into the program. List the lesson day or number next to each. Indicate the sound(s) taught for each letter.
2. Select one letter-sound correspondence. Indicate the lesson on which it is introduced. Indicate how often this letter is presented over the next 10 lessons.
3. Are students initially introduced to one sound for each letter or multiple sounds?
4. Are the vowels introduced as short, long, both, or multiple sounds?
5. How often is a new letter-sound correspondence introduced? Is this consistent with the 2- to 3-day guideline?
6. Describe the teaching procedure for introducing letter-sound correspondences. How explicit are these presentations? How clear are these presentations?
7. Do the students respond frequently so that the teacher can get information to determine if students can pronounce the correct sound for a letter?
8. What corrections are specified for student errors?
9. Are letter-sound correspondences practiced daily?
10. What modifications would you make based on your answers to the previous questions?

At a Glance   Teaching Letter-Sound Correspondence

Materials	• Sounds written out—on overhead, whiteboard, or flashcards.
What to Do	• Introduce new letter-sound correspondence with a teacher model: "This sound is mmm. What sound?" Hold continuous sounds 1 1/2 to 2 seconds, and stop sounds for an instant.
	• Provide discrimination practice with other previously taught sounds—with the new sound appearing several times. Practice until students can respond correctly to all the sounds.
	• Give individual turns to several students.
Correcting Mistakes	• Immediately model the correct sound—don't let students guess.
	• Test students on the missed sound, then alternate with other sounds they've correctly identified in the format. This alternating pattern is very effective for firming missed sounds.
Rate and Practice	• Teach only one new sound at a time.
	• Introduce new sounds every 2 to 3 days if sounds are firm.
	• Present letter-sound correspondence exercises with six to eight sounds at a time several times during your reading lesson.
Selecting Examples	• Begin with the most common sounds.
	• Separate letters that are visually and/or auditorily similar.
	• Introduce more useful letters before less useful letters.
	• Introduce lowercase letters before uppercase letters.
	• Give extra practice on new sounds and vowel letters.
Strategic Integration	After students can identify a new sound in a discrimination format for 2 days, the sound can then appear in sounding-out exercises.
One Possible Sequence	*a, m, t, s, i, f, d, r, o, g, l, h, u, c, b, n, k, v, e, w, j, p, y, x, q, z*

CHAPTER 8

Letter-Sound Correspondence— Primary Stage

During the beginning stage, the focus of phonics instruction is on words in which each letter represents one sound. During the primary stage, the focus is on combinations of letters. Some of these combinations can be taught in isolation prior to being introduced in words.

Letter Combinations

Table 6.4 lists the letter combinations that we suggest presenting. We recommend presenting a sound for a letter combination if it represents that sound in over half the words in which the letter combination appears and if the letter combination appears in five or more common words.

Sequence

Two factors should determine the order in which letter combinations are introduced in a reading program. The first is the number of common words in which the letter combination appears. When planning a sequence for introducing letter combinations, the number of words containing the letter combination should not only be considered in terms of total occurrence, but also in terms of how many words are common in primary grade literature. For example, although the digraph *ph* appears in a large number of words, many of these words are fairly uncommon words (words that would not appear in primary grade books).

Consequently, *ph* would not be introduced as early as indicated by its frequency of occurrence. However, the letter combination *ol* appears in relatively few words, yet the words are very common (*hold, told, cold*). Thus, *ol* would be introduced relatively early.

The second sequencing consideration is the similarity of letter combinations. If letter combinations make similar (but not identical) sounds, they should be separated by at least three other combinations. Letter combinations to be separated include:

1. *sh* and *ch*. These consonant digraphs are both made by forming the lips in a very similar manner. This factor, along with their similar sound and appearance (both contain the letter *h*), can cause confusion.

2. *oa, oi, oo,* and *ou:* In addition to the fact that these letter combinations sound somewhat similar, they are part of a bigger group of letter combinations that begin with *o* (*oa, oi, ol, oo, ou, ow,* and *oy*). The large number of combinations beginning with the same letter and having similar, but different, sounds can confuse students.

3. *r*-controlled vowels. The three sounds produced by *r*-controlled vowels (/ ar / as in *arm;* / er / as in *fur, bird, her;* and / or / as in *sport*) all sound similar.

Letter combinations representing the same sound (*ee* and *ea, ai* and *ay, ir* and *ur, oi* and *oy, au* and *aw*) need not be separated. Only letter combinations that represent similar, but different, sounds should be separated.

Table 8.1 shows a sample order for introducing letter combinations. Keep in mind that the order suggested is not meant to represent the only order for introducing letter combinations. It is only an example of how the sequencing guidelines can be applied.

Here is the rationale for determining the placement of specific letter combination, in Table 8.1.

1. *Th, wh,* and *ol* are introduced early because they appear in very common, high-frequency words (e.g., *this, that, when, where,* and *sold*).

2. -*Er* and -*ing* are introduced early because, in addition to serving as letter combinations, they also function as affixes (e.g., *cutter, cutting*).

3. *Sh* and *ch* are separated by nine other combinations because, if introduced too near each other, they might be confused by some students.

Table 8.1

Sample Order for Introducing Letter Combinations

1. th	**10.** ea	**19.** ir
2. er	**11.** oo	**20.** ur
3. ing	**12.** ee	**21.** kn
4. sh	**13.** ai	**22.** oi
5. wh	**14.** ch	**23.** oy
6. qu	**15.** or	**24.** ph
7. ol	**16.** ay	**25.** wr
8. oa	**17.** igh	**26.** au
9. ar	**18.** ou	**27.** aw

Table 8.2

Isolated Sounds for Letter Combinations (This Format Introduces the Letter Combination *ea*)

Teacher	Students
Teacher writes on the board: *ea, or, ee, ea, th, sh, ea,* and *ing.*	
1. Teacher models by saying the sound of the new letter combination and tests by having the students pronounce it. Teacher points to *ea.* "These letters usually say /ē/. What sound?" (Signal.)	"ē"
2. Teacher alternates between the new combination and other combinations. Teacher points to a letter combination, pauses 2 seconds, says "What sound?" and signals with an out-in motion.	Say the most common sound.
3. Teacher presents the remaining letter combinations using an alternating pattern similar to this: *ea, or, ea, ee, th, ea, sh, ing, or, ea.*	
4. Teacher calls on several individual students to identify one or more letter combinations.	

Rate of Introduction

Learning to decode words containing a new letter combination is more difficult than simply learning the sound of a letter combination in isolation. When reading a word that contains a letter combination, the student can no longer decode by looking at the word letter by letter, but must see the word as being composed of one or more combinations of letters. For example, to decode the word *sheet,* the student must see that *sh* and *eet* are units within the word. This transition, from decoding letter by letter to decoding words as units, requires extensive practice. The students' performance in decoding words containing previously taught letter combinations determines when to introduce a new letter combination, rather than their ability to identify a letter combination in isolated sound tasks.

As a general rule, students should be able to read a list of words containing previously learned letter combinations introduced to that date with no errors on the first trial at a rate no slower than every 2 seconds with 95% accuracy before a new letter combination is introduced. There are exceptions to this rule. If a student has developed confusion between two letter combinations, the teacher (while working on alleviating the confusion) might introduce another letter combination. The new letter combination should not be similar to the ones with which the student is having difficulty. For example, if a student is having difficulty with the combinations *oo* and *ou,* the teacher might introduce the combination *ir,* which is not similar to either of the pair the student has confused. If, however, a student is having difficulty with more than one pair of previously introduced combinations, the teacher should work on firming up the student's knowledge of these combinations before introducing a new one. In a developmental program being taught to average-ability students, nearly all letter combinations can be introduced by the end of the second year of reading instruction. This translates into a new letter combination being introduced about every 5 to 10 days.

Teaching Letter Combinations Through Explicit Instruction

The letter-combination sounds format (see Table 8.2) is similar to the formats used to teach the most common sounds of individual letters. The teacher writes the new letter combination, along with several previously introduced letter combinations, on the board. The teacher models the sound of the new letter combination and tests the students on saying the sound. The teacher then alternates between the new letter combination and previously introduced letter combinations.

Critical Behaviors

Signals and pacing.   The teacher uses the same signaling procedures and alternating procedure discussed previously. The teacher points to a letter combination, pauses to let the student recall the sound, then signals with an out-in motion. The pacing should be rapid from letter to letter. When the students respond correctly to a signal, the teacher quickly moves to another sound, allows the students time to recall the sound, and then signals.

Correcting mistakes.   If a student misidentifies a letter combination or responds late, the teacher tells the student the correct sound, has the student say the sound, and then alternates between the missed letter combination and other letter combinations the student knows. Extra practice should be provided on that combination in the next lessons.

Selecting examples.   The format should include six to eight letter combinations. The following are guidelines for selecting examples:

1. Review the most recently introduced letter combinations daily until students correctly produce the correct sound for the letter combination on the first trial for three consecutive lessons.

2. Exclude previously taught, similar letter combinations the first day a new letter combination appears. On the second day after the new combination appears, include any previously introduced letter combinations similar to the newly introduced combination. For example, on the second day *ch* is introduced, the combination *sh* should be included because it sounds similar. Similarly, on the second day after

the letter combination *or* is introduced, the letter combination *ar* should be included. Do not, however, include a similar letter combination unless it has been taught earlier.

Application to Your Curriculum

Evaluate Teaching of Letter Combination in Your Core Reading Program

1. List the letter combinations in the order of introduction into the program. List the lesson day or number next to each. Indicate the sound(s) taught for each letter.
2. Select one letter combination. Indicate the lesson on which it is introduced. Indicate how often this letter is presented over the next 10 lessons.
3. Are students initially introduced to one sound for each letter combination or multiple sounds? Is the order potentially problematic?
4. How often is a new letter combination introduced? Is this rate potentially problematic?
5. Describe the teaching procedure for introducing combinations. How explicit are these presentations? How clear are these presentations?
6. Do the students respond frequently so that the teacher can get information to determine if students can pronounce the correct sound for a letter combination?
7. What corrections are specified for student errors?
8. Are letter-combination correspondences practiced daily?
9. What modifications would you make based on your answers to the previous questions?

At a Glance   Teaching Common Letter Combinations

Materials	Write new combination and five to seven review combinations on a whiteboard, overhead, or on flashcards (*ea, or, ee, ea, th, sh, ol, ea,*).
What to Do	• Teacher models by saying sound of the new combination and has students say it. Teacher points to *ea*. "These letters usually say the sound /ē/. What sound?"
	• Teacher alternates between new combination and other combinations and asks, "What sound?"
	• Give individual turns to several students.
Correcting Mistakes	• Teacher tells students the correct sound, then has students repeat. "These letters say 'sh.' What sound?"
	• Go back to a combination previously identified correctly, then back to the missed combination. Use alternating pattern until firm.
Rate and Practice	• Present a new combination every 5 to 10 days.
	• Present for 2 to 3 minutes with six to eight letter combinations at a time prior to word-reading and text-reading exercises.
Selecting Examples	• Begin with high-frequency letter combinations in primary reading (*ol, th, sh,* etc.)
	• Separate similar sounding letter combinations (*sh, ch oa, oi, oo, ou / ar, or, ir*).
	• Letter combinations that sound the same need not be separated (*ai, ay / ir, er, ur*).
Strategic Integration	After students can identify a new sound combination in a discrimination format for 2 days, the sound combination can then appear in word-reading exercises.
One Possible Sequence	*th, er, ing, sh, wh, qu, ol, oa, ar, ea, oo, ee, ai, ch, or, ay, igh, ou, ir, ur, kn, oi, oy, ph, wr, au, aw.*

CHAPTER 9

Word Reading—Beginning Stage

This chapter presents information on how to teach the initial steps in word reading and includes (a) teaching sounding out regular words, (b) making the transition from sounding out to sight-reading, and (c) introducing irregular words.

The procedures in this section may prove very helpful to teachers working with struggling readers and at-risk students in kindergarten and first grade, as well as older students who are nonreaders. Many commercial reading programs do not provide children with clear explicit teaching of how to read regular words during the beginning stage, as they assume that students will be able to internalize a sounding-out strategy with relatively little teaching. The reality is that many struggling readers and at-risk children need highly explicit and systematic instruction that begins with sounding out words orally and gradually transitions to a stage where students can recognize words without sounding them out orally. Hopefully, this section will provide teachers with useful information for making the first steps in reading a more successful experience for their struggling readers and at-risk students.

Teaching Sounding Out Regular Words Through Explicit Instruction

Regular words are words in which each letter represents its most common sound. For example, the word *sat* is regular because the letters, *s, a,* and *t,* each represents its most common sound.

Regular word-reading instruction can begin when students have mastered four to six letter-sound correspondences and the auditory skills of segmenting and blending the easiest word types to decode (i.e., CVC words beginning with continuous sounds).

Sounding out instruction for regular words begins with word-list exercises in which students are taught to sound out regular VC and CVC words that begin with continuous sounds. The teacher prompts the students to read a word by pointing to the letters in the word. As the teacher points to the letters, the children say and blend the sounds in the word. After blending the sounds, the children say the word at a normal rate. Word lists are the vehicles the teacher uses to initially teach and provide practice on sounding out regular words.

Guidelines for Constructing Word Lists

■ The initial word-list exercises (first week) should include only two to four words since in these initial exercises the students will be learning the mechanics of sounding out and are likely to need a good deal of repetition before they can follow the teacher's signal and sound out words correctly.

■ The number of words in word lists should increase gradually. The number can be determined by the students' performance. A general rule is to include the number of words the student can be brought to mastery on within a 5 to 7-minute period. Mastery is reached when the students are able to respond consecutively to all the words in a list without making an error.

■ Words should include only letters students have mastered in letter-sound correspondence tasks. Mastery is demonstrated when a student does not make an error on a particular sound for two consecutive lessons.

■ When a new letter first appears in word-list exercises, that letter should appear in about one-third to one-half of the words in the list.

■ Word lists should be constructed in an unpredictable manner. Generally the same letter should not appear in the same position for more than two words in a row. For example, a list such as *sit, mat, rut, fat* would be inappropriate since the same letter, *t,* appears in the same final position in all the words. The problem with lists such as this is that such predictability may inadvertently encourage student nonattentiveness as the students anticipate rather than examine letters.

The chart in Figure 9.1 illustrates the integration of these word-list construction guidelines into daily lessons. The chart shows instances presented in the letter-sound format and the word-list sounding-out format over a four-lesson

Lesson	31	32	33	34
Letter-Sound Intro	u	u		c
Letter-Sound Disc	h l g a i r d f	u a i g h l t	u i r d h l a o	c r o u l h t d
	fill	ran	lot	rug
	if	fill	mad	in
Word-List Sounding Out	lot	it	lid	lad
	lad	lit	if	mud
	am	mom	Sam	mat

Figure 9.1
Integration of Example-Selection Guidelines, into Daily Lessons

period during the sixth week of instruction. The students already know about 15 letter-sound correspondences and have been sounding out words for about 3 weeks. The letter *u* is introduced in the introductory format for letter-sound correspondences in lesson 31. Previously introduced letters are reviewed in the letter-sound discrimination format. The words in the word-list exercise in lesson 31 include only previously mastered letters. Note that the letter *l* appears in three words; it was recently introduced and receives more practice. Note also that the letter *u* does not appear in word-list exercises until lesson 34. There is a 3-day period for the students to practice the letter-sound correspondence for *u* before reading words with these letters. Remember that student performance dictates when new skills are introduced. If the students are having difficulty with *u* in the letter-sound correspondence format, words with *u* should not be presented. A final note concerns the word *fill.* Even though *fill* is technically a CVCC word, it is included as an easier word type since it includes only three sounds.

Teaching Procedure for Sounding Out Words in Lists

Introductory Format.   The format for introducing sounding out appears in Table 9.1. The teacher introduces sounding out by demonstrating (modeling) how to sound

Table 9.1

Introductory Format for Sounding Out Words in Lists (Illustrated with the CVC Word Type)

Teacher	Students
(Teacher writes on board: *am, fit.*)	
1. Teacher states instructions. I'm going to sound out this word. When I touch a letter, I'll say its sound. I'll keep saying the sound until I touch the next letter. I won't stop between sounds."	
2. Teacher *models* sounding out the first word. "My turn to sound out this word. Get ready." Teacher touches under each letter that represents a continuous sound 1 to 1 1/2 seconds and under letters that represent stop sounds for only an instant. "Aaaammm."	
3. Teacher *leads* students in sounding out the word. Teacher points to left of word. "Sound out this word with me. Get ready." (Signal.) Teacher touches under letters. The teacher sounds out the word with students until they respond correctly.	"Aaaammm."
4. Teacher *tests* the students on the word. Teacher points to left of word. "Your turn. Sound out this word by yourselves. Get ready." (Signal.) Teacher touches under letters.	"Aaaammm."
5. Teacher has several students sound out the word individually. Alberto, sound it out. Get ready." (Signal.)	"Aaaammm."
6. Teacher repeats steps 2 through 5 with the word *fit.*	

out a word. The teacher points to each letter for about 1 1/2 seconds and says the sounds for the respective letters, not pausing between the sounds. Note the similarity between this task and the auditory segmenting skills tasks. The students have learned in the auditory skills task to pronounce a series of sounds without pausing between each sound, and to follow a teacher's signal indicating when to switch from sound to sound. In the sounding-out task, the students say the sounds when the teacher points to the letters. After the teacher models sounding out a word, the teacher has the students respond with him or her (lead). The purpose of responding with the students is to ensure that they hear the correct response. People who have not worked with young students usually do not realize how difficult sounding out is for them. To read a word, the student says the first sound. Then, while saying the first sound, the student must examine the next letter to determine its sound. The student then says the next sound without distorting either sound. This is a difficult coordination task for young students. The teacher responds with the students since it is predictable that they will make errors at first. The teacher repeats responding with the students until they appear able to respond correctly without prompting. Then the students respond without any leading (test).

The introductory format is presented daily until the students are able to sound out the words correctly in the format with no more than two practice trials for each word.

Critical Behaviors

Signaling.   An illustrated explanation of the signaling procedure for sounding out appears in Figure 9.2.

Monitoring.   The teacher monitors by watching the students' eyes and mouths and by listening to their responses. Coordinating signaling and monitoring is difficult. The teacher should quickly glance at the letters to determine where to point next, and then look at the students before pointing to the next letter. All these movements are done in an instant. The key is to watch the students' mouths when they say a new sound, since the position of their mouths provides feedback about the correctness of their responses and also informs the teacher whether students are responding.

Pacing.   The teacher should point to each letter long enough for the students to say its sound and look ahead to the next letter. This will be between 1 and 1 1/2 seconds for each continuous sound. Not pointing to a sound for a long enough time is probably the most common mistake teachers make in early sounding-out teaching. The importance of allowing adequate time cannot be overstated.

Students may have to sound out a word several times before they can blend the sounds in the word without error. The pacing of these repetitions is important. For each repetition, the teacher points to the left of the word, pauses about 2 seconds, then says, "Again, get ready," then begins the signal. Shorter pauses before beginning signaling may not give the students time to focus on the beginning of the word.

1. Instructions: Teacher points about an inch to the left of the first letter in the word. "Get ready."

2. The signal for the first sound: Teacher looks at the students to see if they are attending, then quickly touches under the *m*. Teacher holds finger under *m* for about 1 to 1½ seconds.

3. The signal for the second sound: Teacher *quickly* makes a loop, moving his finger from the first letter to the second letter, *a*, and holds his finger under *a* for about 1 to 1½ seconds.

4. The signal for the third sound: Teacher loops *quickly* from *a* to *d* and instantly removes his finger from the page. When signaling for the students to say a stop sound, the teacher touches under the letter for an instant and then moves his hand quickly away from the letter.

Figure 9.2
Signaling Procedure

The teacher can expect more instructionally naive students to need 10 to 15 repetitions on the lead step during the first lessons when sounding out is taught. A great deal of teacher skill is needed to give the children adequate practice and still make the reading lesson enjoyable for the students. One way to keep lessons enjoyable is to provide a short 5- to 10-second change-up after each five or so practice trials. During the change-up, the teacher encourages the students: "You kids are working so hard. These are really hard words and you've almost got them." When the students finally sound out all the words correctly, the teacher should act very excited and proud of the students. "You did it! I'm so proud of you. Give yourself a big pat on the back."

Providing the practice students need to respond correctly to all words consecutively in the early days will result in steadily improving student performance. Not providing adequate practice will result only in minimal daily improvement.

Table 9.2

Discrimination Format—Sounding Out Words in Lists

Teacher	Students
1. Teacher states instructions. "You're going to sound out each word. After you sound out the word correctly, you'll say it fast."	
2. Teacher points to left of first word. "Sound it out. Get ready." Teacher touches under each letter for 1 to 1 1/2 seconds. After the student sounds out the word correctly, the teacher moves her finger back to the beginning of the word immediately says, "What word?" and signals.	
3. Teacher repeats step 2 with remaining words written on the board.	
4. Teacher gives individual tests. Teacher calls on several students to sound out a word.	

Discrimination Format. In the discrimination format (see Table 9.2) for sounding out words in lists, the teacher provides the children with practice on sounding out a set of words. The teacher does not model the words before the children are to read them. The discrimination format replaces the introductory format when students' performance in the introductory format indicates they no longer require the teacher to lead. Specifically, after the teacher models sounding out a word in the introductory format, the students can (with generally only one or two practice trials) sound it out correctly. In the discrimination format, a new step is introduced. After sounding out the word, the students say the word at a normal rate.

Critical Behaviors

Pacing. The students should not be asked to say the word at the normal rate until they have sounded out the word acceptably (i.e., saying each sound correctly and not pausing between sounds). The teacher should say, "What word" immediately after the students correctly sound out the word. Any pause makes translating the blended sounds into a word said at a normal rate more difficult. Likewise, the teacher should not praise after the students sound out the word, but should hold the praise until after the students say the word at a normal rate.

Individual Turns. Remember, individual turns are given only when the students responding in unison appear to have mastered all the words. Keeping all the students in a group attentive while one student is given an individual turn is very important. The more students are attentive and actively practicing word reading, the faster they will progress.

During individual turns the teacher should tell the other students to read the words to themselves. The teacher can encourage students to read to themselves by initially using specific praise: "Ravi and Ginger are reading to themselves. They are going to be good readers because they are practicing."

Correcting Mistakes.   Two common errors made during sounding out are paus-ing between sounds and saying a sound incorrectly. Pausing errors involve the students' stopping between sounds, which can result in the student leaving out a sound when saying the word the fast way. For example, in sounding out the CVC word *sat,* a student pauses between the first and second sounds, "sss (pause) aaat." When translating these blended sounds into a word, the student may leave off the sound preceding the pause, translating "sss (pause) aaat" into "at."

Below is the correction procedure for pausing errors. The teacher:

1. *Models.* As soon as the teacher hears the error, she says: "Don't stop between sounds. Listen to me sound out the word without stopping." (Teacher points to letters and sounds out the word.)
2. *Leads by responding with the students.* "Sound it out with me. Get ready." (Teacher responds with students.) "Again, get ready." (Teacher responds with students.)
3. *Tests by having the students sound out the word themselves.* "All by yourselves. Sound it out. Get ready."
4. *Returns to the first word in the list and repeats all the words in the list until the students can sound out all the words consecutively without an error.* *
5. *Gives individual turns.* At the completion of the list, individual turns are given to students who missed the word.

The teacher should sometimes begin the correction procedure by prais-ing one of the students who responded correctly. "Nice job, Ravi. You didn't stop between the sounds."

Sound errors involve the students saying a sound that is not the most common sound of a letter. For example, in sounding out the word *fat,* a student says the sound /ĭ/ when the teacher points to the letter *a.*

The correction for sound errors is somewhat different. In correcting a sound error, the teacher uses a limited model, which involves first modeling and testing only the sound missed rather than the entire word. For example, if the teacher points to the letters in *sip* and the student responds "sssaaa," the teacher immediately says "iiii." Next, the teacher points to *i* and asks, "What sound?" The teacher then tests students on sounding out the entire word. The following text presents a sample sounds correction for a student who said /ă/ for *i* in sounding out the word *sit.*

1. *Limited model.* As soon as the teacher hears the sound error, the teacher says the correct sound, "/iiiii/."
2. *Tests.* The teacher tests the whole group on the missed sound, care-fully monitoring individuals who originally made the error. The teacher points to *i.* "What sound?" The teacher signals by touching *i.*

---

*Note: If there are more than four words in a list, the teacher simply returns to a word four words earlier in the list rather than to the beginning of the list.

3. *Tests.* The teacher tests the whole group on sounding out the word. "Sound it out. Get ready. (Signal.) What word?" (Signal.)

4. *Firms. The teacher returns to the first word in the list and repeats all the words until the students can correctly sound out each word in the task.* *

5. *Individual turns.* At the completion of the list, individual turns are given to students who made errors.

Teachers sometimes cause pausing errors and sound errors by not pointing long enough to each letter. If the teacher moves too quickly from one letter to the next, some students will not have time to look ahead to the next letter and, consequently, will guess or pause. If students make many of these errors, the teacher should consider whether he or she is causing the error and try pointing longer. Teachers also sometimes cause student errors by not signaling clearly. Teachers should make certain their signals are not causing student errors.

A third type of error that occurs when the teacher is presenting the discrimination format involves the student saying the word incorrectly after sounding it out, usually leaving out the initial sound. For example, the student sounds out "sssaat" and when the teacher asks "What word?" the student says "at."

This type of error is usually the result of the student pausing between the first two sounds when sounding out the word (e.g., *sat* is sounded out "ssss [pause] aaaat"). The steps in the correction procedure for this type of error are:

1. The teacher says the word. "That word is *sat*."

2. The teacher models sounding out and saying the word. "My turn. Sssaaat. What word?" "Sat."

3. The teacher tests and leads if necessary. "Sound it out. Get ready. (Signal.) What word?" (Signal.)

4. The teacher returns to the first word in the list and repeats all the words until the students can correctly sound out each word in the task. *

5. At the completion of the list, individual turns are given to students who made errors.

Teachers should record the errors students made. Table 9.3 shows a simple recording form that can be used over a week's time. The names of the students in a group are written in the spaces in the left column. Across from each student's name are boxes for each day of the week. The teacher records errors the student made in the appropriate box. If a student makes an error in a letter-sound-correspondence task, the teacher writes the letter and over the letter writes the sound that the student said. In a sounding-out task, the teacher can write the word the student was reading, then write the response the student said over it. This information is used in lesson planning. Missed sounds would be reviewed and practiced during letter-sounds correspondence exercises.

---

*Note: If there are more than four words in the list, the teacher just goes back four words.

Table 9.3

Weekly Record-keeping Form

WEEKLY RECORD-KEEPING FORM					
Student	**Monday**	**Tuesday**	**Wednesday**	**Thursday**	**Friday**
Bill	(n) m				
Francine	(sad) sid	(t) (mit) d mid			
José					
Elwin	(i) e	(i) (lid) e led			
Marcy					

Precorrecting.   Precorrecting involves the teacher prompting the student on a pre-requisite skill a student is having difficulty with just before presenting a task that calls for application of that preskill. Precorrecting is a valuable technique for minimizing errors students make in a lesson. In a sounding-out precorrection, the teacher prompts the students on a letter that has caused them difficulty in earlier lessons before having them sound out a word with that letter. For example, if the students were having difficulty with *e,* the teacher would point to *e* in the word *met* before having the students sound out the word and ask, "What sound?" After students identify the letter, the teacher would then have the students sound out the word.

Precorrections are particularly appropriate when new, difficult letters appear in words or when a letter that is causing students difficulty appears in a word. A possible danger with using precorrections is in using them too much, making some students dependent on them. If precorrections are overused, the students will not try to remember difficult sounds because they expect the teacher to identify them. Teachers can avoid developing dependency by precorrecting a sound only for a few lessons.

Introducing New Word Types

Regular words can be classified by type according to their relative difficulty to decode. The types are illustrated in the following list, according to what appears to be their relative difficulty—easy to difficult:

- VC and CVC that begin with continuous sounds (e.g., *at, man*)
- CVCC that begin with continuous sounds (e.g., *runs, lamp, fist*)

■ CVC that begin with stop sounds (e.g., *hot, cap*)
■ CVCC that begin with stop sounds (e.g., *cast, hand*)
■ CCVC in which both of the initial consonants are continuous sounds (e.g., *slap, frog*)
■ CCVC in which one of the initial sounds is a stop sound (e.g., *crib, stop*)
■ CCVCC words (e.g., *brand, clump*)
■ CCCVC and CCCVCC words (e.g., *split, sprint*)

Sounding-out instruction begins with VC and CVC words that start with continuous sounds. Instructionally naive students may require 20 to 30 lessons of practice with this type of word before they are able to sound out a set of these words with relative ease. Teachers often underestimate the amount of practice needed by instructionally naive students to become proficient in sounding out words. During the first months of instruction the students will be learning many new letter-sound correspondences. Integrating all the new correspondences when sounding out words requires a great deal of practice, although the amount needed will vary from student to student.

The students' performance tells the teacher when the student is ready to learn a new word type. When a student can sound out a set of four CVC words beginning with continuous sounds without error on the first trial for two consecutive days, CVCC words beginning with continuous sounds can be introduced. No special teaching procedure is required for introducing CVCC words. The teacher writes three CVCC words on the board and uses the introductory sounding-out format. This format is repeated daily until the students can sound out the three words with no more than one error during the format. Then the introductory format is dropped and CVCC words are included in the discrimination format. Half the words in the discrimination format should be CVC words while the other half should be CVCC words.

Words Beginning with Stop Sounds.* CVC words beginning with stop sounds can be introduced when students master CVCC words that begin with a continuous sound. Remember, student performance is always the key factor that determines when something new can be introduced.

Several modifications in the teaching procedure are necessary for words that begin with a stop sound. First, the sounding-out signaling procedure has to be modified slightly. The letter for the initial stop sound is touched for just an instant, followed by a quick movement to the next letter, which is pointed to for slightly longer than usual, about 1 1/2 to 2 seconds. When modeling how to sound out the word, the teacher does not pause at all between the initial stop sound and vowel. The word *can* would be modeled "caaaannnn" with no pauses.

Note: Words beginning with the stop sound /h/ often cause students particular difficulty. When words beginning with *h* are introduced, include at least three such words in a format, such as *hit, hug,* and *him,* to provide massed practice.

During the first week when words that begin with stop sounds first appear, the teacher can use a precorrection in which she has the students say the sound of the letter following the stop sound before they sound out the word. For example, before the students sound out the word *cut,* the teacher points to *u* and asks, "What sound?" If this precorrection is used, the teacher should have the students sound out the entire word list again later without using the precorrection so that students do not become overly dependent on the precorrection. Furthermore, the precorrection should not be used for more than 1 week.

CVCC words beginning with stop sounds (e.g., *camp, hunt, test*) can be introduced when students are able to sound out CVCC words beginning with continuous sounds and CVC words beginning with stop sounds.

Words Beginning with Blends. Words that begin with initial blends (two consecutive consonants) are introduced next. This type can be divided into words that begin with two continuous sounds (e.g., *snap, frog, sled*), and words in which one of the initial consonants is a stop sound (e.g., *stop, club, grab, spin*). There are not many regular words that begin with two continuous consonants; moreover, these words will usually not present difficulty for students. Words in which one of the two initial consonants is a stop sound, such as *step* and *skin,* will require careful teaching and a great deal of practice.

In addition to providing sounding-out practice, the teacher can also present several supplementary exercises. First is the auditory blending and segmenting task in which students say the sounds in a word slowly without pausing and then say the word at a normal rate (see page 43.). This auditory exercise can be started a week or so before students begin reading words containing initial blends, then can be continued daily for about 2 weeks. When presenting the auditory format, the teacher includes words the students will be asked to decode within the next few days.

Precorrections can also be used when words containing blends are first introduced. The precorrection involves the teacher pointing to the letter following the stop sound (e.g., in the word *skim,* the teacher would point to *i,* and in *cram, r*). If the word does not contain a stop sound, the teacher would point to the second consonant in the blend (e.g., the teacher would point to *l* in *flap* and *r* in *frog*).

Example Selection

Example selection criteria are very important. Discrimination format word lists should contain a mix of words from the various types introduced to the current day. About half the words should be of the most recently introduced type and half a mix of words from earlier types. The purpose of the mix is to buttress against students not attending carefully to the letters in a word. For example, if students read lists of words all having the letter *l* as the second letter, some students might become careless and often include the /l/ sound when sounding out a word.

Making the Transition from Sounding Out to Sight-Word Reading

In sight-reading exercises, the students do not sound out words vocally, but say them at a normal rate when the teacher signals. Sight-word reading is introduced in word-list exercises. Students initially sight-read several words they sounded out earlier in the lesson. The number of words in sight-reading exercises increases gradually until the students sight-read all of the words in a list.

Sight-word reading in lists may be introduced when students can consistently sound out a set of four CVC words with continuous sounds without error. Two formats—an introductory format and a practice format—can be used to teach sight-reading.

Introductory Format for Sight-Word Reading

The introductory format is really a transition format from sounding out words to reading the whole word (see Table 9.4). For each word, the teacher has the

Table 9.4
Format for Introducing Sight-Reading Words

Teacher	Students
Teacher writes on board: *sat, mud, fit, sad.*	
1. Teacher models.	
a. "You are going to read these words without saying the sounds out loud."	
b. "My turn. Watch my mouth. I'll say the sounds to myself, then I'll say the word." Teacher points to the first word, moving lips and whispering each sound as she points to each letter. After saying the sounds subvocally, she says "What word?" signals, and says the word "sat."	
c. Teacher models with one more word.	
2. Teacher tests group on all the words.	
a. "Your turn." Teacher points to left of first letter. "As I point to the letters, sound out this word to yourselves." Teacher loops from letter to letter touching under each continuous sound letter for about 1 second. "What word?" (Signal.)	Students sound out words, whispering sounds. "Sssaaat." Students say word at normal rate. "Sat."
b. Teacher repeats step 2(a) with remaining words in list. Teacher presents the list until students correctly identify all words.	
3. Teacher presents individual turns.	

students sound out the word to themselves (subvocally) instead of sounding it out vocally. When the teacher signals, the students say the word out loud at a normal rate. This format begins with the teacher modeling how to sound out words subvocally, then say the words out loud at a normal rate. The model is followed by a step in which the teacher instructs the students to sound out a word to themselves (as the teacher points to the sounds), and then say the word out loud at a normal rate when the teacher signals. This step is very important, especially for instructionally naive students. It overtly shows them what to do in sight-reading exercises. Without this step, some more passive students might not sound out words but rather rely on guessing. The format is presented daily until the students are able to respond correctly to all words on the first trial for 2 consecutive days. Then a sight-reading practice exercise where the students practice sight-reading without any teacher prompting replaces the introductory format.

Practice Format for Sight-Reading in Lists

Table 9.5 contains the format for practicing sight-reading in word lists. In this format, the teacher tells the students to sound out the words to themselves, then say the word the fast way out loud when the signal is given. The students read the list of words at least two times. The goal of the first reading is to have students identify each word within 3 seconds. The goal of the second reading is to have students identify each word with only a 2-second pause.

Table 9.5

Practice Format for Sight-Reading Words in Lists

Teacher	Students
Teacher writes on board: *sad, not, fit, am, sun, fin.*	
1. "You're going to read these words the fast way. When I point to a word, sound it out to yourself. When I signal, say the word the fast way."	
2. Students read words with a 3-second pause.	
a. Teacher points to left of the first word, pauses 3 seconds, then says, "What word?" and signals.	"Sad."
b. The teacher continues the same procedure, as in step 2(a), with the remaining words.	
3. Students read entire word list again with a 2-second pause.	
a. Teacher has the students read words again with only a 2-second pause.	
4. Teacher gives individual turns.	
a. Teacher points to word, pauses 2 seconds, then calls on a student.	
b. Teacher repeats step 4(a) with the remaining words.	

Critical Behaviors

A critical teaching behavior is deciding how long a pause should be given to enable the students to figure out a word. The goal of the first reading of a list is to enable the students to respond to each word with no more than a 3-second pause before the signal. Some students may need longer than 3 seconds to sound out a word to themselves. During the first several weeks, up to 5 seconds can be allowed to let the students figure out a word. After 5 seconds, the teacher should give the signal for the students to respond, even if it appears that not all students have figured out the word. Allowing the students too much time may inadvertently reinforce student indecisiveness. Some students take a long time to figure out a word because they start to sound it out, say one or two sounds to themselves, then stop and start over again. Remember, the teacher can usually determine what a student is doing by watching the student's mouth.

If any student in the group needs more than 3 seconds to figure out a word in a list, the teacher should either return to the beginning of the list or continue with the other words in the list, then present the entire list again. The extra practice of doing the list again is critical to enabling the students to develop adequate fluency.

A problem with repeating a set of words several times is that the students may memorize the words on the page according to their position. To minimize the possibility of students memorizing the position of words, the teacher can present the words in a random order each time the list is repeated. The teacher can also keep the student's motivational level high by using praise. Remember, praising students when they respond correctly is a very powerful motivator for young students. When returning to an earlier word in a list, the teacher can make a comment such as, "You certainly are working hard. Let's go back and see if we can read a little faster." Be certain to praise effusively when a student who has had difficulty finally succeeds.

Signals.   The teacher points just to the left of a word, pauses to let the students figure out the word, then says, "What word?" and signals by either tapping the word or moving his or her finger quickly under the word in a slashing movement.

The teacher should be watching the students when he or she gives the signal for the students to respond. Watching the students is critical. It enables the teacher to see if the students are attentive (look at students' eyes) and helps to determine if the students made a correct response (look at students' mouths).

Individual Turns.   Keeping students attentive during individual turns is very important and a challenge for the teacher. Pacing is also very important. The teacher should not call on students in a predictable order. The teacher points to a word, pauses long enough for all the students to figure out the word, then calls on an individual student to respond. After the student responds, the teacher praises then points to the next word. The critical behaviors involve allowing enough time for all the students to figure out the response before calling on an individual student and calling on students in a random order so students don't know who is going to be called upon to answer.

The teacher can make up an activity game such as "I'm going to see if I can trick you. I'll point to a word and give you time to figure it out, then I'll call on someone. You won't know who until I call on you. Don't get tricked." The teacher should strongly praise students who answer correctly immediately when their name is called. "That was great. You are a hard-working reader."

Sometimes teachers inadvertently cause students to be inattentive by calling a student's name before pointing to a word for individual turns. The problem with doing this is that once a student knows that he or she won't be called on, the student is much less likely to be attentive.

Correcting Mistakes.   There are two types of errors that occur in sight-reading exercises: a signal error in which the student does not say the word when the teacher signals, and a misidentification error in which the student makes an incorrect response. The correction procedure for misidentification errors involves (a) giving a limited model by identifying the missed sound (e.g., if student says "fat" for *fit,* teacher points to *i* and says, "This says ĭ"); (b) having the students sound out the word vocally and say it at a normal rate; then (c) returning to an earlier word in the list. The teacher goes back three or four words and re-presents the words. At the end of the lesson, the teacher retests students individually on any words they have missed.

The following text shows an example of a limited model-correction procedure. A student said "fat" for *fit.*

1. Teacher gives limited model: (Teacher points to *i.*) "This says ĭ. What sound?" (Signal.) "ĭ."
2. Teacher has students sound out word: "Let's sound out the word. Get ready." (Teacher points to the left of the first letter, pauses, then loops under each letter.) "What word?" (Signal.) "Fit."
3. Teacher goes back several words in the list and repeats the list. "Let's read these words perfectly."*

Example Selection

The criteria for constructing word lists to be sight-read is basically the same as for selecting words for sounding-out exercises.

- Words should include only letters that students have demonstrated mastery on in letter-sound correspondence tasks.
- Words should be listed in an unpredictable order. The same letter should not appear in the same position in more than two consecutive words.
- Words of a new type should make up one-third to one-half of the list.

---

*Note: If there are more than four words in the list, the teacher just goes back four words.

Sounding out words in word lists should be continued after sight-reading is introduced. When sight-word reading is first introduced, the introductory sight-reading format should be presented with just three or four words the students sounded out earlier in the lesson. The number of words to be sight-read increases gradually over a period of weeks until the students sight-read all the words sounded out earlier in the lesson. In future lessons, the teacher can change the pattern by gradually reducing the number of words that are sounded out. Word-list reading exercises, near the end of the beginning stage, might include 15–20 words. The students sound out five words of the newest type introduced, then sight-read all the words. Continued practice in sounding out throughout the beginning stage is important to buttress against the possibility of students adopting guessing strategies.

Introducing Irregular Words

Irregular words are words that a student cannot read by applying the letter-sound correspondence knowledge that the student has learned in the reading program because one or more letters in the word does not represent the sound that the student has learned for the letter(s). For example, the word *was* is irregular because the letters *a* and *s* both do not represent the sound typically associated with the particular letters.

In designing or teaching a reading program, the teacher needs to be aware that words that are irregular at one point in a reading program may not be irregular at a later point in the reading program. For example, the word *park* would be irregular early in a reading program when the students have only been taught to associate the letter *a* with the short-a sound. In the word *park,* the letter *a* does not represent the short-a sound. Later in the program, students will be taught the letter correspondence for the letter combination *ar.* The letter combination *ar* is highly consistent in representing the *r*-controlled vowel sound heard in words like *park, hard,* and *start.* Once students learn the /ar/ sound, the word *park* would no longer be considered an irregular word.

Some words will always be considered irregular because they contain letter-sound correspondences unique to that word or a few words. Examples of this type of irregular word include *was, they, said,* and *break.* In these words, one or more letters represent a sound that is not common for that particular letter.

The manner in which irregular words are introduced in a reading program can be an important factor in determining if students develop confusions regarding how to apply word attack strategies. This section will present suggestions for introducing irregular words when using a program that uses a systematic and explicit phonics approach.

When to Introduce

Learning to decode irregular words is an important step for beginning readers because a different strategy than the strategy for reading regular words is required.

The reader cannot simply sound out a word, working from left to right, then translate the blended sounds into a word. For example, *was* is sounded out as "www ăăăsss" but is pronounced "wuz."

For teachers working with instructionally naive children, we recommend delaying the introduction of irregular words until students can read regular CVC words in a list at a rate of about a word every 3 seconds. This rate, though quite slow in terms of the advanced reader, is adequate at the beginning stage to indicate student mastery of the sounding-out skill. The reason for delaying the introduction of irregular words is to make initial reading instruction easier for the students by simply letting them initially concentrate on the mechanics of sounding out regular words.

Because of the complexity of decoding irregular words, struggling readers and at-risk students are likely to need a great deal of practice to master each individual word. Therefore, the introduction of the first several irregular words should be carefully spaced out—one every four to six lessons. The next 10 or so irregular words can be introduced at a somewhat faster rate of about one new word every three lessons. The students' performance, of course, is the key determinant of how quickly new irregular words can be introduced. During the introduction of the first 10 irregular words, a new irregular word should not be presented if students miss any previously introduced irregular words in word-list reading or in passage reading.

After several weeks, a new irregular word can be introduced even if a student is having difficulty with a previously introduced irregular word. However, the new word should not be similar to the word the student is having difficulty with. For example, a teacher would not introduce the word *where* if students are having difficulty with *were,* but could introduce *where* if students are having difficulty with *said.* If students are having difficulty with more than one previously introduced word, no new words should be introduced.

Sequence

If a teacher is using a commercial program, the words in upcoming passages will dictate the order that irregular words are introduced. The teacher will introduce irregular words according to the order they appear in the program.

If a teacher is constructing a program, the following factors should be considered when making a sequence: frequency, similarity, type of irregularity, and presence of related words.

Frequency. As a general rule, words that appear more often in children's literature should be introduced before words that appear less often. The sequence of words is not particularly critical as long as the general rule is followed. Appendix B contains a list of 400 high-frequency words.

Similarity. Some irregular words are very similar to other irregular words (e.g., *saw-was, of-off, were-where*). The introduction of these pairs should be planned so that one of the two words is introduced at least 15 lessons before the other.

The separation allows students to master the first word before encountering the second and, thus, decreases the probability of the students confusing them.

Type of Irregularity.   As the students progress through a reading program, they will begin to learn the letter-sound correspondences for letter combinations (e.g., *ar* in *shark, ea* in *seat;* a list of common letter combinations appears in Table 6.4) and patterns of letters such as the VCe pattern, which produces a long-vowel sound, as in *hate, like,* and *note.*

As a general rule, words that contain a VCe pattern in which the vowel is long and words containing a letter combination representing its common sound should not be presented as irregular words during the beginning stage, with the exception of very common words such as *name* and *told.* The reason is that later in the program students will learn generalizable strategies that allow them to decode these words. Spending time in the beginning stage teaching a word as an individual word is not efficient if soon thereafter the students learn a strategy that allows them to decode a wide range of words, one of which is that word.

Related Words.   Some irregular words will be related because parts of the word are the same. Examples of some common related irregular words appear below:

some	*talk*	*mother*	*most*	*to*	*live*	*none*
come	*walk*	*bother*	*post*	*do*	*give*	*done*
	chalk	*other*	*ghost*			

As a general rule, related words should be taught one after another or introduced together.

Teaching Irregular Words Through Explicit Instruction

The teaching procedure to use when introducing irregular words should (a) require the student to examine all the letters in a word and (b) point out to students the irregularity in one or more of the letter-sound correspondences.

If teachers are using a reading program in which regular words are introduced first and practiced a good deal before irregular words instruction begins, the strategy we recommend for introducing the first 15 to 25 irregular words involves the teacher alerting the children that the word is a "funny" or "tricky" word. The teacher then has the student sound out the word as it is written, saying the sound they have been taught for each letter, then translating that series of sounds into the correct pronunciation. *Was* is sounded out as "wăăăsss," but is pronounced "wuz." The word *walk* is sounded out as "www ăăălllk," but is said "wauk." Even though this procedure is somewhat cumbersome, it has several advantages. First, it increases the probability that students will carefully continue to attend to all the letters in the word in a left to right progression. It shows students that the same basic sounding-out strategy (i.e., to start with the first letter, say the sound, then blend the sounds for the remaining letters in left to right sequence, one sound for one letter) can be used to decode all words, even though some are pronounced differently from what the blended sounds indicate. Without this demonstration, some students may develop the misrule that since sounding out does not work on some words, it will no longer work on many words, so guessing is the best strategy to use. Second, the sounding-out strategy prepares students for later spelling exercises by demonstrating that students cannot rely solely on how a word sounds to spell words.

   Table 9.6 contains the format for introducing irregular words with this sounding-out strategy. The format starts with a model: The teacher says the irregular word, then sounds it out saying the most common sound for each letter, then says it again as a meaningful word. The teacher then tests the students, asking them to say the word, sound it out, then say the word again as it is pronounced.

Critical Behaviors

Modeling.   The teacher must clearly demonstrate that the irregular word is pronounced differently than it is sounded out. When sounding out the word, the teacher must say the most common sounds. As a precorrection, to prevent students from making errors when sounding out a word, the teacher can point to a letter in the word that is pronounced differently from its most common sound, and ask the students "What sound?" before having the students sound

Table 9.6
Introductory Format for Irregular Words

Teacher	Students
1. Teacher tells students a new word, then sounds it out. Teacher points to *was*. "Everybody, this is a funny word. The word is 'was.' What word?" (Signal.)	"Was."
"Listen to me sound out the word." Teacher touches each letter. "Wwwwăăăsss. That's how we sound out the word. But here's how we say it: *was*. How do we say it?" (Teacher touches word.) "Yes, *was*."	"Was."
2. Teacher has students sound out the word and then say it. Teacher points to the left of *was*. "Now you are going to sound out *was*. Get ready." Teacher touches under each letter for about a second.	"Wwwwăăăsss."
"But how do we say the word?" (Signal.)	"Was."
"Remember, how do we say the word?" (Signal.)	"Was."
3. Teacher gives individual turns on step 2.	

out the word. For example, before sounding out *was,* the teacher points to *a* and asks, "What sound?"

Correcting Mistakes in the Introductory Format.   Students make two types of errors in step 2 of the introductory format: (a) when sounding out the word, they may say the sounds for how the word is pronounced, rather than saying the most common sound for each letter (e.g., when sounding out the word *was,* the students say /ŭ/ instead of /ă/ for *a*); and (b) after sounding out the word, they may say the word as it is sounded out, rather than as it is said (e.g., after sounding out the letters in *was* as "www ăăăsss" student says "wăs" instead of "wuz").

The correction procedure for both errors is (a) to model by repeating the task and saying the correct answer, (b) to test by returning to the beginning of step 2, and (c) to retest by repeating the format later in the lesson. For example:

■ *Error.* Student says /ŭ/ when sounding out the word *was.*
Teacher models. "My turn to sound out *was.* Listen: Wwwăăasss."
Teacher tests. "Sound out *was.* Get ready." (Signal.) "Wwwăăass."
"How do we say the word?" (Signal.) "Was."
Later in the lesson, the teacher repeats the format.

■ *Error.* After sounding out *of,* student responds "off" when the teacher asks, "What word?"
Teacher models. "We say *of.* What word?" (Signal.) "Of."
Teacher tests sounding out and saying word.
"Sound out *of.* Get ready." (Signal.) "ŏŏofff."
"How do we say the word?" (Signal.) "Of."
Later in the lesson, the teacher repeats the format.

Modified Introductory Format

A procedure for introducing irregular words after the first 15 to 25 words have been presented has the teacher tell the students the word, then has the students repeat the word, spell it by letter names, and say the word again:

1. "This word is *giant.* What word?" (Signal.) "Giant."
2. "Spell *giant.*" (Signal.) "G-i-a-n-t."
3. "What word did you spell?" (Signal.) "Giant."
4. "Yes, *giant.*"

The purpose of having students spell words is to ensure they attend to the letters in the word. Obviously, this format would not be introduced until the students know the names of all letters.

Facilitating Retention. Students will require considerable exposure to an irregular word before they can be expected to recognize it on sight. New irregular words should be systematically introduced and practiced.

A new irregular word should be presented daily for 3 to 4 days using one of the introductory formats. On the third day, the new irregular word is incorporated into a practice sight-word-list exercise (see Table 9.5) along with regular words and previously introduced irregular words. The new irregular word appears daily in the word-list exercise until the students are able to identify it correctly for 2 consecutive days. Then the new irregular word is incorporated into stories to be read in passage-reading exercises; the new word appears at least every second day for several more weeks in either a word-list or passage-reading exercise.

Correcting Mistakes in Word-Reading Exercises. When the teacher asks students to identify an irregular word in a word-reading exercise, students may make two types of misidentification mistakes: (a) saying the word as it is sounded out (saying "wăs" instead of "wuz"), or (b) saying a different word (saying "saw" instead of "wuz"). The correction procedure for either error is the same:

1. The teacher tells students the word and asks them to repeat it. "This word is *was*. What word?"
2. The teacher has students sound out the word or say its letter names, depending on what procedure was used to introduce the word.
3. The teacher asks how the word is pronounced. "How do we say that word?" or "What word?"
4. The teacher backs up four words in the list and has the students reread that part of the list.
5. Later in the lesson, the teacher retests by calling on the student who missed the word to identify it.

If a previously introduced irregular word is missed more than once, it should be reintroduced in the next lesson and stressed in the word-list exercise for several days. For example, if students had trouble with the word *put* in Monday's lesson, the teacher should reintroduce *put* in an introductory format on Tuesday and include it in sight-word-list exercises daily until the students correctly identify the word for 2 consecutive days on the first trial.

The teacher can incorporate a more powerful correction technique into a word-list exercise by using an alternating pattern: The teacher presents the missed irregular word, one of the other words, and then returns to the missed word. She returns to the missed word several times during the task, but each time only after having presented more review words. For example, if the irregular word *said* is in a word list with *was, the, walk,* and *lamp,* and the student misread *said,* the teacher could present the words in this order: *said, was, said, walk, the, said, walk, the, lamp, said.* Note that more words appear between each successive presentation of *said*. The teacher keeps alternating between the missed word and review words until the student is able to identify the new irregular word correctly three times.

Commercial Reading Programs

The manner in which word reading is introduced in many commercial core reading programs can be problematic for the struggling reader and at-risk child. The problems may stem from the presence of one or more of the following characteristics:

No or little explicit teaching of sounding out. Some reading programs do not teach sounding out. These programs begin with whole word reading. Some programs teach sounding out, but do so for a limited number of days.

Rapid and early introduction of irregular words. Most core reading programs introduce irregular words very early in the kindergarten and first grade levels before students have mastered reading regular words. When a high proportion of the words first introduced in the early lessons are irregular words, struggling readers and at-risk children may develop confusions that lead to habitual guessing and lack of attending to all the letter-sound relationships in a word.

Rapid introduction of more difficult word type before children have mastered reading easier word type. Many reading programs will introduce words with stop sounds very early in the program even though students have had little practice with words that begin with continuous sounds.

Absence of daily practice. Some programs will not provide for daily work on word reading because too many other activities are included in the program. Other programs will not clearly point out that word-reading exercises are to be presented daily.

Solutions

The problems related to the reading regular words of: no or too little explicit teaching of sounding out, the rapid introduction of word types, and the absence of daily practice can be solved by the teacher supplementing daily lessons with word-reading exercises and/or creating new lessons when necessary. During the first months of instruction in the beginning stage, daily lessons should include phonemic awareness exercises, letter-sound correspondence exercises, and once the students have learned six to eight letter-sound correspondences, word-reading exercises. Initial sounding out is done with VC- and CVC-regular words that begin with continuous sounds, the easiest type of word. Sight-reading would be introduced when students develop accuracy and ease with sounding out. The amount of extra practice to be provided depends on the students' performance. If the students have difficulty with a particular skill, new related skills should not be introduced the next day; more practice is needed.

The problem of a too rapid and/or too early introduction of irregular words is more difficult to solve. If irregular words are introduced before a child knows most letter-sound correspondences or letter names, the child is not likely to use a strategy of looking at words in a left to right direction and attending to all the letters in the word. While more instructionally sophisticated children can overcome the confusion that occurs when irregular words, are introduced too early or too quickly, the more at-risk instructionally naive children are likely to develop confusions that may be difficult to clear up.

For teachers who are working with children who have little knowledge of letter-sound correspondences when irregular words are introduced in their reading program, we recommend that the introduction of irregular words be slowed up dramatically while the teacher instructs children how to read regular words. During the time that children are learning to read regular words, the teacher can tell the child any irregular word they don't yet know when the word appears in a story. Once irregular words are introduced, the teacher should concentrate on providing extra review and practice on the more important irregular words, those that will appear more frequently. When a new irregular word is presented during the beginning stage, that word should appear in a word-list exercise and/or a story for the next 10 or so consecutive lessons and thereafter periodically at least every second or third lesson.

The previously described solution is not an ideal solution. The ideal solution would be to obtain a program in which the introduction of irregular words is delayed until students master reading regular words and the introduction of irregular words is carefully controlled. More on this topic will be presented in Part 3.

Application to Your Curriculum

Evaluate Beginning Word Reading Instruction in Your Core Reading Program

Reading Regular Words

1. When is regular-word reading introduced? What literacy-related skills have been introduced prior to its introduction?
2. What strategy is specified to teach students to read regular words?
3. Is this strategy explicit? Does the teacher model how to sound out words?
4. Locate and list the first 30 regular words introduced in the program. Does the program begin with CVC words that start with a continuous sound?
5. Do students only sound out words that contain sounds they have mastered?
6. Is there a transition from sounding out to sight-reading regular words?
7. What corrections are specified for student errors?
8. Is there daily practice provided in reading regular words in word-list exercises?
9. What modifications would you make based on your answers to the previous questions?

Reading Irregular Words

1. When is irregular-word reading introduced? Locate and list the first 15 regular words introduced in the program. What letter-sound relationships have the students learned prior to the introduction of the words?
2. What strategy is specified to teach students to read irregular words?
3. Does this strategy focus on students examining all letters in the word?
4. Does the strategy used to read irregular words during the first months of reading focus on cues such as pictures or context instead of examination of all letters in the word?
5. What corrections are specified for student errors?
6. Is there daily practice provided in reading irregular words in word-list exercises and passages?
7. What modifications would you make based on your answers to the previous questions?

At a Glance   Sounding Out Regular Words

Materials	Write out words on an overhead, whiteboard, or flash-cards.
What to Do	Say "You're going to sound out each word. After you sound out the word correctly, you'll say it fast."
	Start at the left side of the word and say, "Sound it out. Get ready." Touch under each continuous letter for 1 to 1 1/2 seconds and stop sounds for an instant.
	After the students sound out the word correctly, immediately say, "What word?"
	Note: You may have the students sound out the word several times before asking them, "What word?"
	Repeat with remaining words.
	Give individual turns to several students.
Correcting Mistakes	Use a model-lead test correction—don't let them guess.
	Model and lead if necessary until they sound out and say the word correctly.
Rate and Practice	Present sounding out for up to 5–7 minutes with six to eight words at a time.
	Use only words in which the students know the sounds.
	The first several days show the students how you sound out each word, then have students do it with you, then by themselves.
Suggested Sequence	VC and CVC that begin with continuous sounds (*at, sun*).
	CVCC that begin with continuous sounds (*sand, lamp, fist*).
	CVC that begin with stop sounds (*hot, cap*).
	CVCC that begin with stop sounds (*cast, hand*).
	CCVC in which both of the initial consonants are continuous sounds (*slap, frog*).
	CCVC in which one of the initial sounds is a stop sound (*crib, stop*).
	CCVCC words (*brand, clump*).
	CCCVC and CCCVCC words (*split, sprint*).
Strategic Integration	After students have mastered words in list-reading exercises, they should appear in connected text passage reading exercises.

At a Glance   Sight-Word Reading with Regular Words

Materials	Use the same lists from sounding-out exercises for initial sight-word reading exercises during the beginning stage. As students become more skilled, increase the number of words in exercises. Not all words need to be sounded out first.
What to Do	Say "You're going to read these words the fast way. When I point to a word, sound it out to yourself. When I signal, read the word the fast way."
	Point to the left of the word. Pause 3 seconds, then say, "What word?" and signal.
	Continue with all the words in the list. After the students read the list correctly, go back to the top and read the list again with a 2-second pause.
	Give individual turns to several students.
Correcting Mistakes	Model or ask students to identify any sound that resulted in an error. Have students sound out the word out loud, then say it fast.
	Return to the first word (or 4 words earlier) in the list and read the words again the fast way.
Selecting Examples	Word lists include a mix of words from most recent types and previously introduced types.
Strategic Integration	After students read words the fast way, the words should appear in connected text passage reading exercises.

CHAPTER 10

Phonics and Word Attack During Primary Stage

During the beginning reading stage, students learn how to read phonetically regular words and some high-frequency irregular words. As the students progress through the beginning reading stage, they should receive adequate practice to enable them to read one-syllable words relatively quickly, without laboriously sounding out the word subvocally first. The nearly instantaneous decoding of words indicates that the students are seeing words as composed of units of letters rather than single letters. This ability to see words as composed of units of letters prepares students for the primary stage of learning to read words.

During the primary stage, the focus is no longer on words in which each letter represents a particular sound: the focus of the primary stage is on learning the relationships between groups of letters and the sounds they represent in words. Students learn to read:

- Words that contain common letter combinations such as m<u>ai</u>d, b<u>ee</u>t, cl<u>ou</u>d, f<u>ar</u>m, and c<u>ol</u>d.
- Words that have a VCe pattern. In these words, the initial vowel makes its long sound and the final vowel is silent (*like, hope, came*).
- Words formed by adding a common suffix to a base word. The suffixes *-ed, -er, -est, -ing, -y,* and *-le* are common (*hopped, bigger, smartest running, funny, single*). Some words formed by adding a suffix to a word are more difficult because of spelling changes when parts are combined (*hope + ing = hoping*).
- Multisyllabic words formed by adding a prefix and/or suffix to a base word or base morpheme (*reporting, unhappy, carefully*).
- Irregular words that contain one or more phonic elements the students do not know because the phonic element has not yet been taught or because the phonic element is not consistent enough to warrant teaching as a phonic element (*fuel, thought, reign*).

The primary stage, for children who entered school with a good deal of literacy-related knowledge, may begin just a month or two into the school year. For struggling readers and at-risk children who entered school with few literacy skills, 6 months or more of instruction on beginning stage skills may be necessary for them to be ready for the primary stage skills. The children's performance is always the indicator of when new skills can be introduced. Some children who enter school with few skills will progress very quickly. Remember, it is not what a child knows when entering school that dictates how quickly skills are introduced, but the student's performance as teaching occurs.

Teaching Words with Common Letter Combinations Through Explicit Instruction

A letter combination is a group of consecutive letters that represents a particular sound(s) in a number of words. In Chapter 8, we discussed procedures for teaching the most common sound of common letter combinations. In this chapter, we will present procedures for introducing words with the letter combinations.

Words with letter combinations can be introduced when students have developed basic fluency in reading regular words (reading words at about 20 words per minute).

Letter combinations should first be introduced in isolation as specified in Chapter 8 (see pages 81–85 for a discussion on how to introduce letter combinations in isolation). After 1 to 2 days of practice with the letter combination in isolation, words with that letter combination can be introduced as long as the students are not having difficulty with that letter combination in the isolated sound format.

A word-list format for introducing and practicing words with letter combinations appears in Table 10.1. In the format, the teacher prepares two lists of words, with each list containing six to eight words. In the first list, the letter combination is underlined in all the words (sp<u>ea</u>k f<u>ol</u>d, <u>th</u>at). In the second list, the letter combinations are not underlined. The first list provides intensive practice with the newest letter combination. The first three words in the first list should contain the newest combination. One to two more words in the first list would also contain the new letter combination while the other words would contain recently introduced letter combinations. For example, let's say that words with the letter combination *ai* are appearing in the word list for the first time and that the letter combinations *oo* and *ee* were the combinations introduced just previously. The first word list could include these words.

b<u>ai</u>t

m<u>ai</u>d

t<u>ai</u>l

b<u>ee</u>t

w<u>ai</u>t

m<u>oo</u>n

The students read the first list two times. On the first reading, the students say the sound for the letter combination, then say the word. On the second reading, the students just say the word.

Table 10.1

Words with Letter Combinations

Teacher	Students
Teacher writes on the board:	
b<u>ai</u>t *aim*	
m<u>ai</u>d *weed*	
t<u>ai</u>l *cart*	
b<u>ee</u>t *bait*	
w<u>ai</u>t *boat*	
m<u>oo</u>n *tool*	
fair	
First Column	
1. a. Students identify the sound of the letter combination, then read the word. Teacher points under the underlined letters and asks, "What sound?" (Signal.)	"a."
b. Teacher points to left of word. "What word?" (Signal.)	"Bait."
c. Teacher repeats step 1(a–b) with remaining words.	
2. a. Students reread the list without first identifying the sound of the letter combination. Teacher points to *bait,* pauses 2 seconds, and asks, "What word?" (Signal.)	"Bait."
b. Teacher repeats step 2(a) with remaining words.	
Second Column	
3. a. Students read the list without first identifying the sound of the letter combination. Teacher points to *aim,* pauses 2 seconds, and asks, "What word?" (Signal.)	"Aim."
b. Teacher repeats step 2(a) with remaining words.	
4. Teacher calls on individual students to read one or more words.	

The second list provides practice on the new combination and previously introduced combinations. This list should include two to three words that have the new combination and three to four words that have previously introduced combinations. Here is a sample list:

aim
weed
cart
bait
boat
tool
fair

For the second list the students would read the words without first identifying the sound of the letter combination.

Appendix A includes words the teacher can use in constructing word-list exercises for words with letter combinations.

Critical Behaviors

Signals.   When having the students say the sound for the letter combination, the teacher points under the letter combination and says, "What sound?" then signals the students to respond by moving her finger out several inches from the board and back to touch just under the letter combination in an out-in motion. When having students say the word, the teacher points to the left of a word, pauses 2 seconds to let students figure out the word, then signals by using the out-in motion. The signaling procedure must be clear. The teacher signals for the students to respond by moving her finger away from and then back towards the board. This out-and-in motion is done crisply with the finger moving away from the board (about 3 inches) and then immediately back to the board (see Figure 7.1). When the finger touches the board, the students are to respond. The out-and-in motion is done the same way every time it is used. Any hesitation or inconsistency makes a unison response difficult because the students cannot tell when they are supposed to answer.

Monitoring.   The teacher monitors the students by watching their eyes and mouths as they respond. The teacher has the group respond in unison for each list. When she believes the group is able to correctly read all words, she gives individual turns. When giving individual turns, the teacher points to a word, pauses to let all students figure out the word, then calls a student's name. This procedure increases the probability of high student attentiveness. If the teacher called the student's name first, other students might not attend to the word.

Correcting Mistakes.   If a student misidentifies a word or does not respond on signal, the teacher points to the letter or letter combination pronounced incorrectly, tells the students the sound made by the letter or letter combination, then asks the student to say its sound. For example, if a student says "boot" for *bout,* the teacher points under *ou* and says "These letters say /ou/. What sound?" After the student produces the correct sound for the letter (or letter combination), the teacher pauses for a couple of seconds and says, "What word?" After the students say the word, the teacher returns to the beginning of the list or four words earlier in the list, whichever is fewer, and re-presents the words.

Teaching Words with a VCe Pattern Through Explicit Instruction

In a VCe pattern word, a single vowel is followed by a consonant, which, in turn, is followed by a final *e*. Note the VCe patterns in the following words:

> *lake*
>
> *stripe*
>
> *smile*

In approximately two-thirds of the one-syllable words containing VCe patterns, the initial vowel represents the long sound (the letter name). In the other one-third of the words in which there is a VCe pattern, the vowel sound is sometimes the most common sound of the initial vowel (*give*) and sometimes a sound that is neither the most common sound nor the long sound (*done*).

Since the initial vowel represents its long sound in many one-syllable VCe pattern words, we recommend teaching students a strategy of saying the long vowel sound for the initial vowel when a word ends in *e*. The one-syllable, VCe pattern words in which the initial vowel makes a sound other than its long sound should be treated as irregular words.

The strategy to decode VCe pattern words can be introduced after students have been taught to identify six to eight letter combinations and can decode words containing those combinations. Reading words with letter combinations gives students practice in looking at units of letters. This skill will prepare students for VCe words in which the initial vowel sound is determined by a letter at the end of a word (the final *e*).

Preskills

Students need to be able to discriminate vowel letter names from vowel letter sounds before VCe pattern words are introduced. Many students will already know letter names for the vowels and be able to tell the sound and letter name for each letter. For these students, instruction on VCe pattern words can begin right away. For students who do not know the name of the vowel letters, the teacher will need to make a mini-program to teach vowel letter names and provide practice in discriminating the name from the sound of the letter.

The mini-program for teaching the discrimination between vowel names and sounds would begin with teaching letter names for the vowels. On the first day, the teacher writes two vowels on the board, then tells the students the names of each vowel. "You know the sound these letters make. Today you're going to learn their names." (Points to *a*.) "This letter's name is *a*." (Points to *o*.) "This letter's name is *o*." The teacher then tests the students asking, "What's the name of this letter?" for each letter. The next day, the teacher begins by testing the students: (Points to *a*.) "What's the name of this letter?" (Points to *o*.) "What's the name of this letter?" If the students know both letter names, the teacher can introduce another letter name, then test on all three letter names. The procedure is repeated daily until the students can say the letter names for all vowels.

When the students know all vowel letter names, a discrimination format including the name and sound for the letter should be introduced. The teacher writes two letters on the board: *o* and *a*. The teacher models, points to the *o*, and says, "This letter's name is o. Its sound is /ŏ/." The teacher then tests the students by asking, "What's its name? What's its sound?" The same procedure is followed with the letter *a*.

The next day the teacher begins by testing. She writes *a* and *o* on the board and for each letter asks, "What's its name? What's its sound?" If the students are able to produce the name and the sound correctly for each letter, the teacher introduces the third letter: *i*. The teacher models saying the name and sound for *i*, then tests for that letter. Afterwards, the teacher tests all three letters (*a, o, i*) by asking students to say the name and sound for each letter. The teacher provides daily practice on saying the name and sound of the vowels, *a, i,* and *o*. When the students can respond without making any errors for two consecutive days, the teacher can introduce VCe pattern words. Note that we did not include the letters *e* and *u* in the discrimination format. There are relatively few VCe pattern words in which these letters are the initial vowel. We recommend delaying the introduction of VCe pattern words with either *e* or *u* as the initial vowel. This delay reduces the initial demands on the students. Words with the letters *e* and *u* as the initial vowel can be introduced when students can decode VCe words that have *a, i,* or *o* as initial vowels.

Introductory Format for VCe

In the introductory format (see Table 10.2), the teacher tells students about the VCe rule and prompts its usage. For each word, the teacher first has the students say the name of the initial vowel, then say the word. Note that the teacher does not use the term *initial vowel,* but instead points to the initial vowel and says, "An *e* at the end tells us to say the name of this letter." This wording is used to keep the strategy simple. The VCe concept can be taught without first teaching the meaning of the terms: *vowel* and *initial*.

Discrimination Format for VCe

The discrimination format (see Table 10.3) is presented when students can respond to all questions in the introductory format without error for two consecutive lessons. Included in the discrimination format is a six-word list with three CVCe words: one with *i* as the initial vowel, one with *a* for the initial vowel, and one with *o* for the initial vowel. The remaining three words should consist of regular CVC words: one with *i* as the initial vowel, one with *a* as the initial vowel, and one with *o* as the initial vowel. One or two minimally different pairs should

Table 10.2

Introductory Format for VCe Words

Teacher	Students
Teacher writes on the board: *game, rope, mine, tape, note.*	
1. Teacher states the rule: "An *e* at the end tells us to say the name of this (pointing to *a*) letter."	
2. Teacher guides students in applying the rule.	
a. Teacher points to *game.* "Is there an *e* at the end of this word?" (Signal.)	"Yes."
b. Teacher points to *a.* "So we say the name of this letter."	
c. "What's the name of this letter?" (Signal.)	"A."
d. "Get ready to tell me the word." Teacher pauses 2 seconds, then says, "What word?" (Signal.)	"Game."
e. Teacher repeats step 2(a-d) with the remaining four words.	
3. Students read all the words without prompting from the teacher.	
a. "You're going to read these words."	
b. Teacher points to *game,* pauses 2 seconds, then signals.	"Game."
c. Teacher repeats step 2(b) with remaining words.	
4. Teacher calls on individual students to read one or more words.	

Table 10.3

Discrimination Format for VCe Words

Teacher	Students
Teacher writes on board: *make, sit, hope, like, ram, hop.*	
1. Teacher reminds students of the rule: Remember, an *e* at the end of a word tells us to say the *name* (points to initial vowel) of this letter.	
2. Teacher guides students.	
a. Teacher points to *make.* "Is there an *e* at the end of this word?" (Signal.)	"Yes."
b. Teacher points to *a* in *make.* "Do we say /ā/ or /ă/ for this letter?" (Signal.)	"/ā/."
c. Teacher points to left of *make,* pauses, then says, "What word?" (Signal.)	"Make."
d. Teacher repeats step 2(a-c) with remaining words.	
3. Students read words without teacher prompting.	
a. "When I signal, tell me the word."	
b. Teacher points to *make,* pauses 2 seconds, then asks, "What word?" (Signal.)	"Make."
c. Teacher repeats step 3(b) with remaining words.	
4. Teacher calls on several individual students to read one or more words.	

be included (e.g., *hope-hop, dime-dim*). The list would be constructed in an un-predictable order (a CVCe word is not always followed by a CVC word). A list might include these words: *make, sit, hope, like, ram, hop.* Words beginning with consonant blends (e.g., *globe, crime*) should not appear in the introductory or discrimination format for the first 2 weeks of practice with VCe pattern words in order to let students concentrate on applying the new rule.

The students read the list twice. During the first reading, the teacher guides the students, asking about the presence of an *e* at the end of the word, then asking if the initial vowel says its name. In the second reading, the students simply say the word without teacher prompting. The discrimination list is presented daily (not using the identical words from day to day) until the students are able on the first trial to respond correctly to all the words for at least three consecutive days. Thereafter, VCe pattern words are incorporated into passage-reading stories and mixed into sight-word-list exercises that contain words with letter combinations, as well as irregular words. VCe pattern words with *e* and *u* can be introduced at this time.

Correcting Mistakes.   The most common error is the students saying a CVC word for the CVCe word (e.g., saying "pan" for *pane*). The correction procedure is illustrated in the following text:

1. The teacher asks, "Is there an *e* at the end of this word?" and prompts rule "Remember, if there is an *e* at the end, we say its (pointing to vowel) name."
2. The teacher asks "What's the name (pointing to initial vowel) of this letter?"
3. The teacher has students say the word. "What word?"
4. The teacher returns to the beginning of the list and re-presents the words.

If the student says the long sound when a CVC word is presented, the teacher uses the same wording except in step 2 asks, "What's the sound of this letter?"

Teaching Words with Common Suffixes Through Explicit Instruction

During the primary stage, an increasing proportion of word-reading instruction will be devoted to reading words formed by adding affixes to base words. A first step in this sequence is to teach students to read words formed by adding the most common suffixes to base words. The most common suffixes are *-s, -er, -est, -ing, -le, -ed,* and *-y.* These suffixes are introduced early in the primary stage.

Words formed by adding a common suffix can be introduced at about the same time that letter combinations are introduced. Students should be able to read regular words at about a rate of 20 words a minute.

Words with the common suffix *-er, -ing, -est, -y,* or *-le* can be introduced with a procedure similar to that used for teaching students to read words with letter combinations. The basic procedure for teaching students to read words formed by adding a common suffix to a base word ending in a consonant is to (a) introduce the suffix in isolation, (b) practice the suffix in isolation for several days, (c) introduce words containing that suffix in a word-list exercise, and (d) then include words of that type in passage-reading stories.

The procedure begins with the teacher introducing a new suffix in isolation. The teacher writes the new suffix on the board along with several other suffixes that have already been introduced.* The teacher:

1. *Models the sounds made by the suffix.* (Teacher points to *-er.*) "At the end of a word, these letters usually say *-er.*"
2. *Tests the students.* (Teacher points to *-er.*) "What do these letters say?" "*-Er.*"
3. *Provides practice.* Teacher alternates between the new ending and other letter combinations and endings. "What do these letters say?"

Note that the teaching procedure is similar to the procedure for teaching isolated letter-sound correspondences and letter combinations.

The new word ending is practiced for several days in isolation, then words with that suffix are presented in a word-list exercise. In the word-list exercise, the teacher makes two lists. The first list contains six words, the first three of which contain the new suffix added to a known base word. Two of the other three words have recently introduced suffixes and one has the new suffix. In the first list, the base word of each word is underlined.† The base word is underlined through the double consonant. The following sample list might be used to present words with the suffix *-est.* Assume that the endings *-er, -ing,* and *-y* have previously been introduced.

<u>bigg</u>est

<u>fast</u>est

<u>hott</u>est

<u>hott</u>er

<u>madd</u>est

<u>hopp</u>ing

The teacher has the students read the list twice. On the first reading, for each word, the teacher first has the students say the underlined part ["Say the

---

*Note: The suffixes *-er* and *-ing* also function as letter combinations in one-syllable words (*sing, fern*).

†Note: In many words there will be a double consonant (*bigger, running*). This double consonant occurs because of the spelling rule requiring doubling the last letter when adding a suffix that begins with a vowel (*bat* + *-ing*= *batting*).

underlined part." (Signal.)], then say the entire word ["Say the whole word." (Signal.)]. After completing the list, the students reread the list without reading the underlined part.

In the second list, the newly introduced word ending should appear in about half the words. The other words should have previously introduced endings the first teacher has the students identify the words without saying any part of the word. Below is a sample second list.

> *softest*
>
> *funny*
>
> *smartest*
>
> *hopping*
>
> *better*
>
> *smallest*

The most important criteria in selecting words is that base words must be words the student is able to read (i.e., either an irregular word that has been previously taught or a regular word that contains letter-sound correspondences the student has been taught). A list of words containing common suffixes can be found in Appendix A.

Words Formed by Adding *-ed*

The *-ed* suffix is often troublesome for students because it may represent one of three pronunciations. When *-ed* is added to a word that ends in *d* or *t,* the *-ed* is pronounced as a separate syllable (e.g., *handed, batted*). When *-ed* is added to other words, the *-ed* sometimes represents the /t/ sound (e.g., *jumped, tricked*), and sometimes, the /d/ sound (e.g., *hummed, begged*). The suffix *-ed* can be introduced when students are able to read words formed by adding the suffix *-ing* and *-er* to a base word.

The teaching procedure for words that contain the *-ed* suffix needs to help students with the complexity of *-ed*. We recommend preparing students for reading words with *-ed* endings by first presenting a verbal format (see Table 10.4) in which the teacher writes *-ed* on the board, says a word, then says the word with the *-ed* ending (e.g., "I'll say *hop* with this ending. *Hopped.*"). The teacher repeats this procedure with two more words, each ending with a different sound (*filled, handed*). Then the teacher tests the students on a set of six words. (Say *hop* with this ending.) In two words, the *-ed* represents the /d/ sound (e.g., *filled, hummed*); in two other words the /t/ sound (e.g., *jumped, hopped*); and in the remaining two words an extra syllable (e.g., *handed, landed*). The words are not presented in a predictable manner. A sample list might include: *hand, jump, fill, land, hop,* and *hum.*

The advantage of using this verbal format is that it clearly demonstrates the different sounds the *-ed* ending can represent. Because the students do not have

Table 10.4

Format for Verbally Presented *-ed* Words

Teacher	Students
1. Teacher writes *-ed* on the board. Teacher then models and tests, saying different words with the *-ed* suffix.	

a. "Say hop." (Signal.)
      "I'll say hop with this ending."
      Teacher points to *-ed*. "Hopped."
	"Hop."

b. Teacher points to *-ed*. "Say hop with this ending." (Signal.) Teacher repeats step 1(a-b) with *hum* and *lift*.	"Hopped."
2. Teacher tests students.	
a. Teacher points to *-ed*. "Say hop with this ending." (Signal.)	"Hopped."
b. Teacher repeats step 2(a) with *hum, jump, lift, hand,* and *rub*.	
3. Teacher calls on individual students.	

to read the base word, they can concentrate on saying the ending appropriately. The *-ed* ending is not presented in an isolated-sounds task; doing so would be inappropriate since *-ed* can represent one of three sounds.

When the students can do the verbal *-ed* format without errors for two consecutive days, a format with written words can be presented (see Table 10.5). The teacher writes on the board a set of six regular words to which *-ed* has been added. (The same example selection procedure as previously described for the verbal format is used; two words in which the *-ed* will represent a separate syllable, two words in which *-ed* represents the /d/ sound, and two words in which *-ed* represents the /t/ sound are included in the set. The base words are all words that the student can decode.)

    hand̲ed

    fill̲ed

    jump̲ed

    batt̲ed

    hopp̲ed

    humm̲ed

In part 1 of this format, the students read the list of words two times. The first time through the list, the students say the base of each word, which is underlined, then say the entire word. The second time through the list the students just say the entire word. The teacher presents part 1 for 2–3 days. Part 2 is introduced on day 2 or 3 when the students can read the words in part 1 without

Table 10.5
Format for Presenting Written *-ed* Words

Teacher	Students
Teacher writes on the board:	
hum<u>m</u>ed be<u>gg</u>ed	
jum<u>p</u>ed tri<u>pp</u>ed	
lif<u>t</u>ed han<u>d</u>ed	
Part 1—Introducing *-ed* Words (presented for 2-3 days only)	
1. Students read each word by first identifying the root word and then saying the whole word.	
a. Teacher points to <u>*hum*</u>*med.* "Say the underlined part." (Signal.)	"Hum."
b. "Say the whole word." (Signal.)	"Hummed."
c. Teacher repeats step 1(a-b) with remaining words.	
2. Teacher tests students on reading words.	
a. Teacher points to *hummed.* "What word?" (Pauses 2 seconds, then signals.)	"Hummed."
b. Teacher repeats step 2(a) with remaining words.	
3. Teacher gives individual turns.	
Part 2—Discrimination Practice (begins on third day)	
Teacher writes on the board:	
lifted stopped handed	
handing skipper running	
hummed picked lifting	
biggest picking tagged	
1. **a.** Teacher points to *lifted,* pauses 2 seconds, says "What word?" (Signal.)	"Lifted."
b. Teacher repeats step 1(a) with remaining words.	
2. Teacher gives individual turns.	

error. In part 2, a list of 8–12 words is presented. Half of the words have one of the various-*ed* endings, while the other half of the words would end with other previously introduced endings. Different words are presented each day until the children can read the list for several days in a row without error.

Common Endings Added to VCe Pattern Words

Words formed by adding a common suffix that begins with a vowel (*-ed, -ing, -er*) to a VCe pattern word can be troublesome for students because of the effect of a spelling rule: When a suffix that begins with a vowel is added to a word that ends with *e,* the *e* is dropped (e.g., *hope + -ing = hoping, time + ed = timed use + -ed = used*). The difficulty that results from this spelling rule is that students may see a CVCe + suffix word as a CVC word plus an ending (e.g., *hoping* is seen as *hop + -ing* rather than *hope + -ing*).

Words of this type should not be introduced until students are firm on (can accurately read) words formed by adding a common suffix to a regular word (*batting, hammer, biggest*) and are firm on discriminating CVCe words from CVC words (*hope* vs. *hop* and *tap* vs *tape*).

Two formats can be used to teach students to read words formed by adding the suffixes *-er* or *-ing* to a CVCe word. The first format (see Table 10.6) is a format that illustrates how these words are created by applying the spelling rule. The teacher writes a set of three CVCe base words, each followed by a plus sign and a suffix that begins with a vowel, then an equal sign and the combined word (e.g., *tape + -ed = taped*). The teacher first presents the rule that *when you add the ending (-ing), you drop the final e* and then shows application of the rule with each set. The students read the base word, the suffix, and the new word formed by adding the suffix.

A format for discriminating CVCe and CVC derivatives (*hoping* vs. *hopping*) appears in Table 10.7. In this format, the teacher shows the students

Table 10.6
Format for Introducing CVCe Derivatives Formed by Adding *-ing*

Teacher	Students
Teacher writes on the board:	
hope + -ing = hoping	
care + -ing = caring	
ride + -ing = riding	
1. Teacher tells students the spelling rule: "Here's a rule about spelling words that end with an *e.* When you add the ending *-ing,* you drop the final *e.*" (Points to *hoping, caring,* and *riding.*) "These are words formed by using this rule."	
2. (Points to *hope.*) "What word?" (Signal.)	"Hope."
(Points to *hope.*) "Spell *hope.*" (Signal.)	"H-o-p-e."
(Points to *-ing.*) "What ending?" (Signal.)	"-ing."
(Points to *-ing.*) "Spell *-ing.*" (Signal.)	"i-n-g."
(Points to *hoping.*) "What word?" (Signal.)	"Hoping."
(Points to *hoping.*) "Spell *hoping.*" (Signal.)	"H-o-p-i-n-g."
3. Teacher repeats step 2 with remaining sets.	
4. Teacher has students read two-syllable words.	
a. (Points to *hoping.*) "What word?" (Signal.)	"Hoping."
b. Repeats step 4(a) with remaining words.	

Table 10.7
Discrimination Format—CVCe Derivatives vs. Regular Word Derivatives

Teacher	Students
Teacher writes on the board:	

h*o*ping   _t*a*ping_
t*a*pping   _b*a*tting_
f*i*lling   _r*o*bbing_
f*i*ling   _r*o*ping_

Teacher	Students
1. Teacher models presence of double consonants. "Some of these words have double letters after the underlined letter. Some of these words have single letters after the underlined letter." Teacher points to _hoping_. "There's one _p_ after the underlined letter. That's a single letter." Teacher points to _tapping_. "There's two _p_'s after the underlined letter. Those are double letters."	
2. Teacher tests on presence of double letters.	
a. Teacher points to _hoping_. "What comes after the underlined letter? A single letter or double letters?" (Signal.)	"A single letter."
b. Repeat step 2(a) with remaining words.	
c. Teacher gives individual turns.	
(_Note:_ Steps 3 through 5 are not introduced until students are firm on step 2.)	
3. Teacher presents rules about what to say.	
a. "Here are the rules about what to say for the underlined letter.	
b. If double letters come next, say the sound. If a single letter comes next, say the name.	
c. What do you say if a single letter comes next?" (Signal.)	"The name."
d. "What do you say if double letters come next?" (Signal.)	"The sound."
4. Teacher leads through steps in applying rule.	
a. (Points to _o_ in _hoping_.) "Does a single letter or double letters come next?" (Signal.)	"Single letter."
b. (Points to _o_.) "Do we say the name or the sound for this letter?" (Signal.) "What word?" (Signal.)	"The name." "Hoping."
c. Teacher repeats steps 4(a) and 4(b) with remaining words.	
5. Teacher tests.	
a. "This time you'll just say the whole word when I signal.	
b. (Points to _hoping_ pauses 2 seconds.) What word?" (Signal.)	"Hoping."
c. Teacher repeats step 5(b) with remaining words.	

how to use the number of consonants in the middle of the word as a cue to the pronunciation of the initial vowel. To discriminate between words such as *tapping* and *taping,* students must cue on the number of consonants in the middle of the word. One consonant in the middle of a word indicates that the word was derived from a CVCe pattern and that the initial vowel will probably represent its long sound. Two consonants in the middle of a word indicate that the word was derived from a CVC-pattern word and that the initial vowel will not represent its long sound.

The format is designed to keep language usage simple. The rule students learn is: *Double letters after the underlined letter (or vowel) tell you to say its sound. A single letter after the underlined letter (or vowel) tells you to say its name.*

Steps 1 and 2 teach students to determine if a word contains a single letter or double letters after the underlined letter (vowel). Step 3 presents the rules, In step 4, the teacher leads students through applying the rules. Appendix A lists words that can be used in this format. Note that if students can readily identify letters as consonants or vowels, the teacher can modify the exercise to say single consonant or double consonant.

This discrimination is not an easy one and may take 5 to 10 days of practice over consecutive days.

Teaching Multisyllabic Word Reading Through Explicit Instruction

A systematic introduction of prefixes and suffixes, and their incorporation into multisyllabic words, should occur throughout the primary stage.

The average number of syllables in the words students read increases steadily throughout second and third grades. At the end of the first year of instruction in beginning reading programs, students are reading primarily one- and two-syllable words. A year later, students will be reading more two- and three-syllable words with occasional four- and five-syllable words appearing. By third grade, many multisyllabic words appear. The following word list might be presented to students reading at a third-grade level:

belonging	*unfairly*	*complaining*
surrounded	*respected*	*enjoyable*
returning	*carefully*	*prevented*

Common prefixes and suffixes should be systematically introduced throughout the primary grades. Table 10.8 presents a possible sequence for introducing prefixes and suffixes. Appendix A includes list of words containing these prefixes and suffixes.

When introducing prefixes and suffixes, teachers need to keep in mind that the pronunciation of some of these affixes will differ from their phonetic representation. For example, the suffix *-able* is pronounced differently than the

Table 10.8
Sample Sequence for Introducing Common Prefixes and Suffixes

	Sample Word	Type		Sample Word	Type
-er	*batter*	inflected ending	-ist	*artist*	suffix
-ing	*jumping*	inflected ending	ad	*address*	prefix
-ed	*jumped*	inflected ending	-ible	*sensible*	suffix
-y	*funny*	suffix	-age	*package*	suffix
un	*unlock*	prefix	-sion	*mission*[a]	suffix
-est	*biggest*	inflected ending	-ence	*sentence*	suffix
-le	*handle*	suffix	-ish	*selfish*	suffix
be	*belong*	prefix	-ation	*vacation*	suffix
re	*refill*	prefix	pre	*preschool*	prefix
de	*demand*	prefix	ex	*expect*	prefix
-ic	*panic*	suffix	over	*overtime*	prefix
-ful	*careful*	suffix	-ion	*million*	suffix
con	*confuse*	prefix	-ship	*friendship*	suffix
-ment	*payment*	suffix	com	*compare*	prefix
-teen	*sixteen*	suffix	-ure	*adventure*	suffix
dis	*distant*	prefix	-ive	*detective*	suffix
-able	*enjoyable*	suffix	ac	*accuse*	prefix
-less	*useless*	suffix	-ous	*joyous*	suffix
-ness	*darkness*	suffix	inter	*interfere*	prefix
pro	*protect*	prefix	-ward	*forward*	suffix
-tion	*invention*[*]	suffix	-ize	*realize*	suffix

[*]The suffix *tion* is often formed by adding *ion* to a word ending in *t* (interruption). We list *tion* as a high-frequency suffix for convenience. In addition, *sion* is formed by adding *ion* to a word ending with *s* (miss + ion = mission).

word *able*. Also some of the items in the table are not truly affixes. Note that in the table, we list *-tion* and *-sion* as suffixes. In fact, they are not suffixes. Both *-tion* and *-sion* are formed by the affix *-ion* to a base word (*state* + *-ion* = *station*; *impress* + *-ion* = *impression*). For decoding purposes, introducing *-tion* and *-sion* as endings is functional.

The teacher introduces the affix in isolation, telling the students how it is pronounced. After introducing the affix in isolation, a word-list format is presented containing the new affix. Two lists are included in the format. The first list includes six words. The first three words include the new affix. Two of the other three words have other most recently introduced affixes and one has the new affix. In the first list, the new affix is underlined (e.g., inven<u>tion</u>, frac<u>tion</u>, inspec<u>tion</u>). The teacher has the students read the first list twice. On the initial reading, the students first say the underlined part, then read the entire word. On the second reading, they just read the entire word without first saying the underlined part.

In the second list, the newly introduced word ending should appear in about half the words. The other words should have previously introduced endings. When reading the second list, the students just read the entire word without saying the affix or base first.

The following illustrates sample lists for word-list exercises with *-tion* as the newest affix and *-ment* and *dis* being the other most recently introduced:

- *inven<u>tion</u>*   *payment*
- *frac<u>tion</u>*   *action*
- *inspec<u>tion</u>*   *displease*
- *ship<u>ment</u>*   *station*
- *men<u>tion</u>*   *formation*
- *<u>dis</u>miss*   *discuss*

Teaching Irregular Words Through Explicit Instruction

An irregular word is a word that contains one or more letter-sound relationships that the student has not learned. The concept of what is an irregular word is very important for teachers to understand. An irregular word is basically a word that the student does not have the phonic skills to read. As students learn more phonic skills such as letter combinations and the final *e* rule, the number of words that need to be treated as irregular words decreases. However, there are two types of words that will always be considered irregular and that will need to be introduced as irregulars:

- Words containing a letter combination that will not be taught to the students either because of its low frequency of appearance or lack of consistency in representing any particular sound (e.g., *duel, build, ceiling*). (See Table 10.9 for a list of these combinations.)
- Words containing common letters or letter combinations not representing their respective, most common sounds. (For example, in the word *break,* the *ea* is not representing its most common sound.)

Systematic Introduction of Irregular Words

The sequencing guidelines for introducing irregular words remain the same as during the beginning reading stage. More common words should be introduced before lower-frequency words. Also, words that are very similar to each other should not be introduced too near each other (i.e., *were* and *where*).

Table 10.9

List of Letter Combinations NOT to Be Taught

Letter Combination	Sample Word	Percentage of Words with Sound
ae	algae	83
	aesthetic	17
ei	reign	40
	deceit	26
	foreign	13
	seismic	11
eo	pigeon	67
	leopard	20
	people	13
ie	chief	64
	tie	36
gh	rough	45
	ghost	48
oe	foe	59
	shoe	22
ue	clue	75
ui	build	47
	fruit	29
uy	buy	100

Note: The words in this table either appeared in less than 10 words and/or did not represent the same sound(s) in more than half the words in which they appeared. The source for these figures is Burmeister (1968), who also utilized Hanna and Hanna's (1966) computer analysis of letter-sound correspondences.

During the primary stage, words to be introduced as irregular words will be drawn from the irregular words that will appear in upcoming stories that students are to read in the core reading program. The teacher examines the words from upcoming passages to identify irregular words to be taught. Remember, an irregular word is one that contains one or more letter-sound correspondences the student does not know. If there are an overwhelming number of new irregular words in a story, the teacher should select the irregular words from the story that are most likely to occur in future stories to preteach over words that are just unique to that particular story. During story reading, the teacher can tell the students any irregular words that have not been pretaught as they read the story.

New irregular words should appear in word-list exercises for several days before their appearance in a story. The more difficult the irregular word, the more practice is required. Two factors determine the difficulty of an irregular word. First is the difference between how the word is sounded out and how the word is pronounced. The greater the discrepancy between the sounds and the actual pronunciation, the more difficult the word is. The word *though,* for example, is more difficult to decode than the word *put* because several letters in *though* do not represent their most common sound (*ough*); whereas, in *put* only one letter does not represent its most common sound (*u*). The second factor that determines the relative difficulty of an irregular word is familiarity. The more familiar a word is to students, the easier it will be for them to decode. A word such as *tough* will be easier for students to remember than a word such as *agile,* because *tough* is more likely to be in the students' speaking vocabulary. Therefore, *agile* needs more practice and review.

Format

The format for introducing and reviewing irregular words appears in Table 10.10. The format has two parts. In part 1, the teacher presents the new irregular words.

Table 10.10
Format for Introducing and Reviewing Irregular Words

Teacher	Students
Part 1: (Teacher introduces new words.)	
Teacher writes on board:	
New Words Review Words	
ghost *agile*	
pour *fuel*	
zero *anchor*	
weight *chew*	
earth *zero*	
wrong	
1. Teacher models and has students spell words in new word column.	
a. Teacher points to *ghost.* "This word is *ghost.* What word?" (Signal.)	"Ghost."
b. "Spell *ghost.*" (Signal.)	"G-h-o-s-t."
c. "What word?" (Signal.)	"Ghost."
d. Teacher repeats step 1(a-c) with remaining words in the new word column.	
Part 2: (Students sight-read words in new word column and review word column.)	
1. **a.** "When I signal, tell me the word."	
b. Teacher points to *ghost,* pauses 2 seconds. "What word?" (Signal.)	"Ghost."
c. Teacher repeats step 1(b) with all remaining words.	
2. Teacher calls on individual students to read several words.	

These new words appear in the first column. To introduce each new word, the teacher:

- Tells the students the word. "This word is *ghost.*"
- Has the students say the word. "What word?"
- Has the students spell the word. "Spell *ghost.*"
- Has the students say the word again. "What word?"

The teacher repeats the preceding procedure with each word. After the teacher introduces and has the students spell each word in the new word column, the teacher directs the students to return to the top of the new word column and read each word without the teacher modeling or spelling. Then the teacher has the students read the review words from earlier lessons. More difficult words from previously introduced lessons also appear in the review word columns. The students read each word without any prompting from the teacher. Any error is corrected by telling the students the word, having them spell it, saying it again, then returning to the beginning of the column and re-presenting the list.

Table 10.10 shows words that might be presented in a series of mid-third-grade lessons. The new words are introduced in the first column. The words in the review column were introduced prior to the current lesson.

Providing Extra Practice

Some students may need extra practice to develop automaticity in reading irregular words. A peer-practice/testing procedure can be used to provide more practice and to ensure that students are, in fact, mastering irregular words. In this procedure, the teacher prepares a worksheet on which about 30 recently introduced irregular words appear. The words are in lists. Each word might appear two to three times on the paper. Students practice reading the list in pairs. To ensure students are attentive, the teacher directs the student who is not reading to point to the words being read. If the reader misses a word, the checker says "Stop," and tells the student the word. The reader says the word, moves back four words in the list, then continues to read. The teacher can put in a group reward to encourage cooperation and on-task behavior. After several days of practice periods, the teacher has a testing period. Higher-performing students or adults (volunteers or aides) can be the testers. The instructions to the tester are kept simple. If a student misidentifies a word, the tester says the correct word and makes a mark next to the missed word. If a student takes longer than 3 seconds to say a word, the tester tells the student the word, then makes a mark next to the word. The students' goal is to read the list without error at a rate of at least one word per second.

Every couple of weeks, a new set of words can be introduced with 30 new words. The teacher keeps old word lists and has students review them periodically. For example, after the students have been given three worksheets, they might be directed to review worksheets one and two. A danger with this procedure is that the students will memorize the order of words in a list. This danger can be minimized by sometimes having the student begin at the end of the list and read the list from bottom to top.

Putting It All Together

Teachers using a systematic core reading program can follow the sequence of their program for introducing new phonic skills. Most programs will follow a sequence that is somewhat similar to the scope and sequence chart that follows. The solid lines in the chart indicate the time period in which particular skills would be introduced and practiced daily in word-list exercises. The dotted lines indicate periodic review.

	Late first year	*Early second year*	*Mid second year*	*Later second year*
Words with letter combinations	—————————	——————————	———— - - - - -	- - - - - - -
VCe pattern words	—— - - -	- - - - - - -	- - - - - - -	- - - - - - -
Words formed by adding a common suffix	——————	— - - - - -	- - - - - - -	- - - - - - -
VCe pattern word + suffix beginning with vowel		—— - - -	- - - - - - -	- - - - - - -
Multisyllabic words		————————	————————	————
Irregular words	—————————	——————————	————————	————

Daily lessons would include several word-list exercises. For example, during early second-year instruction, a lesson might include the following exercises:

- Introduction of words with a new letter combination (Table 10.1) 12 words
- VCe pattern word introduction format (Table 10.6) 6 words
- Practice with words formed by adding a common affix 6 words
- Practice and review of irregular words (Table 10.10) 8 words

Commerical Programs

There are several characteristics of commercial reading programs that may be problematic for the struggling reader and at-risk student:

Sequencing guidelines violations. Some programs introduce letter combinations in an order that can be potentially confusing for students. Letter combinations that make similar sounds and that have a common letter are sometimes introduced very close together in the program sequence. For example, one program introduced *sh* and *ch* on consecutive lessons.

Too fast a rate of new information. Some programs concurrently introduce all the letter combinations that represent a particular sound, including the VCe pattern for a particular vowel (e.g., *ai, ay, a-e*). For the struggling reader and at-risk child, this can be overwhelming and result in students having difficulties applying knowledge of these elements when reading words in text.

Confusing teacher demonstrations. Some programs use language-ladened presentations that are likely to cause confusion for the struggling reader and at-risk child. In one program, the teacher was directed to display a chart with the letter *i* followed by a space and the letter *e*. The students are told there must be a consonant in the space and that the vowel must say its long sound. The presentation did not focus on the presence of the final *e*.

Lack of discrimination practice. Providing students with discrimination practice is important to help students determine when to use a new strategy or apply new information. Some core programs will provide practice on just the new phonic element, but provide no systematic discrimination practice. For example, when CVCe words are introduced, the word lists will include all words with CVCe, but no lists with a mix of CVC and CVCe words.

Irregular words do not receive sufficient practice. Irregular words need to be introduced and practiced systematically. Irregular words that will be appearing in stories that students are to read should be introduced in word-reading exercises for several days before the words appear in stories. In some programs, not all irregular words are introduced and practiced sufficiently before their appearance in stories.

Solutions

Modifying reading programs at the primary stage is easier than modifying programs at the beginning stage, assuming that students have firmly learned the beginning stage word-reading skills.

Teachers can create extra word-list exercises to provide needed initial and discrimination practice using the procedures discussed in this chapter. If the teaching presentations are unclear, the teacher can use the formats presented in this chapter for initial presentations.

Fixing serious sequencing problems is more difficult. If two letter combinations that are similar to each other are introduced consecutively, the teacher can delay the introduction of one of the combinations until the students are able to read words with that combination accurately when the words appear in a discrimination list.

Teachers should examine stories to be presented in the upcoming lessons, locate all words that students will not be able to decode, and introduce these words as irregular words for several days in word-list exercises prior to their appearance in stories.

Application to Your Curriclum

Evaluate Teaching of Word Reading in Your Core Reading Program (Grade levels 1 to 3 only)

1. Words with Letter Combinations

   a. Examine the first- and second-grade levels of your reading program. List the grade level and lesson when letter combinations are introduced. Indicate the sound/s/ for each letter combination.

   b. Are there problems with the order and rate in which words with letter combinations are introduced?

   c. Examine the lesson/s/ in which the letter combination *ai* is introduced. What is the procedure for teaching students to read words with that letter combination?

   d. Examine 10 consecutive lessons after a particular letter combination. Is there adequate practice on reading words with letter combinations in word-list exercises and/or stories?

   e. Indicate revisions that are needed to make the teaching of words with letter combinations more effective.

2. Words with VCe Pattern

   a. Examine the first five lessons in which words with a VCe pattern are presented.

   b. What is the teaching procedure for reading words with a VCe pattern?

   c. Are revisions needed in the teaching procedure?

   d. Is there adequate word-list practice on VCe pattern words including discrimination practice with CVC words?

   e. When do VCe pattern words begin to appear in stories? Is their appearance in stories coordinated with the word-list introduction?

   f. Indicate revisions that are needed to make the teaching of words with VCe patterns more effective.

3. Words with Common Affixes

   a. Examine the first five lessons in which words with the affix *-ing* are presented.

   b. What is the procedure for teaching students to read words with *-ing* endings?

   c. Examine the first five lessons in which words with the affix *-ed* are presented.

   d. What is the procedure for teaching students to read words with *-ed* endings?

   e. When do words that end with the affixes *-ing* and *-ed* begin to appear in stories? Is their appearance in stories coordinated with the word-list introduction?

   f. Indicate revisions that are needed to make the teaching of words with common affixes more effective.

4. Irregular Words

   a. Select two consecutive lessons from late in the first-grade level or early in the second-grade level. Examine the stories in those two lessons to determine irregular words that appear in the stories.

   b. Examine the teacher presentation book for these two lessons and three lessons preceding the stories. Note if and how the irregular words that appear in the stories are taught in these lessons.

   c. Indicate revisions that are needed to make the teaching of irregular words more effective.

At a Glance   Reading Words with Common Letter Combinations

Materials	Write two columns of words on the board:

b<u>ai</u>t	*aim*
m<u>ai</u>d	*weed*
t<u>ai</u>l	*cart*
b<u>ee</u>t	*bait*
w<u>ai</u>t	*boa*
m<u>oo</u>n	*fair*

Selecting Examples

First column:

- The first three words should contain the new combination.
- In the next three words, the new combination should appear along with two of the most recent combinations.
- Underline all letter combinations in the first column.

Second column:

- Words should contain a mix of new and review combinations.

What to Do

- Students identify the sound, then read the whole word. Teacher points to underlined letters and says, "What sound?" Teacher then points to left of word and says, "What word?"
- Repeat with all the words in column 1.
- Students go back to the top and reread the list without first identifying sound combination ("What word?").
- Students read words in column 2. Teacher points and asks, "What word?"
- Call on individual students to read one or two words.

Correcting Mistakes

- Teacher points to missed letters in word, tells students the sound represented by the letter(s), asks students to identify sound, then the whole word. "What do these letters say?, What word?"
- Go back to the beginning of the list or back three to four words.

continued

| Rate and Practice | • Do this exercise for 3 to 4 minutes with 10 to 14 words with letter combinations prior to text reading exercises. |
| Strategy Integration | • After students read words with letter combinations in words lists, these words should appear in passage reading exercises. |

At a Glance   Reading Words with Affixes

Materials	Write two columns of words on board:
	invention payment
	frac<u>tion</u> location
	inspec<u>tion</u> displease
	ship<u>ment</u> basement
	men<u>tion</u> formation
	<u>dis</u>miss discuss
Selecting Examples	First column:
	• The first three words should contain the new affix.
	• In the next three words the new affix should appear along with two of the most recent affixes.
	• Underline all affixes in the first column.
	Second column:
	• Words should contain a mix of new and review affixes.
What to Do	• Students identify the underlined part, then read the whole word. Teacher points to the underlined letters and says, "What part?" Teacher then points to left of word and says, "What word?"
	• Repeat with all the words in column 1.
	• Students now reread list without first identifying the word part.
	• Students read words in column 2. Teacher points and says, "What word?"
	• Call on individual students to read one or two words.

continued

Correcting **Mistakes**	• Teacher points to the missed word part, tells students what the missed letters say, then asks students to identify the part, then the whole word. "What does this part say? What word?"
	• Go back to the beginning of the list or back three to four words.
Rate and Practice	• Do this exercise for 3 to 4 minutes with 10 to 14 words prior to text reading exercises.
Strategy Integration	• After students read words with affixes in words lists, these words should appear in passage reading exercises.

CHAPTER 11

Overview of Fluency

What Is Fluency?

Fluency is the ability to read a text quickly and accurately with ease and expression. When fluent readers read aloud, it sounds like they are speaking. Fluency is important because it is a bridge between word recognition and comprehension. Fluent readers can focus their attention on the meaning of text because they do not need to concentrate on decoding the words. In contrast, the oral reading of readers who have not yet developed fluency is slow, word-by-word, choppy, and plodding. They do not chunk words into meaningful units. Because less-fluent readers must focus their attention on figuring out the words, they have less attention left to devote to understanding the text. Fluency is essential to comprehension and automatic word recognition is essential to fluency. Thus, fluency is a bridge that the reader must traverse to get from word recognition to comprehension. Although the terms *automaticity* and *fluency* frequently have been used interchangeably, they are not the same. Automaticity refers to fast, effortless recognition of words in isolation or in lists. Fluency refers to fast, effortless reading of words in sentences and passages coupled with the ability to group words quickly to help gain meaning from what is being read. Automatic word recognition is a necessary, but not sufficient, condition of fluency. Some students may recognize words in isolation or in lists automatically and still lack fluency when reading those same words in sentences. These students need instruction in fluency.

Why Fluency Is Important—The Research Connection

Automatic word recognition, fluency, and comprehension are inextricably intertwined reading skills. The main findings of the National Reading Panel (2000) on fluency appear in Figure 11.1. As stated in Figure 11.1, instructional procedures that improve fluency also have a positive impact on word recognition and comprehension.

- Classroom practices that include repeated oral reading with feedback and guidance lead to improvements in reading for good readers, as well as those who are experiencing difficulties.
- Guided, repeated oral-reading procedures that improve reading fluency also have a positive impact on word recognition and comprehension.
- Repeated reading procedures have a clear impact on the reading ability of non-impaired readers through at least grade 4, as well as on students with various kinds of reading problems throughout high school.
- Fluency can be improved by having students read and reread text a certain number of times or until certain levels of speed and accuracy are reached.
- No research evidence is available currently to confirm that instructional time spent on silent, independent reading improves reading fluency and overall reading achievement.
- The lack of demonstrated effectiveness of strategies encouraging independent silent reading suggests that explicit are more important than implicit instructional approaches for improving reading fluency.

Figure 11.1

National Reading Panel Conclusions from Scientifically Based Research on Fluency Instruction

Adapted from the NRP Report of the Subgroups, Chapter 3, "Fluency," p. 29.

Two major instructional approaches to fluency have been investigated by researchers:

1. Repeated reading approaches in which students read passages aloud several times and receive guidance and feedback from the teacher as they read aloud.

2. Independent silent reading approaches in which students are encouraged to read extensively on their own.

The National Reading Panel pointed out that research has not yet confirmed independent silent reading as a means of improving fluency and overall reading achievement. Research has, however, confirmed that repeated oral reading with feedback and guidance improves fluency and has a positive impact on comprehension. In repeated oral reading, students read and reread a text a specified number of times or until specified levels of speed and accuracy are reached. Listening to good models of fluent reading also promotes fluency; however, students must reread the text themselves after listening to the model.

Recent research on the relationship of fluency development in the lower grades and student performance on state reading tests in third and fourth grade has shown strong relationships. Students who meet expected grade-level fluency rates at each grade are more likely to meet or exceed state benchmark standards in reading.

How Fluency Fits into the Reading Program

Story reading is an integral part of reading instruction. The first story-reading exercises begin early in the beginning stage shortly after students learn to sound out words in lists. Story reading is part of each lesson. The first step includes teaching students to use the sounding-out skills they learn in phonics exercises to read words in stories. Initial stories are very short and story-reading exercises constitute just a small part of the reading lesson. During the first part of the beginning stage, students sound out the words in stories. A gradual transition is made during the beginning stage from sounding out to sight-reading. A good deal of the reading during the beginning stage is choral so that students receive the active practice needed to develop fluency.

In the primary stage, story reading consumes a larger part of the reading period as students work on accuracy, fluency, and comprehension. Students continue to orally read text daily.

There is a concurrent emphasis on both accurate and fluent reading in both stages. Teaching students to read text accurately is a critical part of the reading program. An early emphasis on accuracy will enable students to develop the concentration to read accurately without great effort. The need for accurate reading becomes increasingly observable when students encounter more complex scientific materials where misreading one word can change the meaning of a sentence.

In the chapters that follow, we present procedures for teaching fluency. We begin by presenting procedures for conducting passage reading during the beginning stage of reading. We first present procedures to use during the first few months of reading instruction and then present procedures to use during the following years of reading instruction. The procedures incorporate modeling of fluent reading and repeated oral readings to specified levels of speed and accuracy. These procedures are carried out in the context of passage-reading activities.

CHAPTER 12

Passage Reading During the Beginning Reading Stage

The transfer of the skills taught during phonic exercises to the reading of connected text requires a good deal of teacher support, particularly for children at risk because of limited literacy and/or language backgrounds. This chapter includes three major teaching steps to provide this support to the beginning reader.

The first major step is teaching the students to participate as part of an instructional group in sounding out regular words and phrases, which are written as very short decodable passages. The second major step is actually sounding out words in short decodable stories composed of regular words and some irregular words. The third step is the transition from sounding out to sight-reading of stories.

Preskills for Story Reading

Sounding out words that appear in decodable booklets or worksheets is significantly more difficult for the instructionally naive child than word-list sounding out. In word-list exercises, the teacher points to the letters and the students say the sounds. In passage-reading exercises, the student must learn to coordinate independently moving from letter-to-letter and concurrently saying the sounds. This important step is often overlooked in the instruction for instructionally naive beginning readers.

In this section, we present suggestions for the important preskill of teaching children how to sound out single words and phrases written on worksheets.

Reading words on worksheets can be introduced when students know about 8 to 10 letter-sound correspondences and are able to sound out the words in a word-list task with relative ease. This level of mastery would be indicated by the students not making more than one error on a five-word sounding-out word-list task for two consecutive days.

The procedure that we recommend for what is essentially a preskill for story reading involves the children reading in unison as the teacher signals. The format for this step (see Table 12.1) has the students sound out a word while responding in unison, saying the sound and touching each letter as the teacher signals. The students sound out the word until they can sound it out two times in a row without error, then say the word at a normal rate.

A main purpose of this format is to teach children to work as a group, using choral responding. Choral responding can be especially beneficial with

Table 12.1

Format for Sounding Out Words on Worksheets

Teacher	Students
1. "Everybody, touch the big ball of the arrow for the first word."	Students touch ball of first arrow.
2. "We are going to sound out the word. When I clap, touch the first little dot and say the sound above it. Keep on saying it until I clap again, then move your finger and say the next sound. Don't stop between sounds."	
3. "Get ready." Teacher pauses 1 second then claps. After 1 to 1 1/2 seconds, teacher claps for next sound. Then 1 to 1 1/2 seconds later she claps for the last sound.	Students say sounds, pointing to the dots under the letters as they say sounds.
"Again, back to the big ball of the arrow."	Students touch the ball of the first arrow.
"Get ready." Teacher pauses 1 second, then claps. After 1 to 1 1/2 seconds, teacher claps for next sound. Then 1 to 1 1/2 seconds later, she claps for the last sound.	Students say sounds, pointing to the dots under the letters as they say sounds.
Step 3 is repeated until the students sound out the word two times without an error. Then the teacher asks, "What word?"	Students say the word at a normal rate.
4. a. "Touch the big ball of the next arrow."	Students put a finger on ball of next arrow.
b. Teacher repeats step 3 with the next word.	
5. Teacher gives individual turns. Several students sound out a word.	

instructionally naive students, who tend to be very distractible. The touching procedure and unison responding not only keep students actively involved, but also make monitoring easier, since the procedure enables the teacher to more easily see and hear students respond. For teachers working with groups of four or more children, the unison reading procedure is critical if students are to receive enough active practice to develop automaticity. Young children, especially struggling readers and at-risk children, are not likely to be highly attentive when they are not actively involved. The procedures we recommend facilitate very active involvement.

Initial exercises include just one or two words. The words should be ones that the students sounded out in word-list exercises in earlier lessons. Words to be read in these exercises should be written large enough to allow the students to place their finger under each letter. A useful prompt for these exercises is to have an arrow under each word. The arrows would resemble these:

The dots under each sound are prompts to help students know where to touch as the teacher signals.

Critical Behaviors

Signaling. The signaling procedure for unison responding needs to be done precisely. Because the students are looking at their worksheet and not at the teacher, the signal for unison responding must be audible. Students cannot look at the worksheet while simultaneously watching for the teacher's signal. The audible signal we recommend has two parts—a "Get ready" and a series of claps (or taps or finger snaps). The "Get ready" tells the students that they will begin to respond in a second; the first clap indicates that they are to say the first sound. The critical teacher behavior in making the signal effective is a consistent 1-second pause between the "Get ready" and the first clap. Consistency is necessary so that students will be able to use the "Get ready" as an effective cue by expecting the clap 1 second after they hear "Get ready." The teacher pauses 1 to $1^1/_2$ seconds and claps for the next sound, then pauses 1 to $1^1/_2$ seconds and claps again for the next sound.

The students will sound out each word several times. To ensure that repetitions are done quickly and with little confusion, the teacher must use a clear signal for instructing the students to return to the first letter of a word. The teacher can do this by saying, "Again, back to the big ball of the arrow." After giving this instruction several times, it can be abbreviated to "Again." The teacher should make certain all the students are touching the ball of the arrow before signaling the group to sound out the word another time.

Monitoring. The monitoring techniques used in sounding out passages in unison are similar to those a teacher uses in word-list exercises. As in word-list reading, the teacher watches the students' mouth and notes if the students' lip movement is appropriate for each sound. For example, if a students' lips do not come together at the end of the word *ham,* the teacher knows that the student made an error. To say the word *ham,* the lips must be pressed together for the final "mmmmm" sound. The teacher also watches the students' fingers, noting if the student is pointing to the appropriate letter.

Correcting. Initially instructionally naive students will have difficulty following the signal for shifting from letter to letter. The teacher corrects by leading, responding with students and, if necessary, by physically moving the student's finger from one letter to the next. The teacher can expect more instructionally naive students to need 10 to 15 repetitions on the lead step during the first lessons when this new skill is introduced. A great deal of teacher skill is needed to give the children adequate practice and still make the reading lesson enjoyable for them. One way to keep lessons enjoyable is to provide a short 5- to 10-second change-up after each five or so practice trials. During the change-up, the teacher encourages the students: "You kids are working so hard. These are really hard words and you've almost got it." The teacher should praise students who are responding correctly. Remember, it is important to give your attention to children making the response you want. When the whole group finally sounds out a word correctly following the signal, the teacher should act very excited and proud of the students. "You did it! I'm so proud of you. Give yourself a pat on the back!"

Selecting Examples

The number of words in these initial reading exercises can increase gradually. The number of words in an exercise can be determined by the number of minutes a group took to master the words in the previous lesson. Generally, on the initial word-reading activities on worksheets, about 5 to 7 minutes would be allocated to this activity. During the first lesson, just one or two words can be included in the exercise. When students can follow the signal and touch and sound out on signal with few errors, another word can be added to the exercise. Note that the words are not selected to make up a sentence or phrase. In this stage students are simply learning how to sound out and read individual words. Each day different words would be presented on the worksheet. Below is a possible sequence:

- Day 1 *am*
- Day 2 *Sam*
- Day 3 *sad it*
- Day 4 *sit am*
- Day 5 *mad Sam it*
- Day 6 *am fat sad*
- Day 7 *at it rim Sam*
- Day 8 *it fit Sam sad*

For some children, learning how to sound out words on their own copy of a worksheet and responding in unison as part of a group, may only take a couple of days. For some children, several weeks of instruction and practice may be needed.

Sounding Out Passages

Sounding out passages can be introduced when a group is able to read the individual words on worksheets in unison. A format for sounding out stories appears in Table 12.2. The procedure is very similar to that for introducing reading individual words on worksheets. The signaling and monitoring procedures are the same. In the format, the teacher has the students read the story two times in unison. The first time through the story the students sound out the word twice, then say it at a normal rate. The second time through the story, the students just sound out the word one time, then say it fast. Note that when irregular words appear the teacher should remind students that the word is a "funny" word.

The word in the stories that students are given to read must be very carefully controlled. The words should be coordinated with the introduction of phonic

Table 12.2

Format for Sounding Out Passage Reading

Teacher	Students
1. "We are going to sound out the words in this story. Everybody, touch the first word."	Students touch under first letter of word.
2. "First word. Get ready." Teacher pauses 1 second, then claps. After 1 to 1 1/2 seconds, teacher claps for next sound. Then 1 to 1 1/2 seconds later she claps for last sound.	Students say sounds, pointing to the dots under the letters as they say sounds.
"Again."	Students touch under first letter of word.
"Get ready." Teacher pauses 1 second, then claps. After 1 to 1 1/2 seconds, teacher claps for next sound. Then 1 to 1 1/2 seconds later she claps for last sound.	Students say sounds, pointing to the dots under the letters as they say sounds.
"What word?"	Students say the word at a normal rate.
3. a. "Touch the next word."	Students put finger on ball of next arrow.
b. Teacher repeats step 2 with next word.	
4. Teacher repeats step 3 with the remaining words in the sentence.	
5. Teacher repeats steps 2–4 with the next sentence.	
6. Teacher has students sound out the story a second time, having students sound out each word one time before asking students to say the word at a normal rate.	
7. Teacher gives individual turns, calling to several students to sound out several words.	

elements in the phonic word-list exercises. The prime rule of passage construction is that the student should be well prepared through phonic word-list exercises to read all words that appear in passages. During the first weeks of passage reading, the passages students read should contain only words that have previously appeared in word-list exercises. Including previously taught words will help make the transition from word-list reading to sounding-out passage reading easier. Later, words that contain phonic elements the students have practiced a good deal in the word-list exercises can appear in stories without first being presented in word-list exercises.

We recommend that during the first months of reading instruction that struggling readers and at-risk children read stories in which a high proportion of the words are phonetically regular words. Unfortunately in many commercial core programs, a high proportion of the words in beginning books will be irregular words. Suggestions for dealing with this situation appear in Part 3.

The length of stories should gradually increase. The first story might include just one sentence. As the students progress through the beginning stage, more time should be devoted to story reading. Story length should gradually increase.

Passage-reading exercises, during the beginning stage, should be structured so that students attend to the letters in the words and nothing else. Consequently, picture cues should be avoided because some students will try to use them as an aid in decoding words. A student might look at the first letter in a word, then look at the picture to find an object whose name starts with that letter. For example, when reading the sentence "Tom had a rock," a student might look at a picture, then begin reading "Tim had a . . . ," and then, not knowing the /o/ sound in the next word, *rock,* refer to the picture for help in figuring out the word. If the picture shows a child holding a rock, the student is likely to use the picture as a cue for decoding the word. An effective way to avoid problems with pictures is to construct pages so that pictures appear only on the page following the end of the passage. The students see the picture only after they read the passage.

Critical Behaviors

Monitoring Student Performance.   During group unison responding, the teacher monitors by looking at the students' mouths, eyes, and fingers, switching from student to student throughout the exercise.

When the students complete the second unison reading, the teacher gives individual turns. As a general rule, individual turns should not be given until all the children in the group appear to be following the signals and responding correctly in unison.

Individual turns serve as a check to see if students are actual participants in the group reading (students often become quite good at mimicking other students rather than actually reading), and to see if the teacher has provided enough practice. During individual turns, the students who are not reading should follow along, touching the letters as the reader says the sounds. Since the teacher can hear the responses of the student who is reading, he or she watches the eyes and fingers of the other students who are following along. To increase the probability of students being attentive, the teacher can instruct the nonreaders to whisper as they point to the letters.

Corrections.   There are several types of errors that might occur during sounding-out stories. Students might say an incorrect sound for a letter (saying *mmmmiiiii* when sounding out *mad*). The correction is similar to that specified in the word-list sounding-out exercises. The instant the teacher hears an error, he or she models the correct sound, and tests by having the students say the sound, then directs students back to the beginning of the word and has them sound out the word again. As the final part of the correction, the teacher has the students return to the beginning of the sentence and reread the sentence. When the students reach the missed word again (after having returned to the beginning of the sentence), they are receiving a delayed test on that word. If the students miss a sound in a word near the end of a sentence, the teacher can let the students continue reading the sentence, then say, "Let's go back to the beginning of the sentence and read it again with no mistakes."

A second kind of error is the students pausing between sounds when sounding out the word. The correction is for the teacher to first model sounding out the word. The teacher directs the students to touch the sounds on their story while modeling how to sound out without pausing. "My turn. Touch the sounds as I sound it out. Get ready, *mmmmaaad*. Then the teacher has the students sound out the word. The teacher responds with them, then has students sound it out on their own.

A third kind of error might occur when the teacher asks students to say the word fast and the students do not say the correct word; for example, saying "at" when the word is *mat*. The correction is similar to the correction to word-list reading. The teacher says the word, has the students say the word, then leads, responding with the students as they sound out the word again and then say it at a normal rate. Note that this type of error usually occurs because the student paused when sounding out a word, such as sounding out the word "*mmm aaaat.*"

Again, a good deal of teacher skill is required to help students reach a high level of performance and, at the same time, keep the lesson positive and motivating for the students.

Finding the Beginning of a Sentence

A critical part of the story-reading correction procedure is to have the students immediately reread a sentence in which they made an error. After telling the students to sound out the missed word, the teacher instructs the students to go back to the first word in the sentence.

A great deal of time can be saved if the students are able to find the first word of the sentence quickly. A format for teaching this skill appears in Table 12.3. This format should be presented early in the school year. The format has four parts. In part 1, the teacher holds up a story and models how to find the end of a sentence. In part 2, the teacher has the students go through the story, finding the end of each sentence. During this part, the teacher must monitor the students carefully to make certain they move their fingers word-by-word until they get to the period. Part 2 is presented daily until the students are able to find the end of sentences in a story without making any errors.

Parts 3 and 4 teach the students how to go back and find the first word in a sentence. In part 3, the teacher models. The teacher holds up a copy of the story and models how to return to the beginning of sentences. In part 4, the students practice finding the beginning of sentences.

Table 12.3

Format for Finding First Word of Sentence

Teacher	Students
Part 1: Teacher models finding end of sentences.	
1. Teacher holds up a story that is at least four sentences long.	
2. "You can tell where a sentence ends by looking for a little dot, called a period."	
3. (Teacher points to first word in the story.) "This is where the first sentence begins. I'll move my finger and stop at the period."	
4. (Teacher moves finger from word to word and stops at the period.) "This period tells us that this is the end of the first sentence."	
5. "I'll move my finger from word to word; say 'period' when I get to the next period." (Teacher moves finger from word to word, pointing at the space between each word for an instant.)	
6. Teacher repeats step 5 with remaining sentences.	
Part 2: Teacher tests finding end of sentences.	
1. "Put your finger on the first word of the story."	
2. "Move your finger from word to word. Stop when you get to the period at the end of the sentence."	
3. Teacher repeats step 2 with remaining sentences.	
4. Teacher repeats steps 1 through 3 if students had any difficulty.	
Part 3: Teacher models finding beginning of sentences.	
1. "I'll show you how to find the beginning of a sentence."	
2. (Teacher holds up a story and points to the period at the end of the last sentence in the story.) "Here's the end of the last sentence in the story."	
3. "Watch me find the beginning of that sentence." (Teacher moves finger from word to word until she reaches the preceding period.) "Here's the period." (Teacher points to word after period.) "This is the first word of that sentence."	
4. "Now I'll find the first word of this sentence." (Teacher points to preceding sentence, moves from word to word, and stops just before period.)	
Part 4: Students practice finding the beginning of sentences.	
1. "Look at your stories."	
2. "Touch the period at the end of the story."	
3. "Move your finger back until you come to the first word of that sentence."	
4. (Teacher points to last word of preceding sentence.) "Move your finger back until you come to the first word of this sentence."	
5. Repeat step 4 with remaining sentences.	

Transition to Sight-Word Reading of Passages

The transition from sounding out passages to reading all the words at sight should be a gradual one. Sight-reading in which students say the word at a normal rate and do not sound it out vocally can begin when students are able to read words in a sight-word list with few errors and with no more than a 3-second pause to figure out the word.

When the transition to sight reading stories begins, we recommend that students first read the entire story orally sounding out the words in unison.

The purpose is to buttress against the possibility of students adopting a guessing strategy. The proportion of the story sounded out first can decrease as students show they can apply a careful word-reading approach during sight-reading. We recommend that students continue sounding out the words in stories for several weeks after sight-word passage reading is introduced.

A format for introducing sight-reading passages appears in Table 12.4. This introductory format is presented after students first sound out the story. After sounding out the story, the students choral read by sight. When they complete sight-reading the story in unison, the teacher has the students read the story a third time, calling on individual students to read a whole sentence. During

Table 12.4

Introductory Format for Passage Sight-Reading

Teacher	Students
1. Teacher says, "You're going to read the words in this story the fast way. When I signal, you'll say a word the fast way."	
2. Students read the first sentence, teacher says:	
a. "Touch the first word."	Students touch under first letter of first word.
b. "Figure out the word. Move your finger under the sounds and say the sounds to yourself." (Pause up to 3 seconds.)	Students touch letters and sound out word subvocally.
"What word?." (Signal.)	Students say the first word.
c. "Next word. Say the sounds to yourself." (Pause up to 3 seconds.)	Students sound out word subvocally.
"What word?." (Signal.)	Students say the next word.
d. Teacher repeats step 2(c) with remaining words in the sentence.	
e. Students are to reread the sentence if they need more than 3 seconds to figure out any word in the sentence.	
3. Teacher repeats step 2 with remaining sentences.	
4. Teacher has individual students read a sentence.	

the unison sight-reading, the teacher prompts the students to sound out each word to themselves before saying it at a normal rate. During this unison sight-reading, the students work on a sentence until the students are able to identify each word in the sentence with no longer than a 3-second pause. This format would be presented daily until students are able to read words accurately with no longer than a 3-second pause on the first sight-reading of the story.

When students have gained some fluency in reading passages (one word each 3 seconds), a less-prompted format can be used (see Table 12.5). In this less-prompted format the teacher does not remind students to sound out the word to themselves during sight-reading. The teacher has the students read the story, signaling for each word to be read in unison. After the unison sight-reading, the teacher writes on the board any words the students missed during the passage reading and conducts a sight-word-list reading exercise. Then the teacher calls on individual students to read the story a sentence at a time.

Table 12.5
Format for Practicing Sight-Reading a Passage

Teacher	Students
Part 1: Students sight-read story in unison.	
1. Teacher says, "We're going to read the words in the story the fast way. Each time I signal, say a word the fast way."	
2. "Touch the beginning of the story." (Pause.)	Students touch.
3. "Figure out the first word." (Pause.) "What word?" (Signal.)	Students say first word.
4. a. "Next word." (Teacher pauses while students figure out the next word.) "What word?" (Signal.)	Students say word.
b. Teacher repeats step 4(a) with remaining words in sentence.	
c. (If students need more than specified pause time for any word or make an error, the teacher has students reread the sentence.)	
5. "Touch the first word in the next sentence." (The teacher has the students read the sentences using the same procedure as in steps 3 and 4.)	
Part 2: Teacher firms up missed words.	
1. Teacher writes missed words on the board. The students sound out, then identify each word.	
2. Students sight-read the list.	
Part 3: Individual turns.	
1. Teacher calls on individual students to read a sentence at a time, asking comprehension questions.	

Critical Behaviors

Signaling and Monitoring.   When reading a passage, the students are looking at their stories, not at the teacher. The students are to point to the words they are reading and keep their eyes on their book. The signal for students to respond in sight-word passage reading, as in the sounding-out passage-reading exercise, must be an auditory signal. The teacher gives the children time to sound out the word, then says, "What word?" Then, a second later, he or she makes a noise such as a clap, snap, or pencil tap. The length of time between the "What word?" and the clap should be consistent. Think of it as hitting a drum. The drummer says, "What word?" then lifts his or her drumstick and hits the drum.

The teacher monitors by carefully listening to the students' response, checking whether the students are pointing to each word, and watching their lips and eyes. The teacher looks at the students' eyes to see if they are in fact attending to the words in the story. The teacher looks at the students' lips to determine if they are sounding out the words to themselves.

During unison passage reading, the teacher will say, "Next word," as a cue for the students to point to the next word. The teacher monitors to ensure that the students touch the next word and immediately try to figure out the word by sounding it out to themselves.

When the introductory format is presented, the goal is for students to read each word with no more than a 3-second pause. Teachers may find that some children will initially need more time to figure out a word. The teacher can allow a couple more seconds, but should not allow more than 5 seconds. (Allowing too much time may inadvertently reinforce the student starting over and over rather than trying to figure out the whole word.) If the students need more than 3 seconds to figure out a word in a sentence, the teacher should repeat that sentence.

As the students progress in the reading program, the time allowed for students to figure out a word decreases. More information on developing fluency will be discussed later in this chapter.

Pacing.   During unison reading, the teacher keeps the passage reading well-paced by having the students move quickly from word to word, while allowing them adequate time to figure out words. Immediately after the students say a word correctly, the teacher should say, "Next word." The students are immediately to begin sounding out the next word to themselves. The teacher allows them time to figure out the word, then says, "What word?" and signals. If the students respond correctly, the teacher immediately says, "Next word," then pauses several seconds to let the students figure out the word. (Teachers should allow for longer pauses for words that occur at the beginning of a new line of print, since students must move their fingers down to the next line and back to the left side of the page to locate the next word.) If the teacher hears an error, the teacher immediately corrects and then has the students return to the first word in the sentence.

Individual Reading.   The last part of each sight-reading format has individual students read a sentence or two orally while the other students follow along. No signals are necessary during individual reading since the students are not responding in unison. However, to encourage attentiveness, students who are not reading aloud should point to each word as it is read. (Remember, this procedure is for the beginning reader. In later grades, this pointing is not necessary.) The teacher calls on students in an unpredictable order. If students can predict when they will be called on to read, some are likely not to attend until it is almost their turn. Others may look ahead to find "their" sentence and practice it. Sometimes inattentive students should be called on to read again after only one other student has read. This indicates to students that, even though they may have just finished a sentence, they cannot become inattentive because they might be called upon again soon. Students should read only one or two sentences in a row, since the longer one student reads, the greater the probability some other students will become inattentive. The more inattentive the students in a group, the fewer the number of consecutive sentences any one student should read.

Students should be instructed to stop at periods in order to read in more meaningful units. The pause also enables the teacher to call on a new student to read. The teacher calls on the new student immediately after one student says the last word of a sentence. This quick pace enhances student attentiveness and maintains story continuity.

During individual turns, some students will read in a very quiet voice, making it difficult for other students to follow along. Imploring or nagging a student to read louder will not usually change the student's behavior. Providing strong reinforcement for students who do speak in an acceptably loud voice will often be effective in eliciting louder responses from a student who is reading too quietly. The reinforcement can be in the form of specific praise after a student reads, such as "Great job, Erika. You read with a big voice," or the teacher can reward the student with a tangible reinforcer (e.g., stickers) at the end of the group session for reading in a "big" voice.

The teacher should incorporate motivational steps to encourage accurate reading during individual turns. Each correctly read sentence might earn the student a point. Earning a specified number of points can lead to a sticker.

Correcting Errors.   During unison sight-word reading, the teacher should make a correction if any student says the wrong word. The correction procedure for misread words during sight-passage reading in the beginning stage should always direct the student to use the strategy of sounding out the word. The steps are to (a) tell the students the word; (b) instruct the group to sound out the word, then say it at a normal rate; and (c) direct the students to return to the beginning of the sentence and reread the sentence. For example, if during choral reading the students are reading "A cat went in it," and the teacher hears a student say "want" for *went,* the teacher should say, "That word is *went,* let's sound out the word. Put your finger on the first sound. Get ready." (Signal.) After the students sound out and say the word correctly, the teacher tells the students to return to the beginning of the sentence and has the students reread the sentence.

The words missed during passage reading should be included in the part 2 firm-up and in the next lesson's word-list exercise.

A second type of error is one in which a student does not respond on signal. The student responds after the rest of the group or simply does not respond. For this circumstance, the teacher also has the group sound out the word and return to the beginning of the sentence. Because the teacher doesn't know whether the student didn't know the word or just wasn't attentive, the extra practice is necessary.

Developing Fluency and Accuracy

Students will differ greatly in the amount of practice needed to develop sufficient fluency and accuracy. A major way that the teacher meets these different needs is through providing more practice to children who need it. Generally, if a correction is required for more than two sentences in a paragraph, the teacher should have the students read that paragraph again. Higher-performing groups may make few errors and need less repetition. More instructionally naive students may need a good deal of repetition. Providing this extra practice daily from the early days of reading instruction will help the more instructionally naive students progress at an accelerated rate.

Requiring students to reread a sentence after a correction or to reread a paragraph if too many words are not read correctly is necessary for students to begin developing fluency while also demonstrating to students that the teacher places an importance on reading accurately. Teachers must be prepared to use a combination of techniques to make passage reading a motivating activity and keep students from viewing reading as a dull, repetitive task. As mentioned earlier, a key to successful passage reading is to ensure careful alignment between word-list exercises and passages to ensure that the passage has only words that students have the skills to decode. A key teaching technique when presenting passage reading is for the teacher to be positive and supportive. When a student makes an error, the teacher needs to monitor the tone of his or her voice, not making it a blaming or punishing tone, but a matter-of-fact supportive tone. Rather than nagging students who make errors, the teacher should praise children who respond well, and respond very enthusiastically when lower performers perform well. When directing the students to reread a sentence, the teacher is supportive. The teacher might say, "Let's read this sentence again. You're working hard. I bet you'll do it perfectly this time." When students read a sentence with no errors, the teacher responds enthusiastically, "Great, perfect reading!" When students read several sentences in a row without error, the teacher would respond with even more enthusiasm. "Wow, that was great. Pat yourselves on the back for a great job."

Increasing Fluency During Year-One Reading

Throughout the beginning stage, the teacher works to steadily increase the rate at which students can read. The teacher gradually decreases the number of seconds provided to students to figure out words when conducting sight-word-unison passage reading. During the first weeks of passage sight-reading, students repeat sentences until they are able to read all the words with no longer than a 3-second pause. This translates to an appropriate rate of 20 words per minute. Higher-performing students may require few, if any, rereadings to read at this rate. Lower-performing students, however, may require numerous repetitions. When the students are able to read at the rate of 20 words per minute without the need of rereading, the teacher can decrease the pause time to about 2 to 2 1/2 seconds (a rate of about 25 to 30 words per minute). This rate in turn can be increased later by decreasing the pause time to 1 1/2 to 2 seconds between words.

Teachers working with lower-performing students may note that students need repetitions on virtually every sentence before they are able to read at the specified rate. We strongly recommend scheduling another 15- to 20-minute reading period later in the day for such students. This practice is necessary to enable the students to develop adequate fluency. Without the extra practice, the students will fall behind their peers. The importance of providing extra practice for students during first grade cannot be emphasized too much. Beginning in second grade, an increasing proportion of school activities (e.g., social studies, science, etc.) are conducted with the whole class. Students who read too slowly may not be able to keep up. Not only may they be subjected to frustration, but they will not be able to benefit from the practice other students receive during these activities.

Individual Checks for Rate and Accuracy

After students begin reading passages, we recommend doing a weekly 1-minute timed oral reading of story text. The individual checkouts will provide valuable information to the teacher, and will show if the student is receiving adequate practice in developing rate and accuracy. The students should read a story that contains the words in the stories currently being read. The teacher times the student for 1 minute and records the number of words read and any errors the student made. Table 12.6 shows a chart that can be used to record student performance over a period of several weeks. The teacher should closely monitor whether the students are increasing in fluency and are on a path to reach the target of reading 60 words per minute by the end of first grade. Likewise, the accuracy should be at least at 95%. As noted in the previous section, students who are not developing adequate accuracy or fluency should be identified early and provided with an extra period of reading instruction.

Table 12.6

Record Form—Individual Checkouts

Student Name	Date		Date		Date	
	Words per Minute	Errors	Words per Minute	Errors	Words per Minute	Errors

Commercial Programs

The story reading components in the kindergarten and first-grade levels of most core reading programs often have characteristics that can cause problems for the struggling reader and at-risk child. Some of the more serious problems are listed below:

Story reading is not practiced daily. In a number of programs, the teacher's guide does not provide directions for conducting daily story reading. The teacher's guide may only call for reading stories several times a week. There will not be sufficient numbers of stories for students to read in which the vocabulary is aligned with the introduction of phonic elements.

Too many irregular words in stories. The stories that students are to read at the beginning of some core reading programs contain a high percentage of irregular words, words that are irregular because the word contains a letter that does not represent its most common sound or words that are irregular because the word contains a letter-sound correspondence the student has not yet learned. Students become overwhelmed, not knowing when sounding out can and cannot be used.

No explicit instruction in applying phonic skills. Few programs teach students how to apply what they have learned in phonics instruction when they read stories. The programs do not provide directions to the teacher for prompting students to use their knowledge of letter-sound corre-spondences reading text. The programs rarely provide specific correc-tion procedures.

Procedures that do not foster high level of student involvement. Most pro-grams do not provide guidance to teachers in how to conduct story read-ing in a manner that keeps all children highly involved in the reading of the story. The programs provide general statements to teachers about calling on students to read.

Reliance on picture and/or context cues. Some programs encourage the student to use the strategy of looking at pictures or relying on the context to read a word. Both of these strategies are likely to cause the struggling or at-risk beginning reader serious confusions. While the use of context as a cue in reading to figure out words is useful when students are past the beginning stage and have learned most phonic elements, the early introduction of reliance on context cues can be very problematic.

Solutions

If teachers have a program in which the beginning stories contain a high pro-portion of irregular words, we recommend that teachers construct worksheets with sentences composed of regular words or short stories composed of regu-lar words to use during the early part of the program to provide the children with practice in using their sounding-out strategy to read stories. When intro-ducing stories from the program, do not expect students to read all the irregu-lar words. Prioritize the most useful words. When coming to a word in the story that has not been taught, the teacher reads the word.

Once children begin reading stories, story reading should be part of daily lessons. We recommend incorporating the unison reading procedures in this book during the beginning stage, beginning with sounding out and then mak-ing the transition to sight reading. If there are not enough stories, the teacher can create lists of sentences for the students to read using the words that have been introduced so far. Creating sentences is less time-consuming for the teachers than trying to write stories.

Irregular words should be introduced at a rate that is not too over-whelming for the students. The students' performance will tell the teacher what that rate is. Remember, if children are able to read previously introduced irreg-ulars, new irregulars can be introduced. If the story has irregular words that the teacher has not yet taught in word-list exercises, the teacher can tell the stu-dents the word when they encounter it in the story.

The chapters in part 3 will provide additional recommendation for deal-ing with creating solutions to problem related to instructional materials.

Application to Your Curriculum

Evaluate Beginning Passage Reading in Your Core Reading Program (Kindergarden and First Grade)

1. What procedures does your reading program provide for introducing passage reading?
2. Does the procedure for reading stories keep students highly engaged?
3. What correction procedure is specified for student errors?
4. How often do students get to practice reading stories?
5. Are there criteria given for when students require extra practice on story reading?
6. What motivation system is provided to encourage accurate and fluent reading?
7. Are the words in the stories carefully aligned with the word-list exercises to ensure that students have the skills to read all the words?
8. Based on your previous answers, what modifications would you make to your reading curriculum?

CHAPTER 13

Story Reading and Fluency Development—Primary Stage

The teacher's challenge in conducting passage-reading instruction during the primary stage is to (a) provide adequate practice for all students to develop fluency; (b) continue stressing accurate reading; (c) provide instruction in specific skills, such as reading with expression; (d) incorporate vocabulary and comprehension activities; and (e) present text-related activities in a manner that provides motivation and fosters high levels of student engagement.

The following teaching and motivation procedures are based on the assumption that the students in a reading group have received sufficient teaching to decode all the words appearing in the stories, and the stories are at the students' instructional level. Text at a student's instructional level contains about two to three words per hundred that the student would not know without adequate prior decoding instruction on those words. With adequate word-list exercises just before reading the story, the children can read the story with few errors. Not every word appearing in the story must have appeared in an earlier word-list exercise. If a word contains a phonic element the students have already mastered in earlier word-list exercises, the word need not be presented in a word-list exercise prior to its appearance in a story. For example, after the students have read about 10 to 15 words containing the letter combination *ar* in word-list exercises, a word containing *ar* that has not appeared in a word-list exercise could appear in a story. Any word containing a phonic element the student does not know should be presented as an irregular word in word-list exercises for several days prior to its appearance in a story.

Teaching Procedure for Story Reading

The basic procedure for conducting story reading during the primary stage has the students read a story three times. In the first reading, the focus is on accurate reading. If the students perform at an acceptable accuracy level on the first reading, the teacher then focuses in the second reading on comprehension as well as accuracy. A third reading would focus on fluency with students rereading the story chorally or in pairs.

The teacher conducts the first and second reading by calling on individual students to read one to four sentences as the others follow along. The teacher calls on different students to read several sentences until the passage is completed. The teacher records any errors the students make. During the first reading, in order to concentrate on accurate reading, the teacher asks few comprehension questions. If the group reads the passage with an acceptable number of errors (a 97% criterion—no more than 3 errors per 100 words), the teacher has the students reread the story and asks comprehension questions as the students read. If the group makes too many errors on the first reading (more than 3 per 100 words), the students reread the story with the teacher solely concentrating on accuracy, not asking comprehension questions.

A format for introducing this primary-stage reading procedure appears in Table 13.1. The format begins with the teacher telling the students they will be reading individually when called upon. When other students are reading, the students are to point to the words being read. We still recommend requiring students to point to words as other students read as a means to increase the probability they will stay actively involved throughout the entire lesson, not only when they are called upon to read. When students read for several weeks without losing their places, the teacher can give them the privilege of not pointing.

Before the first reading, the teacher presents the error limit for the story. This is a motivational technique to encourage accurate reading. [The error limit is determined by multiplying the number of words in the story by

Table 13.1
Format for Introducing Passage-Reading Decoding

---

1. Introducing story-reading procedure

   a. "You're going to read this story out loud. I'll call on different students to read. When you're reading, talk in a big voice so everyone can hear you. Pause when you come to a period. If I don't call on another student, read the next sentence. If it's not your turn to read, point to the words that are being read."

   b. "I'll show you how I want you to read. You point to the words as I say them." (Teacher reads several sentences. Students touch words as teacher reads.)

   c. Teacher repeats step 1(b) until all students follow along as she reads.

2. Students read story—decoding

   a. "Your turn to read. When I call on you, read in a mature voice. Pause when you come to a period. If I don't call on another student, read the next sentence. If it's not your turn to read, point to the words that are being read."

   b. "Our error limit for today's story is 8. If you read the story with only 8 errors or fewer, we'll read the story again, and I'll ask comprehension questions."

   c. Teacher calls on students to read individually. Teacher calls on a new student each one to read three sentences.

3. Students read story—comprehension*

   a. Teacher calls on student to read individually. Teacher asks comprehension questions. "We're going to read the story again. This time I'll ask questions about the story."

---

*Note: If the students consistently read the story accurately on the first reading, the teacher can begin asking comprehension questions during the first reading.

.03 (250 × .03 = 8 word error limit)] The students read the story first with the teacher asking few or no comprehension questions. If the students read the story and make fewer errors than the specified error limit, the teacher congratulates the group, then has the group read the story again. During this second reading, the teacher asks comprehension questions. If the students make more errors than allowed on the first reading, they read the story for a second time with the teacher concentrating again on accuracy. After the students read the story accurately and answer comprehension questions, the teacher works on fluency. Procedures for this work on fluency will be discussed in a later section in this chapter.

Critical Behaviors

Pacing and Monitoring

- Call on students to read in an unpredictable order. Students will be more attentive when they do not know when it will be their turn. Have a student sometimes read one sentence, sometimes several sentences.

- Watch the students carefully to make certain they are following along when another student is reading.

- Good timing will facilitate the transition from student to student. When the teacher wants a new student to read, the teacher says the name of the next student as the student who is reading finishes the last word in the sentence. The teacher should keep his or her talk to a minimum.

Corrections. The correction procedure a teacher uses depends on the group size the teacher is working with.

When a teacher is working with more than three students, the teacher must consider how his or her actions affect the group's attentiveness. If the teacher spends too much time with an individual student correcting an error, this extended time increases the probability of the other students becoming inattentive. The following correction procedure is designed for use with a group of more than three students and is used when a child misidentifies a word.

1. When a student makes an error, the teacher tells the student the missed word. "That word is *astounded.*" The teacher should not use an abrupt or loud voice.

2. The teacher has the student say the correct word. "What word?"

3. The teacher tells the student to read the sentence from the beginning. ("Go back to the beginning of the sentence and read the sentence again.")

4. The teacher records the missed word and provides review on that word before students reread the story as well as in the next day's word-list exercises.

Other types of errors require a variation in the preceding procedure. If the student error was not a misidentification error, but was one that involved inserting a word, or omitting a word, the teacher tells the student the error that was made and has the student read the sentence again. "You left out a word. Please read the sentence again."

If a student is unable to identify a word within a reasonable amount of time, no more than 3-5 seconds, the teacher tells the student the word. Allowing the student to struggle for too much time can be punishing for the student who is unable to figure out the word and can disrupt the flow of the lesson. However, not allowing sufficient time for a student to attempt a word can also be frustrating to the student. The teacher must use his or her judgment. If the student seems on the verge of figuring out the word, the teacher can allow the student several more seconds.

If a student is called on to read, but the student has lost his or her place, the teacher should immediately call on another student to read and assist the student to find the correct place. The teacher should call upon this student again after several other students have read. Losing a reading turn is often motivation enough for students to carefully follow along. Some students may not start reading when called on because their reading rate is slow. If it is obvious a student has been following along, the teacher should allow more time. The teacher must, however, make it clear to the students that she expects them to actively follow along when other students read.

As a general rule, the less said by the teacher when making corrections during passage reading, the smoother the lesson will progress. However, in a one-to-one situation or with a small group, the teacher can use a more sophisticated correction strategy when a student makes an error. The teacher points to the missed word and attempts to prompt the student with the appropriate decoding strategy. If a student misidentifies a word with a certain letter combination, the teacher points out the letter or letter combination missed and asks the student the sound of the letter(s). If the student can identify the sound(s) correctly, the teacher asks the student, "What word?" For example, if a student says "beat" for *beach,* the teacher would point to *ch* and ask, "What do these letters say? What's the word?" If the student cannot identify the letter combination, the teacher tells the student the sound, has the student say the sound, then asks, "What word?" If the student misidentifies an irregular word, the teacher simply tells the student the word, because a phonic or structural cue will not help to figure out an irregular word. For all errors, the student should go back to the beginning of the sentence and reread the sentence.

Occasionally, one or two students in the group may have more difficulty decoding the words in the story or read at a significantly slower rate than the other students in the group. The teacher should provide extra instruction to increase the student's likelihood of having a successful experience during passage-reading exercises. The most practical procedure involves having the student preread stories to a volunteer or peer before reading it as part of a group.

Recording Errors

During oral passage-reading instruction, the teacher should maintain a record-keeping system. A recording system should provide maximum information with minimum disruption of the group, enabling the teacher to record student performance without becoming distracted from teaching the group. At a minimum, the teacher records the number of errors made and writes down any word that was missed so the teacher can reteach that word.

A more extensive recording system can be used for struggling and at-risk readers. The teacher can record student performance on a photocopy of the passage the students are reading. The teacher can code who made the error by writing the reader's initials over the word. The teacher can also note the type of error by using reading error marking notations. The teacher needs a consistent system for describing student errors. The following is one possible system for recording various types of decoding errors.

Type of Decoding Error	Notation
Misidentification or word substitution (student decodes word incorrectly). Slash through the word and write the word the student said.	march mom ma/rk mot/her
Hesitation [student is unable to identify the word within a reasonable amount of time (3 to 5 seconds)]. Slash through the word and mark H over the word.	H l/eft
Reversal (student says "said he" for "he said"). Mark the transposed part with a loop.	he/said was
Omission (student leaves out word). Circle the omitted word.	She (had) smiled
Self-correct (student says "dot," then self-corrects and says "dog"). Write SC over the word.	SC dog
Insertion (student adds a word). Mark a caret (^) and write in the word added.	had He ^ said
Lost place (student is called upon to read but has lost his/her place). Write LP above place where the student got lost.	LP .. went home. He was. . .

Motivation System

A motivation system to maximize attentiveness and accurate reading should be integrated into the procedure for conducting story reading.

Accurate Reading.   A motivation system to foster careful reading begins with the teacher setting up rewards based on the number of errors a group makes when reading stories. The fewer the number of mistakes, the greater the reward.

The criteria for accurate reading should be set at a high level. We recommend a 97% accuracy goal (no more than 3 errors per 100 words). This high-accuracy criterion is based on the assumption that the teacher has constructed word-list exercises that have adequately prepared students to read all the words in the assigned stories and the teacher has provided students with adequate practice to master the word-list exercises. If the students have not had adequate preparation in word-list exercises, the high-accuracy criterion will be unreasonable and cause frustration. If students have had adequate preparation, the 97% criterion will be a realistic goal.

The teacher creates a group chart in which the number of errors are recorded for each lesson. A sample group chart appears in Table 13.2. In the first two columns, the teacher writes the day and the error limit for the story. In the next column, the teacher records how many errors the group made on the first reading of the story. The last three columns are titled, "Excellent," "Good," and "Oops." The teacher makes a check under one of these columns. "Excellent" might be two errors or less, "Good" can be three errors to the error limit, and "Oops" is anything more than the error limit.

The teacher establishes a group reward when the group meets a specified criterion (such as 5 days of meeting the error limit). A variety of rewards may be used. Rewards should be based on the type of students involved. Teachers working with higher-performing, more intrinsically motivated students can rely primarily on verbal and written acknowledgements of performance. Teachers working with less intrinsically motivated students may initially

Table 13.2

Sample Form for Recording Group Story-Reading Performance

Day	Error Limit	How Many Errors	Excellent	Good	Oops
5/12/05	8	2	√		
5/13/05	7	5		√	

need to utilize more powerful pay-offs, such as tokens and tangibles, as well as acknowledgements of good performance. In all cases, the teacher should respond with enthusiasm when students read with high levels of accuracy.

If one child in the group makes significantly more errors than the other children, the teacher will need to take actions to protect that child's self-image. See the section on Protecting a Student's Self-Image that appears later in this chapter.

Attentiveness. If necessary, a motivation system can be designed to keep students attentive throughout the story-reading exercise, particularly when it is not their turn to read individually. A good indicator of attentiveness is the student knowing his or her place when called on to read.

If the group as a whole has lots of lost places, the teacher can set up a reward for improvement in the number of lost places. If one or two students account for the majority of lost places, the teacher can make up individual systems. First though, the teacher should test the student's reading rate to determine if the problem results from the student's reading rate being significantly slower than other members of the group. If the student's rate is not adequate, the teacher should consider placing the student in a different group or providing extra rate practice.

If the student's reading rate is adequate, we recommend setting up a system whereby gradual improvement by the student enables the whole group to earn a reward. For example, if a student loses his place an average of three times a lesson, the teacher might set up a system wherein the student's improvement to only two lost places per lesson earns a small reward for the group. Once the student improves to only two lost places per lesson, the teacher would up the criterion to one lost place per lesson, then two or three per week. It is important to maintain the reward system after the student improves. Paying attention to students when they are performing well and constantly acknowledging their good performance is very important.

Other Behaviors. Two student behaviors are very important to a smoothly run passage-reading exercise: (a) students pausing when they reach a period, and (b) students reading in a loud enough voice for others to hear when called on for an individual turn.

The teacher should rely first on using specific praise when students are not displaying desired behaviors. During the story-reading exercise, the teacher should use specific praise frequently (e.g., "Good stopping at the period," "You talked in a big voice," "Good reading"). This praise will usually be effective with most students in the group. If some students still have difficulty, the teacher can make individual systems with those students (e.g., "Eli, each time you read loud, I'll give you a point. When you get 10 points, you'll earn a bonus point for everyone in the group.").

A motivation system is not a fixed thing. A teacher must continually monitor the motivation system to ensure that each student is feeling successful and competent. The teacher must always resist the temptation to nag students who are having difficulty or implore them to work harder. Neither of these teacher behaviors typically result in student improvement. Instead, the teacher should always test individually to determine if a skill deficit is involved or if motivation procedures need to be strengthened.

Diagnosis and Remediation—Accuracy

Any student whose accuracy rate is below 97% in passage reading should receive extra instruction. The type of instruction to be provided depends on the basic cause of the errors. The teacher should examine student errors over a period of time and look for error patterns. Error patterns may indicate that a student or the group needs extra practice on a previously taught skill.

Accuracy errors can be divided into context-related errors and phonic errors. Context-related errors are usually indicated by inconsistent student performance. The student reads a word correctly in one sentence and, later in the passage, reads it incorrectly. Phonic errors are indicated by a consistent error pattern (e.g., the student misses all words with the letter combination *ou*).

Phonic Errors.   Students whose errors indicate that they haven't mastered previously taught phonic skills should receive daily instruction on the specific deficits. This instruction would include the systematic reintroduction and practicing of the skills the student has not mastered. For example, if the student did not know one or more letter combinations, the teacher would reintroduce the letter combination(s) one at a time in word-list exercises. The teacher would present the letter combination in isolation (see Table 8.2) and then have present words with that combination (see Table 10.1). The teacher would work on words with the particular combination for several days in word-list exercises. While the word-list exercises are being provided, the teacher would prompt the students in passage reading on words containing the unknown elements (e.g., "That word has the letters *o-u*. Remember, those letters say /ou/.").

If the error pattern is specific to an individual student, the teacher can prepare word-list exercises and train a peer tutor or parent volunteer to work with the student having difficulty.

Context Errors.   Context errors may involve either an over- or underreliance on the context of the story. An overreliance on context is indicated by the student misidentifying many words (more than three per hundred), which the student is able to identify correctly in isolation. An overreliance on context error is indicated when the student says a word that makes sense in the context, but is only minimally similar to the actual written word (e.g., reading "The boy was not healthy" as "The boy was not happy").

The remediation procedure for a pattern that indicates an overreliance on context involves prompting a student to read more carefully and providing extra motivation to encourage accurate reading. The accuracy criteria in these exercises depends on the student's current performance. The teacher should set up a system to improve performance in graduated steps. If a student is currently reading at a 90% accuracy level, the system could be set up so that a student is awarded for reading at a 92% or higher criterion. The criterion would gradually be increased as the student's performance improved until the student can read with almost 100% accuracy. The extra motivator can be earning bonus points for the group.

Inaccurate readers often make many self-corrections (misidentifying a word, then immediately saying it correctly). Whereas an occasional self-correct is not important, frequent self-corrects hamper the story flow. If students make too many self-corrects, the teacher should consider a self-correct as an error.

Some students who overrely on context will also have a reading-rate deficit. The teacher should not work on remediating both types of deficits at first, but should initially work on developing accuracy. Only after the student has begun reading accurately on a consistent basis should the teacher work on increasing rate. When working on developing accuracy, the teacher must ensure the passages contain no words that have phonic or structural elements or irregular words the students have not been taught.

An underreliance on context would be indicated by a student saying words that do not make sense in the context of a passage; for example, when reading *The man went to the shop,* a student reads, "The man went to the she." If students make many errors that indicate the student is not attentive to the context of the sentence, the teacher should establish a motivation system to encourage more careful reading. The teacher can also present oral exercises to teach students to identify this type of context error. The teacher says sentences in which a word does not make sense and asks the students to identify in each sentence the word that does not make sense. For example:

"I'll say some sentences. You tell me whether they make sense."

1. "The boy played on the pouch. Does that make sense?"
2. "The girls ran to the sore. Does that make sense?"

Once students learn to identify errors in spoken sentences, they are more likely to identify context errors when they read. Note that English language learners may make errors in which they say a word that does not make sense in the context that results from the student's lack of familiarity with English.

Fluency

Fluency is the ability to read a text accurately and quickly. When fluent readers read, they recognize words automatically, and group words quickly to help them gain meaning from what they read. They read aloud effortlessly and with expression. The remainder of this chapter provides guidance on teaching students to read fluently.

Fluency—Reading with Expression

Training in reading with expression is necessary to demonstrate to students that written passages express meaning in the same way spoken language does. Oral-reading behaviors that characterize reading with expression include pausing at periods and other punctuation marks, dividing text into meaningful chunks, emphasizing the appropriate words, and when reading quotations, using inflections that reflect the mood of the character speaking.

The teaching of reading with expression can begin in kindergarten when teachers read to children. As the teacher reads a story to the children, the teacher selects sentences for the students to repeat orally in unison. The teacher would read the sentence and then have the children repeat the sentence in unison. More instructionally naïve children may need quite a few repetitions before they are able to say the words verbatim. The teacher can make the activity a reinforcing one by repeating the sentence over a number of times just like saying a melody. A good number of the sentences can be ones in which a character makes a statement. The teacher reads the sentence and tells the students to say the sentence just as the character would say the sentence.

Explicit expression training connected with students' text reading can begin when students are able to read at a rate of about 50 to 60 words per minute. A 5- to 10-minute training session can be incorporated into the lesson following the reading of the passage.

We recommend a modeling procedure for teaching students" to read with expression. The teacher says, "We're going to practice reading this story as if we were telling a story. I'll read a sentence. Then you read it the same way as I read it." The teacher then reads the first sentence or two, using slightly exaggerated expression. Students should be instructed to keep their fingers on the first word in the sentence and simply follow along with their eyes as the teacher reads. (Pointing to the first word enables the students to quickly find the beginning of the sentence when it is their turn to read.) After the teacher reads, he or she calls on the group to read the sentence in unison several times. Then the teacher calls on several individuals to read the sentence with expression. If a student does not read with expression, the teacher repeats the model and has the group read the sentence. When the students can read the first sentence(s) with expression, the teacher adds a sentence to the sequence. The teacher reads the first sentence(s) and the next sentence together, then calls on the group and individuals to read with expression from the beginning. This procedure of adding a sentence and having students read from the beginning is repeated for each new sentence, so that the children are able to be brought to mastery on reading a sequence of sentences with expression.

Exercises for teaching reading with expression should be done daily until students read new material with expression without first receiving a teacher model. This can take several months of practice. Teachers can also have children practice reading with expression together in pairs as well as read chorally.

Fluency—Reading Rate

Reading rate refers to the speed at which a student reads a passage. A student's reading rate is usually expressed in words per minute. The question of how quickly children should be reading at various levels is one that is not clearly answered by research. In order to recommend desired reading rates, we examined studies that showed correlations between reading rates and students' performance on reading comprehension assessments (Hasbrouck & Tindal, 1992).

Table 13.3 shows what we consider to be desired reading rates at various instructional levels. These rates are based on examination of reading rates of students who were performing between the 50th and 75th percentiles on standardized tests. We created desired reading rates that are challenging. We recommend setting these challenging rates because in our work with children in high-poverty schools, we have found that helping the children achieve high rates of fluency in early grades leads to more reading by the student and overall makes school a more enjoyable experience since children with high-fluency rates can generally finish assignments more easily.

Exercises to develop reading rate should be part of daily lessons until students are able to read at least 135 words a minute. Remember that during passage reading, the teacher has the students read a passage first for accuracy, then for comprehension, then has the students reread it chorally as a whole group and/or in pairs with a focus on fluency.

Oral Reading Fluency Checks for Rate and Accuracy

We recommend that students be given frequent timed oral reading fluency (ORF) checks that measure rate and accuracy during the primary stage. How often tests are administered depends on the student's relative performance level. Students who are reading significantly below grade level should be tested weekly. Students performing somewhat below grade level should be tested at least every second week. Students performing at and above grade level and who read with desired fluency and accuracy criteria can be tested monthly.

The ORF checkouts will provide valuable information showing if the student is receiving adequate practice in developing rate and accuracy. The students should read a story that is of similar difficulty to the stories currently being read

Table 13.3

Desired Reading Rates for Various Instructional Levels

Instructional Level	Words per Minute on First Reading
Second third of grade 1 materials	45
Last third of grade 1 materials	60
First third of grade 2 materials	75
Second third of grade 2 materials	90
Last third of grade 2 materials	110
First half of grade 3 materials	120
Second half of grade 3 materials	135
Fourth grade and higher	150

in the reading program. One common method of assessing fluency has the students read for 1 minute. The teacher times the student for 1 minute and notes any errors the student made. Two numbers should be recorded: words read correctly in 1 minute (cwpm) and the percent of total words read correctly. Errors of repetitions, and self-corrects are not counted in determining the number of words read correctly. Errors of misidentifications, word substitutions, omissions, and hesitations (after 3 seconds, tell the student the correct word) are counted as errors. The teacher determines the percent correct by dividing the words read correctly by the total words read. If the student read 53 words and read 51 words correctly, the student's accuracy percentage would be 96%.

Teachers should record students' performance on oral reading fluency assessments. Many teachers record students' performance on graph paper (or students graph their own rate and accuracy). Table 13.4 includes a form that can be used to record individual student's performance. For each reading, the teacher records the date, the passage read, the number of words correctly read, the number of errors made, and the accuracy percentage. The student's reading rate is put on the graph. Table 13.5 includes a form that can be used to record the performance of a group of students over time.

Fluency—Providing Extra Practice

Students who read below the desired accuracy or rate criteria levels should receive extra instruction and practice. If a student is reading below a 96% accuracy level, extra work on accuracy is needed. If a student's reading rate is more than 10% below the desired reading rate for the student's instructional level, extra rate-building exercises are needed. Teachers must be aware of the fluency expectations for the student's instructional level. Note that a student's instructional level may be different than the student's grade level. If a student is reading in a book designated for late-second grade, the student's instructional level is at late-second grade, regardless of whether the child is a first, second, or third grader.

Extra work on developing rate can be done through scheduling an extra period each day for repeated readings.

If the children in a group are not very low in their reading rate, the teacher can just do a simple exercise in which the students work in pairs, rereading previously taught passages. For some children a more sophisticated rate-building exercise may be needed.

We have developed a rate-building exercise that may be conducted by a teacher, paraprofessional, volunteer, or a peer. The rate-building exercise involves students doing repeated readings of 100- to 200-word excerpts from previously read passages until the student can read the passage at a targeted higher rate.

To prepare for the rate-building exercises, the teacher first sets a target-rereading rate for each student. The target-rereading rate should be 40% higher than the student's current reading rate. The purpose of setting the rereading

Table 13.4

Individual Reading Rate Record Form

Student Name _____   Class _____

Record of Performance

Date														
Psg.														
WRC														
Err.														
%														

Psg. = Passage WRC = Words read correctly Err. = Errors % = Percent correct

Graphing of Performance

135														
130														
125														
120														
115														
110														
105														
100														
95														
90														
85														
80														
75														
70														
65														
60														
55														
50														
45														
40														
35														
30														
25														
20														
15														
10														
5														
0														

criterion significantly higher than the student's current rate is to foster generalization to first-time reading.

If a student currently reads at a rate of 50 words a minute, the teacher would initially set the target rate at 70 words per minute for the rereading exercise (50 + 20 [40% of 50 is 20] = 70). If a student were reading at a rate of 90 words a minute, the target rate for the exercise would be 126 words a minute (90 + 36 [40% of 90 is 36] = 126).

The teacher prepares the reading material by marking the point in the passage that contains the targeted number of words. The teacher can use the student copy or photocopy the page. A star or bracket is placed at the point corresponding to the target rate. Some teachers will prepare text for the student to read with a running total of words in the text to the right of the row.

■ A young man went to the park near	8
■ his house. Just when he arrived	14
■ at the park, something very strange	20

The student then practices reading and rereading the excerpt to himself or to a partner until the student feels that he is able to read it within a minute. At that point, he raises his hand for the teacher to check him out. The teacher times the student as the student reads the excerpt orally. The student's reading of the excerpt would be deemed acceptable if the student reads the targeted number of words in a minute with three or fewer errors.

If the student reads acceptably, the student may begin practicing another excerpt. If a teacher is working with a group of students, the teacher should structure the session so that while one student is being tested, the other students are practicing reading to themselves. When the student meets the targeted goal on 10 excerpts, the target can be raised by five words a minute.

The teacher should continue to administer the regular oral reading rate checkouts every 2 weeks. Every 2 weeks, the teacher has a student read a passage the student has never read before. The passage should be one that is at the student's independent level (a level at which the student has the skills to read all words correctly). The passage should be of a similar difficulty level to the passages being read in the rate-building exercises. The student's performance tells the teacher if the rate-training exercises are, in fact, working. If the student's rate has improved, the teacher increases the target rate on rereading exercises to the student's new rate plus 40%. For example, if a student had been reading at a rate of 60 words a minute at the beginning of the year and is now reading at 75 words a minute, the target rate for rereading exercises would increase from 84 words a minute (60 + 24) to 105 words a minute (75 + 30).

The exercise just described may be conducted in a small-group setting with three to four students and the teacher, a parent volunteer, a paraprofessional, or a peer tutor. Students might also benefit from a supplemental rate-building curriculum such as "Read Naturally."

The teacher should monitor the rate of student improvement in order to ensure that students are making adequate progress. To monitor progress, the

Table 13.5

Group Reading Rate Chart

Teacher's Name _____ Group _____

Student Name	Date	Date	Date	Date	Date	Date	Date	Date	Date	Date	Date	Date

Words correct / Errors made

teacher determines the weekly average gain the student needs to make to reach the fluency target for the reading level the student will be doing at the end of the year. Let's say a student is reading at beginning second-grade level and by the end of the year the student will be reading at the end of second-grade level. The desired fluency rate is 110 words per minute. The student is currently reading at 70 words per minute. There are 24 weeks in the school year, during which the student's reading rate needs to improve 40 words per minute. We divide the desired improvement (40) by the number of weeks (24) and end up with a goal of improving 1.67 words per minute each week.

Protecting a Student's Self-Image

Teachers have a responsibility to ensure that what occurs during instructional sessions will contribute toward a child forming a positive self-image. The more success a child encounters during instruction, the more likely the instructional sessions will be a contributing factor for the development of positive self-image. Placing a child at the child's instructional level is a critical prerequisite for this success. Still, during instruction, some students may struggle. In addition to providing extra instruction for those students, the teacher should take other actions to ensure that the self-image of lower-performing students is not being hurt. If one student makes a disproportionate number of errors during group passage reading, the other students may react negatively toward that student. One way of dealing with this situation is to not count the student's errors when determining how many errors the group makes when reading a story. The teacher might tell the group, "Kim is working hard now to catch up on some skills. While she is catching up, I won't count any errors she makes when the Group 8 reads the story."

Another action that can protect a lower-performing student's self-image is to arrange for the student to receive a tutoring session on the story before it is presented to the group. The prereading increases the probability of the student performing well when the story is presented to the group. If a student's performance is significantly below other members of the group, and extra instruction is not making it possible for the student to fully benefit from instruction in that group, the teacher should consider placing that student in a group performing at an earlier lesson in the program. Such a situation must be handled with great care.

Reading Outside School

We strongly recommend establishing a program that facilitates a great deal of student reading of books and other forms of written materials outside of the school environment. In order to do this, the teacher will need to have books that are at the student's independent reading level readily available. A book is at a student's independent level when the student can read the book with relative ease and possesses the word-attack skills to figure out virtually all the words in the book. In addition, the vocabulary and sentence structure used in the book should be readily understandable by the child. If possible, some of this reading should be done orally with an adult. Some should also be done silently.

Here is a series of steps the teacher can follow to encourage home reading:

■ The teacher contacts the parent and explains the importance of extra reading. The teacher asks the parent to arrange, at a minimum, a 5-minute daily period during which the student reads a hundred-word excerpt three times to the parent.

■ In addition to the oral repeated readings, the teacher can also send home books that a child can read silently or to the parent. These books must be at the child's independent level.

■ The student brings home a weekly calendar. Each day the parent writes how many minutes the child read. The student brings the calendar to school once a week on a specified day.

■ As a motivator, the teacher can put the minutes read by each student on a chart.

■ A goal with a special event can be planned. "When our class reads 10,000 minutes at home, the principal will come down and give our class a special award."

■ Individual motivation systems might be necessary for some children.

Application to Your Curriculum

Evaluate Story Reading Instruction in Your Core Reading Program (Late First Through Third Grade.)

1. What procedure does your curriculum recommend for conducting story reading. How often does your curriculum have students orally read stories?
2. What types of corrective feedback does your curriculum recommend that you provide for oral reading errors during passage reading? What type of follow-up does your curriculum recommend that you provide for words missed during story reading?
3. Does your curriculum have fluency standards for your grade level? If so, how do they compare with the desired rates in this chapter?
4. Are there materials provided to assess student's reading rates? If so, are these materials adequate? How often does your program recommend assessing rate?
5. What opportunities does your curriculum provide to students to improve reading rate?
6. How does your program specify that you assess accuracy of oral reading? Does your curriculum specify procedures for improving accuracy for students who read below desired accuracy levels?
7. Based on your previous answers, what modifications would you make to your reading curriculum?

## CHAPTER 14

Overview of Vocabulary Instruction

What Is Vocabulary?

Vocabulary refers to the words we must know to comprehend and communicate effectively. In general, vocabulary can be described as oral vocabulary or reading vocabulary. Oral vocabulary refers to words that we use or recognize in listening. Reading vocabulary refers to words we recognize or use in print.

Vocabulary plays a critical role in learning to read and in comprehending what is read. For children to be successful in their classrooms, they must understand the vocabulary used by the teacher in presenting rules, directions, and demonstrations. Furthermore, as they read for comprehension, they must understand the meaning of words in the text.

Children learn vocabulary primarily through indirect means, hearing words used by their parents, teachers, and others in a variety of contexts and through reading.

Direct teaching of vocabulary plays an important role, particularly for the child who enters school with significantly less vocabulary knowledge than is needed for success in school. In the preschool and kindergarten years, great strides can be made by systematically and explicitly teaching children the vocabulary that will be used by the classroom teacher when formal reading instruction begins. Once children learn to read, vocabulary instruction linked to reading must be an integral part of daily lessons.

Why Vocabulary Is Important— The Research Connection

Hart and Risley (1995) followed 42 families for 2 1/2 years to learn why children differ greatly in terms of acquisition of vocabulary and language skills. They found that by the age of 3, children living in deep poverty had acquired less than one-third of the vocabulary of children from high-SES families.

The National Reading Panel reviewed the research in the area of vocabulary instruction. The Panel found that:

■ Teaching specific words before reading helps both vocabulary learning and reading comprehension.

- Children learn words best when they are provided with instruction over an extended period of time.
- Repeated exposure to vocabulary in many contexts aids word learning. Children learn vocabulary when they are explicitly taught both individual words and word-learning strategies.
- Direct vocabulary instruction aids reading comprehension (*Put Reading First: The Research Building Blocks for Teaching Children to Read,* 2001).

How Vocabulary Fits into the Reading Program

During the beginning stage, vocabulary instruction can be presented orally. During this stage, students will be able to read only a small fraction of the words in their receptive and expressive vocabularies. Oral instruction makes it possible to teach a much wider range of concepts than if the teacher limits the instruction to the words students are taught to decode.

The scope of skills presented depends on the students' language skills. Many at-risk students enter school without adequate understanding of many words commonly used in directions given by teachers (for example, find the letter *under* the *last* row, touch the *narrow stripe* in the *first column,* find the letter in the *lower right-hand corner*). For these students, instruction will begin with instruction in basic language concepts. For children who enter school already knowing the basic concepts, vocabulary instruction will start with more sophisticated words.

As students progress through the grades, vocabulary instruction becomes more related to the stories that children read. Teachers select vocabulary words from upcoming stories. The intensity of instruction on a particular word depends on the student's familiarity with the concept. If the vocabulary word represents a concept that is new to the student, a great deal more has to be done than in teaching a synonym for a known word. Vocabulary teaching is not a one-time event. For a word to be learned, it needs to be reviewed over time and presented in a variety of contexts.

In addition to teaching the meaning of particular words, independent word-learning strategies such as using word parts, contextual analysis, and teaching independent use of the dictionary should also be taught.

CHAPTER 15

Vocabulary Instruction During the Beginning Stage

Teaching Vocabulary Through Explicit Instruction

The procedures for teaching vocabulary to at-risk children in preschool, kindergarten, and first grade are very important. These young children are instructionally naive. They will not know many common words, will have difficulty remembering and applying new words, and are likely to be confused by unclear demonstrations.

All vocabulary instruction during the beginning stage is oral because the children will not be able to read sufficient numbers of words. Vocabulary can be taught orally by the use of three different procedures: modeling, synonyms, and definitions.

Modeling is used when verbal explanation of a new word would need to include words students do not understand. For example, when teaching the preposition *over,* the teacher cannot explain why something is over without using the term *over* or a synonym for *over* such as *above.* If a student did not know the word *above,* modeling would be needed to teach *over.* Modeling is used primarily to teach the word labels for common objects, actions, and attributes.

Synonyms are used when a student knows a word(s) that can explain the meaning of a new, unknown word. For example, a student knows the word *over* but does not know *above.* Instead of introducing *above* through modeling examples, the teacher tells the students that *above* means *over* and then tests the students to make sure that they understand the synonym. Similarly, if a student knows the meaning of *wet,* the teacher can use a *little wet* to explain the meaning of *damp.*

Definitions are used when students have adequate language to understand a longer explanation and when the concept is too complicated to be explained through a synonym. The teacher constructs a definition by specifying a small class to which a new word belongs and then by telling how the word differs from other members of the class. For example, a simple definition of *service station* might be "a place where gasoline is sold and cars are repaired." *Service station* is in the class of *places.* It differs from other places because gas is sold

---

Note: Initial synonyms do not have to be precise. They must, however, be designed to give students an approximate meaning that can be refined as they encounter the word in later reading.

and cars are repaired there. After a definition is given, examples are presented to test the students' understanding of the definition.

Example Selection

The most important aspect of teaching vocabulary, regardless of the procedure used, is selecting a set of appropriate examples. A set of examples is appropriate only if it demonstrates the teacher's intended meaning. A set of examples is inappropriate if the student can learn an interpretation other than the intended one; for example, if only a thick pen and a thick pencil are presented as examples of *thick*. Since both of these objects are writing tools, some students might interpret *thick* as having something to do with writing rather than width.

Learning a vocabulary word implies applying the word correctly to a set of examples. When a baby first learns the word *dog,* the baby may think that the word *dog* refers solely to the dog in his house. Through further experience, the child learns to expand her definition of *dog* to a whole set of dogs, many with different appearances. For learning to take place in the classroom, a teacher must provide enough positive examples of a new word so the student can respond to a full range of examples.

Selecting examples that show the range of *positive examples* is the first step in constructing a set of examples. To teach the word *container,* the positive examples might be a garbage can, a cardboard box, a drawer, and a glass vase. Having this wide variety of positive examples rules out the possibility of the student misconstruing the concept of *container* as being something square or something made of metal. The examples also set a base for fostering generalization to things not presented in the lesson (e.g., a plastic can or metal box). When teaching the preposition *over* (as in "the pencil is over the table"), the pencil should not just be presented above the center of the table, since young children might think that *over* has something to do with "in the middle" or a height of about 1 foot. To illustrate the full range of possibilities, the teacher presents the pencil in many different positions by holding it an inch or two above the table, then several feet above it, and then over the table's left and right side.

In addition to positive examples, an appropriate set of examples should also include *negative examples*. Negative examples rule out incorrect generalizations. For example, in teaching the concept *pet,* if only positive examples of *pet* were presented (dog, cat, goldfish, canary), some students might generalize that all animals are pets. In presenting the term *vehicle,* some positive examples might include an airplane, truck, boat, train; negative examples might include a kite and a buoy. When possible, negative and positive examples, which are exactly alike except for the presence or absence of the new concept, should be presented. The positive and negative examples form a pair. Each pair of examples can be referred to as a *minimally different pair.* Minimally different pairs focus student attention on the characteristics that determine whether an example is positive. The advantage of using minimally different pairs is illustrated in the following examples for teaching the color *orange*. A teacher might use these minimally different pairs of objects for teaching *orange:*

1. Two identical shirts, except that one is orange and one is red.
2. Two identical pieces of paper, except that one is orange and one is blue.
3. Two identical plastic disks, except that one is orange and one is brown.
4. Two identical crayons, except that one is orange and one is green.

By varying just the color in each pair of objects, the teacher demonstrates the critical characteristics. Misinterpretations that *orange* has something to do with shape, texture, or size are ruled out. Likewise, any confusion between *orange* and *red* is ruled out by including *red* as a negative example.

Teaching Vocabulary Through Modeling

Modeling is used when it is impossible to use language to explain the meaning of a word. Modeling is used primarily to teach basic language concepts and attributes covered in preschool and kindergarten. The basic procedure for modeling involves three steps:

1. Modeling positive and negative examples of the new concept.
2. Testing the students on their mastery of the examples for the new word.
3. Presenting different examples of the new word, along with examples of other previously taught words.

Review should be cumulative. Newly introduced words should be reviewed heavily at first by appearing daily for at least two or three lessons, then less frequently by appearing every other day for a week or two, and then intermittently thereafter. Also, as in the case of introducing new decoding skills, the introduction rate of vocabulary words is dependent on the students' mastery of previously introduced words.

Table 15.1 includes formats for using modeling to teach basic vocabulary: objects, colors, adverbs, and adjectives. Each format has three basic steps: model, test, and integrated test. Each format contains positive and negative examples and instructional wording. The examples in each presentation were selected to show the range of positive examples and eliminate possible incorrect generalizations. For example, in teaching *mitten* the positive examples vary in color and material, showing that color and material are irrelevant to whether an object is a mitten. Also, minimally different positive and negative pairs are included (e.g., a mitten and a glove of the same color, material, size, and shape). Similarly, the positive examples of the color *orange* in Table 15.1 include a range of objects and minimally different positive and negative examples.

Table 15.1

Format for Teaching Vocabulary: Modeling Examples

	Object	Adjective (Color)	Adverb	Adjective (Texture)
Step 1: *Teacher models positive and negative examples.*	"This is a mitten" or "This is not a mitten." *Examples:* brown wool mitten brown wool glove red nylon glove red nylon mitten blue sock blue mitten	"This is orange" or "This is not orange." *Examples:* 2" red disk 2" orange disk 4 × 4" orange paper 4 × 4" brown paper	"This is writing carefully" or "This is not writing carefully." *Examples:* write on board, first neatly, then sloppily hang up coat, first carefully, then carelessly arrange books, first carelessly, then carefully	"This is rough" or "This is not rough." *Examples:* red flannel shirt red silk shirt piece of sandpaper piece of paper smooth book cover rough book cover
Step 2: *Teacher tests.* Present positive and negative examples until the students make six consecutive correct responses.	"Is this a mitten or not a mitten?"	"Is this orange or not orange?"	"Is this _____ carefully or not carefully?"	"Is this rough or not rough?"
Step 3: *Teacher tests by asking for names.* Present examples until students make six consecutive correct responses.	"What is this?" glove mitten sock mitten mitten glove	"What color is this?" orange brown orange red	"Show me how you _____ carefully" or "Tell me about how I'm writing" (quickly, slowly, carefully, etc.).	"Find the _____ that is rough" or "Tell me about this shirt" (rough, red, pretty, etc.).

Also, note the minimal use of language. Teacher talk is minimized to facilitate pacing and student attentiveness.

The students are tested by asking them to respond to the object as an example or not an example of the new concept (e.g., *heavy* vs. *not heavy*). Requiring students to say "heavy" or "not heavy" provides better practice than a "yes/no" response when the question "Is this heavy?" is presented.

Critical Behaviors

Modeling. When modeling, examples must be presented briskly in order to keep a student's attention. The teacher should present the examples in a lively fashion, stressing the key words: "This is a *mitten*." "This is *not* a *mitten*."

Testing the new word. The teacher presents the set of examples until students can respond correctly in consecutive order to a group of at least three positive and three negative examples (six in all). A teacher can conclude only *after* students make correct responses to all the positive and negative examples that the students understand the new word. Examples should not be presented in a predictable order. Never use a yes-no-yes-no-yes-no pattern. Vary the number of consecutive positive and negative instances.

Teaching Vocabulary Through Use of Synonyms

Teaching new vocabulary through synonyms is similar to the procedure of teaching through modeling examples, except that the teacher first equates a new word (*huge*) with a known word(s) (*very* big) rather than modeling examples. The teacher gives the synonym: "Here's a new word, *huge*. Huge means very big." Next, the teacher tests a set of positive and negative examples for the new word saying, "Tell me if it is huge or not huge." Then, the teacher provides practice on several recently taught synonyms: "Is this sturdy? How do you know?" The purpose of this review is to build retention.

The selection of synonyms must be done very carefully. Students must understand the meaning of the familiar word to be used as a synonym because it is intended to "explain" the new word. It is inappropriate to use the term *textile* to explain *fabric* because most students do not understand the word *textile*. However, using the synonym *strong* to explain *sturdy* is reasonable because most students know the meaning of *strong*.

Teachers can find potential words to use for synonyms by referring to a children's dictionary or thesaurus. One or more of the words will probably be familiar to students and appropriate to use.

Table 15.2 illustrates a synonym teaching format with the word *sturdy*. The major steps include the teacher presenting the synonym, testing positive and negative examples, and then reviewing the new word and previously introduced words.

Table 15.2
Format for Teaching Vocabulary Through Synonyms

Teacher	Students
1. Teacher states the new word and the equivalent, familiar word and then tests.	
a. "Here is a new word. *Sturdy. Sturdy* means strong."	
b. "What does *sturdy* mean?" (Signal.)	"Strong."
2. Teacher presents positive and negative examples until the students make six consecutive correct responses. Examples are not repeated in the same order.	
a. "Tom leaned against a pole. The pole fell over. Was the pole sturdy or not sturdy?" (Signal.)	"Not sturdy."
b. "Tom leaned against another pole. The pole didn't move. Was the pole sturdy or not sturdy?" (Signal.)	"Sturdy."
c. "A house didn't shake at all in a high windstorm. Was the house sturdy or not sturdy?" (Signal.)	"Sturdy."
d. "A different house fell down when the wind started blowing. Was the house sturdy or not sturdy?" (Signal.)*	"Not sturdy."
3. Teacher reviews new word and other previously introduced words.	
a. "Is it mild out today? How do you know?"	
b. "Is that bench sturdy? How do you know?"	
c. "Is my desk tidy? How do you know?"	

Note: The teacher can also provide practice by asking the students to generate examples. "Tell me about something that is sturdy."

Teaching Vocabulary Through Use of Definitions

The third procedure for teaching vocabulary is through definitions. Although definitions can be constructed in several ways, we will focus on a procedure that is applicable to most words and suited to most young students. The procedure includes two steps:

    1. Identifying a small class to which a word belongs.

    2. Stating how the word differs from other members of that class.

In constructing definitions, teachers must make them understandable to students, rather than make them technically correct. For example, a *liquid* might be defined as something you can pour. Although scientists might disapprove of this definition, it is adequate to teach the meaning of *liquid* to young children. Definitions are also kept understandable by using words that students understand.

Following are some sample definitions. Note the effort to keep them as simple as possible.

Class	Differs from Other Things in the Class
1. Container:	an object you can put things in
2. Vehicle:	an object that can take you places
3. Seam:	a place where two pieces of material are sewn together
4. Glare:	to look at someone as if you are angry

The format for teaching vocabulary through definitions appears in Table 15.3. First, the teacher tells the students the definition and has them repeat it. Second, the teacher tests the students on positive and negative examples to ensure that students understand the definition and that they are not

Table 15.3

Format for Teaching Vocabulary with Definitions

Teacher	Students
1. Teacher states the new word and its definition and has students say definition.	
a. "An exit is a door that leads out of a building."	
b. "What is an exit?" (Signal.)	"A door that leads out of a building."
2. Teacher presents positive and negative examples.	
a. Teacher holds up a picture or points to an open closet door. "Is this an exit or not an exit?" (Signal.) "How do you know?"	"Not an exit." "It doesn't lead out of the building."
b. Teacher holds up a picture of a movie theater, points to an open exit door, and asks, "Is this an exit or not an exit?" (Signal.) "How do you know?"	"An exit." "It leads out of the building."
c. Teacher continues presenting examples until the students answer six consecutive questions correctly.	
3. Teacher reviews words recently introduced.	
a. Teacher holds up picture of barracks. "What is this?" (Signal.) "How do you know?"	"A barracks." "It's a building where soldiers live."
b. Teacher holds up a picture of an exit. "What is this? How do you know?" etc.	

just memorizing a series of words that has no meaning. Third, a review of previously introduced words is presented.

Commercial Programs

Although all core comprehensive basal reading programs include exercises designed to teach vocabulary and language skills, none of these programs provides for the comprehensive and systematic teaching of language skills and vocabulary that at-risk children will need to learn at an optimal rate. Most programs use inappropriate teaching demonstrations and provide insufficient practice (Jitendra & Kame'enui, 1988, 1994).

Major modifications are necessary to make basal core-reading programs suitable tools for teaching basic vocabulary and oral language skills in kindergarten and first grade to at-risk students. However, modifying the vocabulary and oral language component of a program is much more difficult than modifying the decoding component of a program, since constructing demonstrations to teach the meaning of a new word can require many illustrations or objects. Our suggestion is, rather than trying to modify the vocabulary and language teaching component of an inadequate core reading program, you should obtain a program specifically designed to teach vocabulary and language skills to instructionally naive at-risk students. When selecting a program, teachers should spend most of their time examining how the programs teach skills, rather than determining what skills are taught, since most programs cover basically the same content. Teachers should look at individual lessons, noting the formats and examples used. The wording in the formats should be simple and direct. The examples, as mentioned earlier, are critical. Example selection is the key to effectively teaching vocabulary. Note if positive and negative examples are provided. If the program does not provide adequate examples, it will not be effective with instructionally naive students. After looking at the way several tasks are constructed, teachers should look at 5 to 10 consecutive lessons to see how many times each new word is reviewed. The purpose is to determine the adequacy of initial practice and review. If a new skill or word is not reviewed, many students will not learn it. Programs with inadequate review are difficult to modify.

In summary, examine a beginning language/vocabulary program by looking at *how* it teaches language skills and vocabulary rather than by looking at what it claims to teach. Look at (a) the clarity of teaching presentations, (b) the adequacy of example selection, and (c) the provision for practice and review.

An example of an effectively constructed program designed to teach basic vocabulary and language skills is SRA's *Language for Learning* program written by Siegfried Engelmann (1999). The program uses an explicit and systematic instructional approach, including clear teaching demonstrations, carefully designed example selection, highly interactive formats, immediate error correction, cumulative review, and frequent progress-monitoring assessments. *Language for Learning* is comprised of seven learning strands: actions, descriptions of objects, information and background knowledge, instructional words, problem-solving concepts, classification, and problem-solving strategies. A typical 30-minute class lesson might include a number of exercises drawn from any or all of the strands.

Language for Learning is unique in that it provides for cumulative introduction and practice of skills (as new skills are introduced, previously introduced skills are reviewed) and introduces new material at a realistic rate. For example, prepositions are introduced at the rate of about one each 5 to 10 lessons; *on* appears in lesson 28, *over* in lesson 31, *in front of* in lesson 36, *in* in lesson 47, *in back of* in lesson 57, *under* in lesson 67, *next to* in lesson 76, and *between* in lesson 86. When a new preposition is introduced, previously taught ones are reviewed.

Language for Learning also uniquely emphasizes expressive language. Tasks range from simple identity statements (e.g., "This is a dog," or "This is not a dog") to more complex statements (e.g., "If the teacher touches her arm or her nose, all the girls will stand up"). A companion program, *Language for Thinking,* can be used when children finish *Language for Learning. Language for Thinking* (2002) reviews the vocabulary from *Language for Learning* and presents more complex reasoning tasks like absurdities, descriptions, definitions, multiple classifications, and analogies.

Application to Your Curriculum

Evaluate the Teaching of Vocabulary in Your Core Reading Program

1. Select a vocabulary word from the beginning, middle, and end of the kindergarten program and from the beginning of the first-grade program. For each word tell:

    a. What procedure/strategy is utilized to teach students each word.

    b. Are the procedures/strategies explicit?

    c. Is the language used in the teaching presentation clear?

    d. Are sufficent examples and nonexamples used to clearly communicate meaning?

    e. Are students provided with enough practice over a series of lessons to learn these words?

2. What modifications would you make given your previous analysis?

CHAPTER 16

Vocabulary Instruction During Primary Stage

In this chapter, we discuss strategies for teaching vocabulary during late first, second and third grade. We present strategies for teaching specific word meanings as well as strategies that students can use to help determine meanings of new words they will encounter during independent reading. In addition, we highlight components of vocabulary instruction that promote comprehension of text containing taught words.*

Vocabulary used at the beginning of first-grade is usually controlled in that nearly all words appearing in stories are in the typical student's speaking vocabulary. From mid-first grade on, students encounter an increasingly large number of unknown words. Stories begin to contain difficult-to-read words that may not already be in the students' oral vocabularies. Therefore, teachers must be prepared to spend time teaching vocabulary, especially to children who have limited language backgrounds. They must work on increasing students' general vocabulary, as well as knowledge of specific words that will appear in upcoming reading assignments.

Teaching Specific Word Meanings Through Explicit Instruction

It is reasonable to thoroughly teach about 8 to 10 words per week (Armbruster, Lehr, & Osborne 2001). The words that are taught and the sequence in which they are introduced will primarily be dictated by the text the students are to read. A teacher must review upcoming lessons and select words that are important, useful, and difficult.

Important words are words that are critical to understanding a story. *Useful words* are those that students will find useful in many contexts. Priority is given to words that students are likely to see and use again and again. For example, it is probably more useful for students to learn a word like *increase* or *decrease* than the word *void*. The more likely students are to encounter a word in the future, the more critical it is to teach it.

When selecting words to teach directly, it's important to keep in mind that students do not either know or not know words; rather, they know words to varying degrees or levels (Beck, McKeown, & Kucan, 2002). Beck and colleagues

---

*This chapter is based on the vocabulary chapter written by Dr. Carrie Beck-Thomas, which appeared in *Direct Instruction Reading*.

have identified three levels of word knowledge: *unknown, acquainted,* and *established* (Beck, McKeown, & Omanson, 1987). At the unknown level, the meaning of the word is completely unfamiliar. At the acquainted level, the basic meaning is recognized after some thought. At the established level, meaning is easily, rapidly, and automatically recognized. Although it is enough for students to have a superficial acquaintance with some words in a selection, for most words—and all important words—students must have an established level of knowledge if they are to comprehend what they read (Nagy, Herman, & Anderson, 1985).

Teachers need to be careful in relying on the guidance in basal reading programs for identifying target vocabulary words. Most programs include lists of vocabulary words to teach; however, these lists are not reliable. Sometimes these words are already known by students. However, important words the students do not know the meaning of may not be included in the list of words designated for vocabulary instruction. If a program does not provide reliable guidance on vocabulary, teachers, especially those working with struggling readers and at-risk students, will need to preview selections and locate important, useful words that students are not likely to know at the established level.

Another aspect of word knowledge relates to expressive versus receptive usage. *Expressive* vocabulary refers to how a student uses words to communicate with other people, whether in speaking or in writing. *Receptive* vocabulary refers to a student's understanding of the words another person has said. Receptive vocabulary also includes recognizing words in print. Teachers should keep in mind that expressive usage (using a word properly) is much more difficult than receptive usage (understanding the word).

The current depth of knowledge a student has about the meaning of a particular word will determine how the word should be taught. Researchers have identified four different kinds of word learning: (a) learning a new meaning for a known word, (b) learning the meaning for a new word representing a known concept, (c) learning the meaning of a new word representing an unknown concept, and (d) clarifying and enriching the meaning of a known word (Graves, Juel, & Graves, 1998). These types of word learning vary in difficulty. Each different kind of word learning requires different instructional procedures. In the sections that follow, we discuss each type of word learning and describe explicit instructional procedures appropriate for that level of word knowledge.

Learning a New Meaning for a Known Word

In some instances, students have a word in their oral vocabulary but are learning a new meaning for it. For example, the student knows what a tree branch is, but is learning about branches of government in social studies. It is estimated that 80% of our words have multiple meanings; these words are also known as polysemous words, and include words such as *bank, run, bay, shot,* and *coach.* Consider the meaning of the following sentence: *Coaches not admitted unless booked in advance* (Irvin, 2001). This sentence contains four polysemous words: *coaches, admit, book,* and *advance.* A reader's first interpretation may be that the individuals who train and direct athletes will not be admitted unless they make a reservation. The sentence is actually referring not to individuals, but to motor buses.

Teachers should directly teach students the new meaning of a word before the children read a selection in which understanding the new meaning for the word is needed. One way of teaching a new meaning is to utilize a dictionary. To teach the new meaning, the teacher presents the sentence in which the word appears and has the children find the word in their dictionary. The teacher points out that there are several definitions for the word. The teacher reads the definitions aloud one at a time, and the class discusses which of the definitions would best fit the sentence's context. Students eliminate the inappropriate definitions. The teacher then has students substitute the most likely definition for the word in the original sentence to verify that it makes sense. As a follow-up activity, teachers can have students create their own sentences using a variety of definitions for the polysemous word. For example, consider the use of *booked* in these sentences:

The criminal was *booked* downtown at the police department.

He *booked* a ticket from San Francisco to Washington, DC.

As students become more sophisticated, teachers can provide less guidance. Eventually, students will use this process for independently finding a new meaning.

Many words have different meanings in different content areas. The word *division,* for example, has a very different meaning in math than it does in science or social studies. Students might be learning long *division* in math, studying cell *division* in science, and discussing *divisions* of the army in social studies. Teachers can reinforce different meanings across disciplines by explicitly teaching that they are using "one" meaning of this word, reminding students that other meanings exist.

Learning a Meaning for a New Word Representing a Known Concept

In this type of vocabulary learning, the student is familiar with the concept, but does not know the particular word for the concept. For example, the student knows about *leaves,* but does not know that the *leaf* of a palm tree is called a *frond.* Teachers can present this type word by using synonyms or definitions. In Chapter 15, we discussed teaching through synonyms when students know a word with a meaning similar to a new word. Synonym teaching can be continued throughout all grade levels. Some examples of less common words that can be taught through synonyms are:

- *merge-join*
- *exterior-outside*
- *amity-friendship*

- *assault-attack*
- *secure-safe*
- *brief-short*
- *vary-change*
- *mentor-teacher*

Definitions are used more often than synonyms as students progress through the grades and the meanings of words become increasingly more complex. The major way to define a word involves putting the new word in a class, then specifying the unique characteristics of that word that distinguish it from other words in that same class:

- *decathlon*—an athletic contest that includes 10 track-and-field events
- *pediatrician*—a doctor who works with children
- *slander*—a false report that says bad things about someone
- *cutlery*—tools used for eating
- *nonentity*—a thing that is of no importance

There are two steps to teach the meaning of a new word representing a known concept. First, the teacher communicates the meaning of the word by presenting a synonym or definition. Second, the teacher presents a series of examples, some positive and some negative, and asks the students to tell if the instance is an example of the new word. This step ensures that students really understand the meaning of the word and are not simply memorizing a rote definition. The teaching procedure is illustrated in the format in Table 16.1. In the format, the teacher presents the word *respite* using a synonym (a *short rest*), then tests the students on a series of positive and negative examples. Note that for testing new vocabulary, the teacher asks, "*How do you know?*" after each question (e.g., "*The bear slept all winter. Is that a respite? How do you know?*"). Asking "How do you know" provides additional practice linking the new word to the synonym or definition. Words would be reviewed daily for several days, then intermittently.

Learning a Meaning for a New Word Representing an Unknown Concept

Much learning in content areas requires that students learn a meaning of a new word representing an unknown concept. In this situation, the student is not familiar with either the concept or the word for the concept, and so must learn both. For example, as students learn about *evaporation* and *photosynthesis*, they may be learning both new concepts and new words. Similarly, literature selections in intermediate grades often contain difficult new concepts such as *altruism, pragmatism,* and *homage.*

Learning the meaning of a new word that represents an unknown concept is the most difficult type of word learning and requires the most elaborate instruction.

Table 16.1

Format for New Vocabulary (Respite)

Teacher	Students
1. Teacher models the pronunciation and definition of *respite*.	
a. "Listen, *respite*. Say that." (Signal.)	"Respite."
b. "A respite is a short rest. What is respite?" (Signal.)	"A short rest."
2. Teacher tests definition.	

a. "John worked hard all day. Then he went home and worked
    all night.
    Did he take a respite?" (Signal.)
    "How do you know?"
	
	"No."
	"He didn't take a rest."

b. "Ann worked hard all morning. At 12:00, she stopped and
    relaxed for awhile. Then she went back to work.
    Did she take a respite?" (Signal.)
    "How do you know?"
	
	"Yes."
	"She took a short break."

c. "Sue did 50 push-ups. Then she splashed cold water
    on her face and lay down for 5 minutes.
    Then she did 25 more push-ups.
    Did she take a respite?" (Signal.)
    "How do you know?" (Signal.)
	
	"Yes."
	"She rested for 5 minutes."

d. "Bill did 50 push-ups this morning, then he slept on
    the bed all night.
    Did he take a respite?" (Signal.)
    "How do you know?" (Signal.)
	
	"No."
	"He slept too long."

3. Teacher reviews recently introduced words.	

The teacher can directly present the meaning of the new word by using a definition. However, for more complex concepts simply presenting a definition is not sufficient. Students will need a deeper understanding. Semantic mapping and concept definition maps are two techniques that can be used to more thoroughly teach the meaning of new concepts. Both utilize graphic organizers.

Semantic Mapping. Semantic mapping encourages concept development by graphically displaying characteristics of words in categories and showing how they are related to each other. The teacher prepares a graphic, writing the new word in the middle of the graphic and providing categories under which to list information about that word. For example, if the teacher presented the word *osprey*, the teacher might make these categories: what it looks like, how it hunts, where you find it, what kind of shelter it builds. Figure 16.1 illustrates a graphic that could be used for a presentation on the word *osprey*.

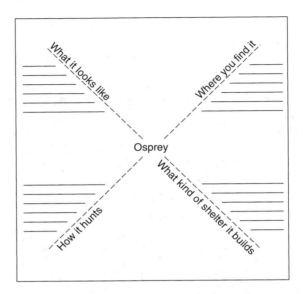

Figure 16.1
Semantic Map for the Word *Osprey*

The teacher presents a source of information about the new concept, either having students read a passage about the new concept, presenting a lecture on the new concept, or (if the concept is one that he or she thinks some children may already be familiar with) conducting a group discussion. The teacher and students would fill out the graphic using the information provided from the text or discussion.

Semantic mapping can also be used to show how related words are the same and different. For example, for a presentation on whales, the teacher could make a graphic with categories that describe all whales and then spaces to tell characteristics of specific whales. Building the map can generate much thought and discussion among students.

Clarifying/Enriching the Meaning of a Known Word

The fourth type of vocabulary learning occurs when students learn more precise definitions for a known word. In many cases the student has some idea of the basic meaning of a word, but needs to learn finer, more subtle distinctions in the meaning and usage. For example, the student knows that the words *jogging, trotting, dashing,* and *sprinting* have something to do with the word *running,* but does not know the specific meaning of each word.

Clarifying meanings of words can be done by explaining the difference between words in a similar category. Instruction would involve presenting more precise definitions and explanations of the words. For example, a teacher can explain, "*Sprinting* is a word we use when a person is running as fast as he or she can. *Jogging* is a word we use when a person is not running anywhere near as fast as the person can run."

Simply telling the students the definition is not adequate. Teachers should also provide practice in applying the definitions. One way to structure this application is by providing sentences and having the child fill in the appropriate word. For example, the teacher would present the sentence *Jason down the street when he saw the school bus door closing* and ask, "What word _____ fits best in the blank, *sprinted* or *jogged?*"

Enriching students' understanding of a word involves providing examples of the word's use in multiple contexts, particularly those that go beyond its use in the story in which it was first introduced. If a student's understanding of a word is limited to one narrow definition or a single context (e.g., *stern* is always used in association with a teenager's father), then students may not be able to comprehend many applications of the word and have limited use of the word in speech and writing (Beck, McKeown, & Kucan, 2002). Teachers can show the range of meaning of a word by presenting the word in a variety of contexts. For example, in enriching the meaning of *stern* as a serious and demanding person, the teacher can present several descriptions of a person as examples of *stern*.

> We had a stern teacher. He was very strict. He never smiled. He demanded that all our work be perfect. If we made any errors at all on our work, he would make us do the whole assignment over again.
>
> Our basketball coach was very stern. She made us practice our plays over and over again until we did them perfectly. She never seemed to be satisfied.

Providing Practice to Reach Established Level

A major goal of vocabulary instruction is to increase the number of words the student knows at the established level (the level at which the student readily and easily understands the meaning of a word). Providing a variety of applications that require students to use words and apply definitions will help students reach the established level of word knowledge. Beck, McKeown, and colleagues have developed numerous activities to enrich students' vocabulary knowledge (Beck et al., 2002). These researchers recommend that teachers have students talk about situations a word would describe. In one activity, "Have You Ever . . . ?", students associate newly learned words with contexts from their own experience. For example, after learning the meanings of the words *covertly* and *impressed,* the teacher can present an activity in which students are asked to describe a time when they might have acted *covertly* or tell about when they *impressed* their teacher. Another activity to promote word usage is to provide students with sentence stems that require them to integrate a word's meaning into a context in order to explain a situation. For example, "The man covertly hopped onto the bus because . . . " or "Nancy's teacher was very impressed because. . . ." Teachers can have students respond to and explain examples as well as creating their own by asking questions such as, "If you had a friend who watched TV all the time, how might you *coax* him into getting some exercise?"

To provide additional practice on word usage, teachers can ask students to determine instances when the word would be an appropriate choice (Beck et al., 2002). For example:

Which of these things might be extraordinary?

Why or why not?

A shirt that was comfortable or a shirt that washed itself?

Teachers can also ask students to differentiate between two descriptions by labeling them as an example or non-example of the target word (Beck et al., 2002).

I'll say some things, if they sound leisurely, say "Leisurely." If you'd need to be in a hurry, say "Hurry."

People taking a walk in the park.

Firefighters getting to a fire.

Runners sprinting in a race.

People sitting and talking to friends.

A dog lying in the sun.

Banter

A husband and wife argue in loud voices about what to have for dinner.

A husband and wife kid each other about who ate more at dinner.

Beck and colleagues recommend presenting words in semantic groups of 6 to 10 words. For example, one semantic group could include words that describe people such as *covert, peculiar, raucous, stern, glum,* and *impatient.* These researchers stress that students' word knowledge is stored in networks of connected ideas. By making the connections between words explicit, teachers provide more opportunities for students to access that knowledge. One way to build connections between new and known words is to ask students to associate one of their new words (e.g., *peculiar, raucous, covert, stern*) with a presented word or phrase, such as "Which word goes with spy?" (covert). Another activity is to present questions that use two target words, such as "Could a raucous presenter covertly leave the room?" The purpose is to make students think about whether a relationship between the words exists. Students generally should be required to justify their answers.

As a culminating activity, the teacher can ask students to place a series of related words on a word line that represents a continuum. The teacher gives students a list of four to eight related words. Students are to rank the words on a continuum based on intensity of meaning. There may not be one correct ordering of the words. The purpose of the activity is to elicit students' explanations that involve target word meanings. See Figure 16.2.

Rank the words on the continuum based on intensity of meaning:

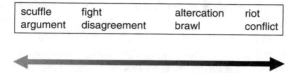

| scuffle | fight | | altercation | riot |
| argument | disagreement | | brawl | conflict |

Figure 16.2

Word Continuum: Shades of Meaning

Developed by MaryBeth Munroe, Southern Oregon ESD.

Teaching Word-Learning Strategies

Skilled reading depends not only on knowing a large number of words, but also on being able to deal effectively with unknown words that are encountered as one reads text. Teachers need to present students with strategies to facilitate independent word learning. Such strategies include (a) teaching students within-word parts, (b) teaching students to be more proficient at figuring out a word's meaning from context, and (c) teaching students how to use a dictionary as an aid to determining meanings of unknown words. Each strategy will be discussed in the sections that follow.

Word Parts

Teaching within-word parts is a productive type of vocabulary instruction. All words are composed of *morphemes,* the smallest linguistic units that have meaning. Morphemes may be free (whole words) or bound (found only as parts of words such as prefixes, suffixes, and nonword bases). Morphemic analysis as a vocabulary aid involves dividing a word into its component morphemes, then using the meanings of the individual morphemes to figure out the meaning of the entire word. Morphemic analysis can be illustrated with the word *unworkable,* which includes three morphemes: *un* (meaning *not*), work, and *able* (meaning *able to*). Through morphemic analysis, *unworkable* can be translated as *not able to work.* Teaching students the meanings of morphemes will give them a strategy for analyzing some unknown vocabulary words. This strategy may be especially important for content-area reading, where many of the words contain identifiable word parts that have the same meaning in different words.

Teachers must realize the limitations of morphemic analysis. Three factors limit the usefulness of morphemic analysis. The first factor is the difficulty of translating individual morphemes into a functional definition. For example, the word *accurate* is composed of three morphemes: *ac,* which means toward; *cure,* which means care; and *ate,* which means that which is. The literal morphemic definition of *accurate* is *that which is toward care.* For a sophisticated reader, this definition might be helpful; however, for the less-sophisticated students, such a definition would be difficult to use.

A second reason why morphemes are of limited value in figuring out word meanings is that many morphemes have dual meanings. For example, the morpheme *dia* sometimes means *through* as in *diameter* and sometimes means *day* as in *diary*.

A third reason for the limitations of morphemic analysis is that students often cannot determine the morphemes that have been combined to make up the word. For example, the word *recognition* is composed of the morphemes *re + cogno + ite + ion*.

Teachers must decide which morphemes are worth teaching. Table 16.2 includes some morphemes that lend themselves to relatively easy translation. Next to each morpheme is a word that illustrates use of that morpheme and the morpheme's common meaning. Note that the meaning we use is designed to be functional rather than technically correct. We tried to construct definitions to make morphemic analysis easier for students.

Two rules for sequencing the introduction of morphemes are: (a) to introduce the most functional ones first, and (b) to separate morphemes likely to be

Table 16.2

Morpheme Meanings[*]

Morpheme	Sample Word	Approximate Meaning
able	*portable*	able to be
bi	*bicycle*	two
dis	*dishonest*	not
	disappear	opposite of
est	*biggest*	the most
ful	*hopeful*	full of
il	*illegal*	not
inter	*interstate*	between
intra	*intrastate*	inside
less	*fearless*	without
pre	*preschool*	before
re	*repay*	again
sub	*submarine*	below
tri	*tricycle*	three
un	*unable*	not
	untie	opposite of

[*] For a more thorough listing of morpheme meanings, see *Dictionary of English Word-Roots* (R. Smith, 1966).

confused. Morphemes are functional when they enable students to understand words they could not understand without knowledge of the morpheme. The morpheme *re*, which means *again*, is an *example of a morpheme that is quite functional*. The morphemes *inter* and *intra* can serve as examples of morphemes that are likely to be confused. The introduction of these morphemes should be separated by at least five other morphemes.

Table 16.3 presents a format for teaching the meaning of new morphemes and reviewing previously taught morphemes. Table 16.4 includes written work that could be used as a review. The rate of introducing new morphemes depends on the students' performance. A new morpheme can be introduced when the students can do the verbal and written exercises that review previously introduced morphemes without error.

Table 16.3
Format for Introducing Morphemes

Teacher	Students
1. Teacher introduces a new morpheme.	
a. "Listen. *Less* usually means *without*."	
b. "What does *less* usually mean?" (Signal.)	"Without."
"So *careless* means without a care."	
"What does *careless* mean?" (Signal.)	"Without a care."
c. "What does less usually mean?" (Signal.)	"Without."
"So what does the word *winless* mean?" (Signal.)	"Without a win."
d. "What does *less* usually mean?" (Signal.)	"Without."
"So what does *homeless* mean?" (Signal.)	"Without a home."
2. Teacher reviews morphemes.	
a. "What does *pre* mean?" (Signal.)	"Before."
b. "What does *un* mean?" (Signal.)	"Not."
c. "What does *tri* mean?" (Signal.)	"Three."
d. "What does *less* mean?" (Signal.)	"Without."
e. "What does *able* mean?" (Signal.)	"Able to be."
3. Teacher applies morphemes to figure out meaning.	
a. "Listen. *Careful*. Tell me the first morpheme in *careful*." (Signal.)	"Care."
"What's the next morpheme in *careful?*" (Signal.)	"Ful."
b. "What does *ful* mean?" (Signal.)	"Full of."
c. "What does *careful* mean?" (Signal.)	"Full of care."
d. Teacher repeats steps 3(a-c) with these words: *preschooler* (one who is before school), *triangle* (three angles), *winless* (without a win).	

Table 16.4

Worksheet for Morphemic Analysis

Part 1: Write the correct meaning next to each morpheme.

un _____   less _____   re _____   mis _____

ful _____   able _____   est _____   er _____

Part 2: Fill in the blanks using these words:

hopeful   hopeless   misspell   winless   preschool

a. Tom did not want to _____ any words on the test.

b. My brother is too young for this school; he goes to a _____.

c. We are _____ our team will win.

d. After trying for 2 months to get his dog to sit, Tom thought it was _____ to continue.

e. The team was sad because it was _____.

The format in Table 16.3 includes several steps. In the first step, the teacher tells the students the meaning of a new morpheme, then tests students on the meaning of several words that contain that morpheme (e.g., the morpheme *less* added to the word *win* creates the word *winless,* which means *without a win*). In the second step, the teacher provides practice on the meaning of the new morpheme and previously taught morphemes. In the third step, students use their knowledge of those morphemes to determine word meanings.

The worksheet practice on morphemic analysis illustrated in Table 16.4 includes two parts. In part 1 of the worksheet, students write the correct meaning for each morpheme. In part 2, students select words for sentence completion items. The students are given a written exercise with 5 to 10 sentences, with a list of words appearing above the sentences. From the list, the students are to select the words that should be in each sentence and fill in the blanks.

Morpheme practice may be extended by asking students to create word journals. Students create one page per morpheme and whenever they encounter a word with that part, they place it on the page and note where they encountered the word. Likewise, teachers can create word walls to reinforce each morpheme. Teachers let students add to the walls as they find words using the morphemes they are studying.

Context Clues

In contextual analysis, a reader uses the words in a sentence surrounding an unknown word to figure out the unknown word's meaning. Contextual analysis is an essential skill for students in grade 3 and above because it allows them to determine the meaning of many unknown words they will encounter. Writers often define words they feel the reader is unlikely to know. Many times the definition is given through the use of an appositive construction containing a synonym or definition that immediately follows the unknown words in the passage:

1. The *drouge,* a small parachute for slowing down an object, shot out of the rear of the space capsule at 10,000 feet.
2. The *surplus,* that is, the amount left over, was so great that the storage bins were full and grain was lying on the ground.

A definition or synonym can also be stated as a negation, a form more difficult for students to understand:

1. The older brother was quite *affable,* not argumentative.
2. Jamie was a *versatile* athlete, while Ann, who was not so versatile, was able to play only one sport.

Contextual analysis is made more difficult not only when negative examples are used, but also when a synonym or definition is separated from the unknown word in a passage. In example 1, which follows the definition immediately follows the new word. In example 2, the definition is separated from the new word, which makes example 2 more difficult:

1. The food is *preserved,* or kept from spoiling, by special refrigeration cars.
2. The food is *preserved* by special refrigeration cars. These specially made cars keep the food from spoiling.

Contextual analysis is also more difficult when the meaning of a word is implied by description rather than by direct use of a synonym. Often a paragraph or series of sentences provides example(s), either positive or negative, that students must use as the basis for inferring the meaning of a new word:

1. Byron's muscles strained as he pulled at the door. He leaned back and pushed as hard as he could. He *exerted* all the force he could.
2. In the sea, bones and shells are not eaten away and harmed by the air. Objects are covered with protective layers of sand so that years from now they will be undamaged. Life from the sea is being *preserved* for the future.

One way to teach students how to use contextual analysis to determine the meaning of an unknown word involves leading students through a series of short passages. For each passage, the teacher (a) points out the unknown word, (b) has the students find the words that tell what the unknown word means, and (c) has the students restate the sentence by substituting a synonym or description for the unknown word. The definition or synonym would be derived through contextual analysis. Table 16.5 shows a format that can be used in the intermediate grades for teaching students to infer meaning from a passage.

Table 16.5
Format for Teaching Vocabulary Through Context

Teacher	Students
An advanced exercise might include four to six passages such as this one: Pioneers saw a dark, living cloud of birds. The cloud was so huge that it almost <u>eclipsed</u> the sun. It seemed like nighttime had suddenly started. People could hardly see.	
1. Teacher calls on a student to read the passage and identify the unknown word.	
a. "Read the passage."	
b. "A new word is underlined, what word is that?" (Signal.)	"Eclipsed."
2. Teacher calls on a student to find the synonym or definition.	
a. "What happened when the birds eclipsed the sun?"	"It got dark and the people could hardly see."
b. "It seemed that nightime has suddenly started. What do you think an eclipse does to the sun?" (Signal.)	"Covers it up."
c. "Yes, it covers it up."	
3. Students say the sentence substituting the meaning of the new word.	
a. "Read the sentence with *eclipse* in it." (Signal.)	"The cloud was so huge that it almost eclipsed the sun."
b. Teacher calls on a student. "Say the sentence using a different word for *eclipse*." (Signal.)	"The cloud was so huge that it almost covered up the sun."
4. Teacher repeats steps 1 through 3 with several more passages.	

A more general way of teaching students to derive word meanings from context is to use a talk-through technique (Stahl & Shiel, 1999). In this technique, the teacher first provides a model by talking through the processes he or she is using to figure out a word's meaning from context. Next, the teacher leads the students through using context to derive the meaning of several words through prompts such as, "What words around you tell you something about the word (_____)?"; "What do you think the word (_____) means?"; "Does that meaning make sense when we substitute it for the word (_____) in the sentence?"

What's important to remember is that effective instruction in contextual analysis incorporates direct instruction procedures, including direct explanation of the purpose of the instruction, modeling, careful transition from guided to independent practice, and extensive practice in deriving word meanings from context with specific feedback (Stahl & Shiel, 1999). Other critical aspects of teaching contextual analysis involve the sequencing of examples from easy to difficult and providing adequate independent practice. Students will learn the skill if they are given enough practice and review on the various types of context construction: synonym or definition (which can be close to or separated from the new word), negation, and inference. Providing sufficient and appropriate examples is as important as the teaching procedure itself.

Dictionary Use.   Using the dictionary to determine a word's meaning is more difficult for the young student than an adult may suppose. First, a dictionary definition may include words a student does not understand. For example, a dictionary may define *habituate* as to *accustom;* unfortunately, many students will not know what *accustom* means. Teachers should try to select dictionaries written at an appropriate level for their students. The dictionary itself should use clear definitions composed of words with which students are familiar.

Second, many words have more than one meaning listed for them (e.g., the word *bark* can mean (a) covering of a tree, (b) a noise a dog makes, or (c) a small sailing ship). Teachers cannot take for granted that students will know how to find the appropriate meaning. Initial exercises should be limited to words in which the differences between the meanings are fairly obvious. For example, two possible meanings for the word *cold* are *low temperature* and *unfriendly.* In the sentence, "I was surprised at how cold my friend acted toward me when we met yesterday," the meaning of *cold* is obvious.

Teachers should encourage students to look up new words they encounter during independent reading. However, they should not require students to look up so many words that reading becomes tedious. Looking up every unknown word makes reading too laborious, while never looking up words can result in students reading without understanding what they read. The decision of whether a word is important depends on the students' purpose for reading the passage. When reading to learn new information, students should look up most unknown words. Yet, students do not need to look up all adjectives or adverbs during pleasure reading. Knowing when to figure out the meaning of a new word is an important skill that is usually not taught.

The basic strategy students need to learn when encountering an unknown word is that they should continue reading the paragraph in which the word appears to see if the context gives the word meaning. If the context does not give the meaning, the students decide if knowing the word's meaning is important to understanding the paragraph. If so, the students look up the word. To demonstrate when looking up a word is necessary, a teacher should conduct exercises where he or she leads students through several passages, helping them to see if the context gives the unknown word's meaning. If the context does not provide the meaning, the teacher asks if knowing the meaning of that particular word is essential to understanding the passage. The teacher then models how to look up the meaning of an unknown word and choose the appropriate definition.

Application to Your Curriculum

Evaluate Vocabulary Instruction in Your Core Reading Program

1. Select two stories from the second- or third-grade levels of your reading program. Inspect the stories to see which words may be unknown to your students. Examine the teacher presentation book for those lessons and several preceding lessons to see if the meanings of those words were taught.
2. Find the vocabulary teaching exercises in two lessons.

    a. What procedures/strategies are utilized to teach students vocabulary words?

    b. Are the procedures/strategies explicit?

    c. Is the language used in the teaching presentation clear?

    d. Are examples and non-examples used to communicate meaning?

    e. Are students provided with enough practice over a series of lessons to learn these words?

    f. What modifications would you make given your analysis?

3. Are students explicitly taught how to use context clues to determine word meaning? Are the teaching presentations clear? How much practice is provided? Is the practice systematic? What modifications would you make given your analysis?
4. Does the reading program teach the use of morphemes (bases, prefixes, and suffixes) to determine the meaning of words? List morphemes that are taught. Are students provided with explicit instruction as to how to use morphemes to determine the meanings of words? Are students provided with sufficient and systematic practice to achieve proficiency with these morphemes?

CHAPTER 17

Overview of Reading Comprehension Instruction

Reading Comprehension—What It Is

Reading comprehension used to be thought of as a natural by-product of learning how to read. Instruction was mainly focused on teaching students how to decode, and comprehension took the form of answering simple questions or responding to more complex tasks such as retelling or interpreting text. Students were provided with lots of practice, but little instruction.

We now know that reading comprehension is a much more complex set of skills and strategies that teachers should actively teach and develop throughout the grades. Recent research has demonstrated a dependent relationship between reading comprehension and prior knowledge, experience, and vocabulary. Explicit instruction in skills and strategies that good readers use also promotes increases in reading comprehension as well as increases in motivation and enjoyment of reading. As students encounter more difficult and complex text in the upper grades, mastery and strategic use of multiple comprehension strategies is essential in understanding and interpreting text.

Why Comprehension Instruction Is Important— The Research Connection

Reading comprehension instruction is necessarily complex and multifaceted. Good instruction is the most powerful means of promoting proficient comprehension and preventing comprehension problems (RRSG, 2002). What we already know about comprehension instruction was summarized by the Rand Reading Study Group in 2002 and converges with the National Reading Panel's research-based conclusions about comprehension instruction.

Both reports emphasize:

- The importance of the teacher determining and developing background knowledge and vocabulary necessary for student understanding of the text.

- Explicit teaching of specific comprehension strategies in which the teacher explains the strategy clearly, models the strategy, guides the students as they learn and apply the strategy, and provides practice with the strategy until students can apply it independently.

- ■ Explicit teaching of how to use multiple strategies in combination.
- ■ Explicit teaching of how to apply strategies flexibly to different types of text.

The National Reading Panel (2002) cited six strategies that were most effective in improving reading comprehension. These are:

1. Answering questions
2. Generating questions
3. Recognizing story structure
4. Summarizing
5. Using graphic and semantic organizers
6. Monitoring comprehension

Overview of Comprehension Instruction for Beginning Stage

Comprehension instruction begins during the beginning stage with oral activities. Comprehension is taught in shared story-reading activities in which the teacher reads a variety of stories and books and engages students in comprehension activities. Four early primary-grade comprehension skills—sentence comprehension, literal comprehension, sequencing, and basic story grammar—will be discussed in this section with attention to specific details that can help instructionally naive children succeed in the early stages of learning. As students learn to read and are able to adequately decode enough words to read simple stories, simple literal comprehension activities should be integrated into text reading.

Overview of Comprehension Instruction for Late Primary Stage

During the primary stage, comprehension instruction expands from the literal to inferential. Students are taught about story structure. Knowledge of text structure fosters comprehension. The NRP reported that story-structure instruction improves students' abilities to answer questions and recall what was read. In addition, inferential comprehension that requires students to determine relationships not directly stated in the passage but rather relies on their prior knowledge, experience, and vocabulary skills is presented. The story-structure exercises incorporate story mapping, main ideas, and comprehension monitoring.

CHAPTER 18

Beginning Comprehension Instruction

During the beginning stage, when children are not able to read longer stories, the teacher can present a variety of oral comprehension activities that, along with oral vocabulary and language instruction, will prepare children for the challenges of text-related comprehension in later grades.

Sentence Comprehension

Introducing Question Words

Oral sentence comprehension begins with teaching students how to identify what happened in a simple-action sentence, who was involved, when the event happened, where the event occurred, and why the event occurred. *Who, what, when, where,* and *why* are referred to as question words.

The rate for introducing new question words is determined by student performance. A new question word is not introduced until the students have mastered questions involving previously introduced question words.

Sequence

Who and what questions (see Table 18.1) should be presented first because they are easiest: "John went to the store. Who went to the store?" "John." "What did John do?" "Went to the store?"

Phrases and questions that tell *where* and questions related to *where* can be introduced next. A phrase telling *where* would be inserted in each sentence and a *where* question asked in addition to the *who* and *what* questions.

For example:

Sentence: A girl played soccer in the park.
Questions: Who played soccer?
              What did a girl do?
              Where did the girl play soccer?

When students are able to answer the *who, what,* and *where* questions without difficulty, *when* phrases can be introduced. Table 18.2 includes a format for presenting *when* and *where* phrases.

Table 18.1

Format for Introducing Question Words *Who* and *What*

Teacher	Students
1. Teacher models. "John ran in the park. Who ran in the park? John. What did John do? Ran in the park."	
2. Teacher provides practice and tests.	
a. "Listen. Tom fell off his bed. Say that." (Signal.)	"Tom fell off his bed."
b. "Who fell off the bed?" (Signal.)	"Tom."
c. "What did Tom do?" (Signal.)	"Fell off the bed."
3. Teacher repeats steps 2(a-c) with these sentences and questions:	
a. "Ann hit the ball. Say that." (Signal.)	"Ann hit the ball."
"Who hit the ball?" (Signal.)	"Ann."
"What did Ann do?" (Signal.)	"Hit the ball."
b. "The cat ate the food. Say that." (Signal.)	"The cat ate the food."
"Who ate the food?" (Signal.)	"The cat."
"What did the cat do?" (Signal.)	"Ate the food."
c. "The dog jumped up and down. Say that." (Signal.)	"The dog jumped up and down."
"Who jumped up and down?" (Signal.)	"The dog."
"What did the dog do?" (Signal.)	"Jumped up and down."

Table 18.2

Format for Introducing Question Words *When* and *Where*

Teacher	Students
1. Teacher models.	
a. "I'll say phrases that tell *when.* Yesterday morning tells when. Last night tells when. Before it got dark tells when. After dinner tells when."	
b. "Now I'll say phrases that tell *where.* In the park tells where. At the beach tells where. On my chair tells where. Under the couch tells where."	
2. Teacher tests. "I'll say a phrase. You say if it tells when or where."	
a. "In the park." (Signal.)	"Where."
b. "After dinner." (Signal.)	"When."
c. "Yesterday morning." (Signal.)	"When."
d. "On my chair." (Signal.)	"Where."
e. "At the beach." (Signal.)	"Where."
f. "Last night." (Signal.)	"When."

After students can discriminate between *when* and *where* phrases, they can be introduced to *when* and *where* questions. The teacher uses all four question words to do this (see Table 18.3).

The next step is to introduce *how*. The procedure for doing this is to model the answer for one or two *how* questions and then test the students on a series of sentences (see Table 18.4).

The last step is to introduce *why* (see Table 18.5). The procedure for teaching *why* is similar to the procedure for teaching earlier question words. The teacher presents examples with *why* and then provides discrimination practice. A teacher should not always include the word *because* in sentences that call for a response to *why* questions, since students may acquire a misrule that *because* is the only word that tells why. To prevent students from learning this misrule, teachers include examples containing *to* (He went home to get his coat), *since* (He ran home since it was late), and finally *and* (He fell down and cried).

After several days of practice on *why* questions, students can be introduced into exercises that include several question word items.

Table 18.3
Format for Using Four Question Words

Teacher	Students
1. Teacher says, "John played in the park yesterday morning. Say the sentence." (Signal.)	"John played in the park yesterday morning."
a. "Who played in the park?" (Signal.)	"John."
b. "What did John do in the park?" (Signal.)	"Played."
c. "Where did John play?" (Signal.)	"In the park."
d. "When did John play?" (Signal.)	"Yesterday morning."

Table 18.4
Format for Introducing *How*

Teacher	Students
1. Teacher models. "She ran like a deer. How did she run? Like a deer."	
2. Teacher tests.	
a. "He worked quickly. How did he work?" (Signal.)	"Quickly."
b. "He wrote carefully. How did he write?" (Signal.)	"Carefully."
c. "They worked like dogs. How did they work?" (Signal.)	"Like dogs."

Table 18.5

Format for Introducing *Why*

Teacher	Students
1. Teacher models. "He cried because he was hungry. Why did he cry? He was hungry."	
2. Teacher provides practice and tests.	
a. "Since she was late to school, she ran. Why did she run?" (Signal.)	"She was late."
b. "He went home to get his coat. Why did he go home?" (Signal.)	"To get his coat."
c. "She tried her best and won the race. Why did she win the race?" (Signal.)	"She tried her best."
d. "They lost because they made mistakes. Why did they lose?" (Signal.)	"They made mistakes."

Story Comprehension—Teacher Read Aloud

During the beginning stage, oral story book reading by the teacher can play an important role in preparing children for later written text-related comprehension. A number of important comprehension skills including story structure, sequencing, inferences, and prediction can be integrated into story-reading exercises.

Story Grammar

A high proportion of narrative stories will have a similar text structure, which is often referred to as story grammar. Stories will often begin by describing the characters and setting and then indicate a particular problem faced by one of the characters. The story will then describe how the problem is solved and conclude by describing how the characters were affected by the events. In presenting stories, the teacher works to enable the students to understand the grammar of the stories.

Presenting Stories

The basic oral story-reading strategy is to read a story several times: the first time for enjoyment and making predictions; then during rereadings—the next day or several days later—incorporating other skills (sequencing, what happened first, next, last; story grammar, who is the story about, where does the story take place, what is the problem, etc.).

Teachers can incorporate a number of techniques to increase the instructional efficiency of story telling:

   1. Select stories in which the sentence structure, vocabulary demands, and background knowledge needed to understand the story are not

overwhelming for the children. This does not mean that all stories read to the children must be simplistic or dull: There are very entertaining stories with controlled language usage that contain realistic vocabulary loads.

2. Preview the story to determine vocabulary, figurative language, or background knowledge that children are likely not to know, but is critical to their understanding of the story.

3. Before reading the story, teach any critical background knowledge or vocabulary that is needed to understanding the story.

4. Read stories multiple times. During one of the readings, make the reading a very entertaining experience with few interruptions. During other readings incorporate a variety of questions and ask the students to make predictions.

5. Use think-aloud modeling to teach causal relationships and how to make predictions. For example, during the story reading, the teacher can make predictions about what she thinks might happen by referring to descriptions of the character. "I think those monkeys might get out of the cage. The zookeeper has forgotten to close the locks on the cages all day long."

6. Work on a particular skill frequently enough to enable all children to master the skill. For example, teaching children how to describe what happened in the beginning, middle, and end of a story is a difficult skill that needs a good deal of practice. It needs to be taught and reviewed over an extended period of time.

7. Make the story reading highly interactive. Do not just call on a small number of students to answer. Involve all children. Address questions that have a specific answer to the group.

Retelling

Retelling is an activity in which the teacher leads the students in describing the story's setting and characters and in summarizing and sequencing the story's events.

Retell exercises would be done after the teacher has read the story to the students several times.

Prior to doing the retell, the teacher reads the beginning of the story again and tells the students he or she is going to ask some questions. "I'm going to read the beginning of the story and then ask you some questions about the beginning of it."

- Who was this story about? (character)
- Where does this story take place? (setting)
- What happened to _____? Or What was _____ trying to do? (problem)

After asking the questions, the teacher summarizes what happened at the beginning of the story (identifying character, setting, and problem). The teacher then calls on several students to tell what happened at the beginning of the story, making sure students included information about character, setting, and problem. If students left out any important information, the teacher can prompt with the question about that element.

The teacher then reads the middle of the story, following the same basic procedure of asking students questions, summarizing the information, then calling on several students to retell these events. Finally, the teacher presents the last part of the story following the same procedures.

When students are proficient in retelling events during the story, the teacher can conclude tasks by asking the questions: What happened in the beginning? What happened in the middle of the story? What happened in the end of the story? The answer to the first question should elicit the main character(s), setting, and problem. The next question addresses the important events in the story and the last question should focus on the outcome or resolution of the story.

If students are unable to correctly answer the questions, the teacher can prompt the students with more specific questions. For instance, if students are not able to tell what happened in the beginning, the teacher can ask, "Who is the story about?" and "What is (the character) trying to do?" After confirming the answer to these questions ("Yes, the story is about a little girl who lost her teddy bear."), the teacher should ask the question again, "What happened in the beginning of the story?"

Because these questions are open ended, students may identify details in the story rather than important story events. The teacher should confirm that the information is in the story, but ask students to describe the "most important" events and confirm student correct responses.

Simple story maps with boxes to indicate the sequence of story events are helpful supports for students learning to summarize and sequence events. The teacher can write the information in the box when students correctly tell what happened in a part of the story.

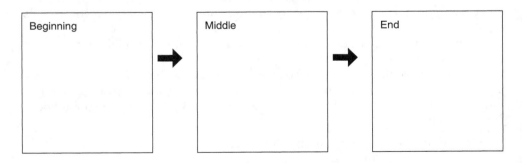

Later, students can use the story map to summarize and retell the main events of the story.

Literal Comprehension

Literal comprehension is the first and simplest form of text-related comprehension introduced in reading programs. In a literal comprehension exercise, the answer is directly stated in the passage. The difference between literal and inferential comprehension is illustrated in the following passage and questions.

> ### Passage
>
> A cat was sleeping in the sun. A dog walked by. The cat jumped up and hid in the can.
>
> *Literal:* Where was the cat sleeping? (in the sun)
>
> *Inferential:* Why did the cat hide? (it was afraid of the dog)

The first question is literal because the answer is directly stated in the passage. In contrast, the second question is not literal since the answer (afraid) does not appear in the passage. In the second item, students must infer that since the cat ran from the dog and hid, the cat was afraid.

Teaching Procedure for Literal Comprehension

In presenting passage-related literal comprehension questions (see Table 18.6), the teacher first has the students decode the passage until they can do so accurately. This is important for early readers as most of their initial efforts will be focused on decoding words rather than constructing meaning. The teacher then has the students reread the passage, pausing at appropriate places, and asks questions. If students cannot come up with the answer, the teacher directs them to reread the part of the passage that contains the answer. The teacher then asks the question again. The teacher then prepares the children to answer written questions. The teacher initially goes over the questions and directions before students work independently.

Difficulty of Literal Comprehension Items.   Several variables affect the difficulty of passage-related items: (a) the length of the passage, (b) the order in which questions are asked, (c) the response complexity, and (d) the use of pronouns.

Passage Length.   Answering questions from longer passages is more difficult. Reading programs often specify questions for the teacher to present following the reading of an entire passage or story. If struggling readers and at-risk students have difficulty retaining this information, teachers should structure passage reading with the teacher asking the questions during the reading of the passage, preferably after the sentence containing the answer. Later in the passage, the teacher can ask the students to answer earlier questions again and praise them for remembering the information. The teacher should gradually increase the amount of reading prior to asking the question until the students can answer the questions at the end of the passage.

Table 18.6

Format for Literal Comprehension

Passage:

A bug lived in a little house. It was made of mud. Yesterday, it rained and rained. The house got wet and fell apart. The poor bug was very sad. It had to fix up its house.

1. Underline the right answer: What got wet and fell apart?
the bug   the house   the rain

2. Circle the right answer: Who had to fix the house?
the bug   the house   the rain

3. Fill in the blank: When did it rain? _____

Teacher	Students
1. The teacher focuses on decoding fluency. **"Touch the first word."** Teacher checks pointing. The teacher alternates between unison and individual responses until the students read the passage accurately.	Students read the passage.
2. Teacher asks literal questions after each sentence or two.	
3. Teacher tests students' understanding of the instructions for written items. Often the instructions for early comprehension activities are not written because the students do not have the decoding skills necessary to read the words that appear in instructions. Whether the teacher gives the instructions or the students read them, the teacher then asks, **"How are you going to answer the question? Tell me what you're going to do. Show me where you put the answer."**	
4. Students read the first item and then mark the answer. If necessary, they find the appropriate sentence in the story that answers the item.	Student reads the question.
a. **"Touch the first question."** Teacher calls on a student to read.	
b. **"Raise your hand if you know the answer to that question."** If the question has only one possible correct answer, the teacher calls on the group to respond. If the question has several possible correct answers, she calls on individuals to respond. **"What's the answer?"**	Students answer.
c. If any students do not remember the answer, the teacher says, **"Let's find the answer in the story. Find the words *got wet* and *fell apart*."** After students find the sentence, the teacher repeats the item. **"What got wet and fell apart?" "Right, *the house*. Circle the answer."**	Students write the answer.
d. The procedure in step 4 is repeated until the students have completed all the items.	

Question Order. Items ordered so that they parallel the sequence of events in a passage are easier to answer than items that do not. When items follow the sequence of a passage, students are encouraged to think about the passage from the beginning and work through the events in order.

Here again, if the reading program specifies questions that do not follow the order of the story, the teacher can present the items in sequence to help students recall and order important story information.

Response Complexity. Instructions indicating how students are to respond range from simple ones in which a student writes a one-word answer or circles the word that goes in a blank to more complex ones in which students must carefully follow directions (e.g., "Circle the word that tells what the boy did. Underline the word that tells what the girl did.")

The teacher should be sure students understand what to do and can read all the words in the questions. Many beginning readers will need to be taught how to answer written questions. The teacher should go over the instructions with students before requiring them to work independently. "Read item 1. . . . What are you going to do to the word that tells what the boy did? . . . Show me what you are going to do. . . . " As the children work, the teacher should provide immediate feedback, focusing first on the students most likely to have difficulty.

Pronouns. Pronouns increase the difficulty of items because students must identify a pronoun antecedent before they can answer the item. In the following example, instructionally naive students or English language learners would be more likely to answer incorrectly if they are not certain what the pronoun "it" refers to.

Tom got a car. It was dirty.

Question: What was dirty?

If students have difficulty because of pronouns, the teacher can provide more structure through asking questions during passage reading.

A sample passage follows.

Passage

Tom and Lisa were sick. They had to stay in all weekend. He cried. She got mad.

Items

   a. Who was sick!
   b. Did Lisa stay in all weekend?
   c. Who cried?
   d. Did Tom get mad?

The teacher or students read the passage. The teacher asks questions after each sentence:

"Tom and Lisa were sick. Who was sick?"

"They had to stay in all weekend. Did Tom have to stay in?"

"Did Lisa have to stay in?"

"He cried. Did Tom cry?" "Did Lisa cry?"

"She got mad. Did Tom get mad?" "Did Lisa get mad?"

If students make errors, the teacher refers to the pronoun (e.g., "She got mad. She tells about a girl. Is Tom a girl?").

Application to Your Curriculum

Evaluate Beginning Comprehension Instruction in Your Core Reading Program

1. Examine the comprehension activities in the beginning of the K or first grade level of the reading program. What comprehension skills are taught? Is there enough direction to the teacher as to how to teach these skills? Is the instruction explicit? Does the program provide for enough practice for students to master the skill(s)? Are skills reviewed and incorporated into subsequent reading lessons? Is background knowledge that is required for understanding the story pretaught?
2. Are comprehension questions specified for story-reading passages? Are these questions asked at the beginning, during, or at the end of the passage? Are your students able to successfully answer the questions?
3. Based on your analysis of comprehension activities, what modifications would you make to your reading program?

CHAPTER 19

Comprehension Instruction for Primary Level

Reading comprehension is a complex cognitive activity that entails a myriad of skills and strategies. Good readers employ a variety of active reading strategies to make sense of text; however, not all readers develop these strategies on their own. Teachers can help students learn and use a variety of comprehension strategies through explicit and systematic instruction.

In the beginning stage, the skills and strategies focused on question answering, literal comprehension, sequencing, and recognizing basic story-grammar elements through a combination of teacher-read-aloud and student-read stories. In the primary stage, the focus shifts to instruction in inferential comprehension, summarization, comprehension monitoring, determining main ideas, and more sophisticated story-grammar strategies.

Preteaching for Text Comprehension

Learning information about a topic or previewing the text before reading stories enhances comprehension and is often critical for inferential comprehension. The general knowledge that students acquire as a result of such preteaching activities can be viewed as "prior knowledge" that prepares the students to better understand and appreciate upcoming stories or passages.

Background Knowledge

Some reading programs provide background information prior to introducing a story. Often, this is in the form of a short paragraph that appears at the beginning of a story. For some students, particularly instructionally naive or at-risk students, the preteaching provided in the core reading program may not be sufficient. Important information may not be taught, taught unclearly, or taught with insufficient detail. The teacher should identify knowledge required for upcoming comprehension activities and preteach any necessary vocabulary or contextual knowledge that students will need to draw upon during comprehension activities.

For example, if students are going to read a story set in Alaska during the gold rush period, the teacher should preteach geographic information about Alaska, the environment, and historical information about the gold rush so students can understand the context for important story elements and events. The amount of this prior knowledge should be based on what the students already know and limited to knowledge that will enhance story comprehension.

The teacher provides this background knowledge in a short mini-lesson(s) prior to reading the text selection.

Previewing Text—Prediction

Prior to reading stories, students should be taught to preview the text. Using a think-aloud procedure, the teacher models how to read the title, review any pictures or illustrations (headings and diagrams for expository text), and predicts what the reading selection is going to be about. As the selection is read, the teacher confirms or modifies the prediction. After modeling with several reading selections, the teacher would scaffold the task, asking students what they should do prior to reading and prompting the steps of previewing and predicting. As the text is read, the teacher can prompt students to revisit their predictions and confirm or modify them. When students can initiate the steps of previewing and predicting independently, these routines should become a regular part of the reading lesson.

Summarization

Summarization is an important comprehension skill that helps students remember important information from their reading. Teaching students to summarize is a first step in comprehension monitoring. The teacher can determine if students understood the main idea or events by having them put these ideas or events into their own words.

As students read longer stories, the teacher periodically stops and prompts students to summarize what they've read so far. The teacher can initially model this procedure as students read stories. For example, after the main character and setting are introduced, the teacher summarizes who the story is about and where the story takes place. As other story events unfold, the teacher can model summarizing these events. An important feature of the teacher's summary is that it focuses on main ideas and key story events, not details. If necessary, the teacher can provide positive and negative examples of summarizing statements and have the students determine whether the statement is a good summary (because it focuses on the main idea) or not (because it focuses on story details). After several instances of modeling, the teacher calls on individual students to provide a summary of the main story features and events as they read the story. The teacher can ask the group if the summary statement tells the main ideas. As students are able to summarize important story information, this routine should also become a regular part of the reading instruction.

Comprehension Monitoring

As previously stated, summarization is an important first step in comprehension monitoring. Students who are good at monitoring their comprehension know when they understand what they read and when they do not. The teacher should stress the importance of constructing knowledge about story events and share that good readers reread when they don't understand parts of stories or when parts or events don't make sense. When the children's response to a teacher's question indicates that the children do not understand what they just read, the teacher can guide students in identifying what information is missing or what doesn't make sense to provide a purpose for rereading. The teacher can then guide the students to the part of the passage that should be reread to gain a better understanding (or fix-up their knowledge) of story events.

As students read and summarize story events, the teacher should direct students to reread whenever a fix-up is needed. Later on, the teacher can prompt the strategy by asking students to identify what to do if parts of the story are unclear. The teacher then guides the students in identifying why they are rereading (what is not making sense or what is missing) as well as where to go in the passage to reread.

Inferential Comprehension

Inferential comprehension requires the student to answer questions in which the answer is not directly stated in the story. To answer the question, the student will have to use clues from information given in the story and/or draw on his or her prior knowledge. For example, let's say that a text referred to Julie's mother as an architect and asked what kinds of tools her mother used when at work. To answer this question, the student would need to know what an architect does and the tools that an architect uses at work.

Students are first introduced to inferential comprehension in the beginning stage with simple questions asking them to predict based on what has already happened in the story. In the primary stage, students should be systematically taught how to make more difficult inferential and evaluative judgments about what they read.

Types of Inferential Questions

Stories can differ in the amount of background knowledge required for students to comprehend the story. When story comprehension or understanding is not highly dependent on the reader's background knowledge, or is dependent on understanding the relationship between two pieces of information presented in the text, it is referred to as *textually implicit.* When story comprehension is heavily dependent on the reader's background knowledge rather than information presented in the text, these types of questions are referred to as *scripturally implicit.* Students who lack the necessary prerequisite knowledge or have difficulty understanding relationships need teacher instruction to develop the strategies needed to comprehend both these types of text.

Teaching Procedure for Inferential Comprehension

When presenting inference questions, the teacher can refer to them as "detective" problems. The students must come up the information (or clues) to figure out the answer to the question.

While reading stories, the teacher presents a question and tells students they can use clues in the passage to "solve" or figure out the answer. If students are unable to find the relevant information, the teacher directs the students to the information needed to answer the question, then present the question.

For example, the following passage is about a fat beagle named Jokey.

> The next day, Jokey went to a health spa. This spa was near a supermarket, but Jokey didn't stop in the back of the supermarket to go through the trash cans. He went straight to the spa. The dogs who ran the spa were poodles who pranced around with their heads up in the air. They seemed to be walking on their tiptoes. One of them pranced up to Jokey, looked at him, and said, "Well, I'm not sure we can help any dog as fat and ugly as you, but we'll try." The poodle said, "Follow me," and pranced down the hallway.

In the early stages of inference instruction, the teacher asks an inference question right after the sentence that gives the relevant information: For example, after reading the first sentence in the previous passage the teacher asks, "What did Jokey usually do when he was near the supermarket? Listen to this sentence and see if you can find the clue to answer the question: '. . . but Jokey didn't stop in the back of the supermarket to go through the trash cans.' So if Jokey didn't stop that time, what do you think he usually did?"

Students:

"He would usually go through the trash cans."

The teacher then asks, "Why would he go through the trash cans?" The students must know that trash cans behind supermarkets are likely to contain food, and that Jokey wanted that food.

When students become proficient at answering these types of questions during the text reading with teacher guidance, the teacher can ask the questions at the end of the story and remind the students to find the clues in the story themselves that help answer the question. If students are unable to answer the question, then the teacher uses the previous procedure as a strategy correction, asking students to identify the necessary information that will help answer the question.

For many inference items, the student is assumed to have the prerequisite information and knowledge needed to answer the question. For example:

Teacher:

"Why do you think Jokey was going to the spa?"

If students were unfamiliar with the term *spa,* they would not be able to infer the relationship between Jokey being "fat" and what he would do at the spa. The teacher would need to preteach the vocabulary word *spa* and then provide instructional scaffolding to help students use this information:

Teacher:

"Remember what we learned about spas. What do people do at spas?" (exercise, work out, get fit) "What does Jokey look like?" (he's fat) "So why do you think Jokey would go to the spa?" (to exercise and lose weight)

Evaluative Questions.   Another type of inferential question requires students to make a judgement or relate story information to their own perspective or opinions.

Teacher:

"What would you do to help Jokey if he were your dog?"

Students would need to utilize knowledge from the passage about Jokey's problem as well as their own ability and resources to solve his problem.

While no single format can prepare students to handle all inference items, the general teaching procedure for introducing students to inferential question answering employs teachers using a think-aloud procedure

1. The teacher poses the question.
2. The teacher models using a think-aloud procedure how the relevant information is used to answer the question.
3. The teacher calls on students to describe how the answer can be determined.

The next step involves the teacher providing the necessary instructional scaffolding in the form of prompting students to find and use relevant information to determine the answer.

1. The teacher poses the question.
2. The teacher prompts students to locate specific information from the passage needed to answer the question.
3. The teacher calls on a student to provide the answer.

As students become proficient with this level of support, the teacher prompts less having the students look for the necessary information if textually implicit, or determine what other information may be needed if scripturally implicit.

1. Teacher poses the question.
2. Teacher asks students to tell what information they need to find or refer to (from their prerequisite knowledge) to answer the question.
3. The teacher calls on a student to provide the answer.

Main Idea

Identifying the main idea of a story or reading selection is a difficult task for students. Condensing the main idea into a single sentence is even more challenging.

Teaching Procedure for Main Idea

The teacher can teach the main idea through presenting a series of positive examples and negative examples. After reading a story, the teacher can provide three possible main idea statements. The teacher tells the students that one of the sentences is a good main idea sentence for the passage. The teacher then has the students read each sentence and asks if it is a good main idea sentence for the passage, asking why or why not after each response.

The teacher should carefully choose passages to scaffold the instruction. Initially, passages in which the main idea can be easily identified should be selected, such as passages in which a main character is doing a particular action (Nicholas tries to make friends at his new school; Sarah learns how to ice skate). Non-examples should focus on details rather than the main thing that happened (The other boys teased Nicholas at lunch; Sarah kept falling down whenever she tried to twirl on the ice).

Later on, passages in which the main idea is related to a lesson or story theme can be introduced (Franklin finds out that hard work pays off). Again, the teacher can provide examples and non-examples for students to evaluate and determine which is a good main idea statement.

Once students can identify main idea statements, the teacher can ask students to identity the main idea by asking, "Who or what is the passage about?" "What is the main thing they did?" or "What is the main thing that happened?" The teacher would model creating single sentences that express the main idea for several exercises, then challenge the students to tell the main idea in one sentence in later exercises. A great deal of practice will need to be provided on these summarization skills.

Narrative-Comprehension Strategies—Story Grammar

Although most commercial core reading programs include both narrative and expository reading passages, a significant portion of the reading selections are narrative stories.

As stated in the previous chapter, narrative stories have their own text structure called story grammar. This structure often revolves around the conflicts or problems faced by the story's characters and the characters' attempts to resolve the problem. The story-grammar components of (a) conflict, (b) goal, (c) resolution of the conflict, (d) plot, and (e) the characters' thoughts and feelings are common to many stories. By keying on the presence of these story components, the reader is better able to comprehend the story. The story's structure can be simple (e.g., the components are few and written in a predictable sequence) or complex (e.g., the components are numerous and their sequence is unpredictable).

Students who do not have problems with literal comprehension may still have problems answering questions about the structure of a story. For example, a student may be able to identify the characters in a story, but not the characters' goals, motives, and actions for achieving those goals. For these students, the teacher needs to demonstrate a strategy for identifying, understanding, and relating these different components of story grammar to each other in comprehending the story's general message.

As discussed in the previous chapter, beginning story-grammar instruction is introduced in kindergarten during story book reading with stories that are textually explicit (i.e., require little or no background knowledge) and structurally simple. There should be few characters, and the conflicts, actions, goals, and resolutions should be rather straightforward. As students enter the primary reading stage, they begin to read longer, more complex stories.

The primary guideline for developing a sequence for introducing stories is to progress from simple stories to more complex stories. Factors to consider are (a) the number of characters, plots, goals, and subgoals; (b) the number of attempts by characters to achieve the goals; (c) the explicitness of the story-grammar components (the main characters, goals, conflict); (d) the length of the story; (e) the readability of the story (structure of sentences, multisyllabic words); and (f) the amount of background knowledge required of students.

Teaching Procedures

The following teaching procedures are based on the assumption that students can decode the words in the stories and are capable of answering basic literal-comprehension questions. To introduce story-grammar instruction, the teacher relies on a facilitative questioning strategy that consists of four basic story-grammar questions: (a) Who is the story about? (b) What is she/he trying to do? (c) What happens when she/he tries to do it? and (d) What happens in the end? These core questions will be used to direct the students' attention to the critical parts of each story. The questions are aligned with the important components of story grammar, such as identifying the characters in the story; identifying their goals, as well as the actions and obstacles related to achieving these goals; a resolution, and the final circumstances surrounding the character's goal-related actions; and the story ending. These four core questions can also be eventually used as a framework for teaching students to retell and summarize the story in either oral or written form.

Table 19.1 contains a format for introducing story grammar. In this format, as students read the story (see Figure 19.1), the teacher stops students at the appropriate points in the story and asks each story-grammar question. The teacher begins the format by telling students the four core questions that they will answer when reading the story. The students read the story orally, with one

Table 19.1

Format for Introducing Story-Grammar Comprehension

Teacher	Students
The teacher writes on the board: Who is the story about? What is the main character trying to do? What happens when the main characters tries to do it? What happens in the end?	
1. The teacher introduces the story-grammar questions: "When we read this story, we are going to ask four questions." The teacher reads and points to each question on the board.	
a. "What's the first question?" Teacher calls on a student.	"Who is the story about?"
b. "What's the next question we're going to ask about the story?"	"What is the main character trying to do?"
c. "What's the next question?"	"What happens when the main character tries to do it?"
d. "What's the last question?"	"What happens in the end?"
2. The teacher calls on individual students to read the title.	
a. "During the reading of the story, I will stop you to ask one of the questions. The answers to the questions can be found in the story. Let's start by reading the title of the story." Teacher calls on a student to read the story title.	"The Mouse and the Hawk."
b. "Yes, the title tells us that the story will be about a mouse and a hawk. So when we read the story, what main characters will we read about?" Teacher calls on a student.	"A mouse and a hawk."
3. Teacher calls on individual students to read the story. Teacher stops students at different points in the story and asks questions.	
a. After reading through the second paragraph, the teacher stops the reader and calls on individual students to answer the following questions: "What is the hawk trying to do?" "What is the mouse trying to do?"	"Kill all the chickens." "Help the townspeople."
b. After reading the next two paragraphs, the teacher stops the readers and asks: "What is the mouse trying to do?"	"Kill the hawk by getting the hawk to fly down on the sharp stick."

Table 19.1

(Continued)

Teacher	Students
c. After reading the last paragraph, the final two questions are asked: "What happens when the hawk tries to get the mouse?" "What happens in the end?"	"It flew onto the sharp stick and was killed." "The mouse is a hero and the people thank the mouse."
4. The teacher has students summarize the story using the four questions. "First, who is the story about?" "What are the hawk and mouse trying to do?" "What happens when they try to do these things?" "What happens in the end?"	 "The mouse and the hawk." "The hawk is trying to kill chickens and the mouse is trying to help the townspeople get rid of the hawk." "The mouse gets rid of the hawk and chickens are saved." "The mouse is a hero."

The Mouse and the Hawk

Long ago in a small western town lived a hawk that attacked almost all the chickens in the whole town. He ate them one by one until finally there were only two chickens left.

Nobody in the town could kill the hawk. They talked about it in the big tent where a little mouse was listening when she heard the bad news. The little mouse was very brave and she also liked to help people. The mouse wanted to help the people in the town, so she worked out a plan.

First, she cut a small hole in the top of the tent. Then she made a very sharp point on one end of a stick. She put that stick through the hole. Next she went outside and sat on top of the tent very close to the sharp stick.

She knew the hawk would see a tiny mouse and come diving down from the sky to get her. Even though she was afraid that the hawk would kill her, she sat there waiting.

Finally, the hawk saw the brave mouse and came flying toward her ready to attack. The mouse waited until the hawk was almost on her. Then she jumped aside and the hawk flew onto the sharp stick and was killed instantly.

The mouse was a hero and everyone in the village came to the big tent to praise and thank her.

Figure 19.1

Example of Textually Explicit Text

student reading several sentences at a time. During the story reading, the teacher asks each story-grammar question at the appropriate place in the story. In addition, the teacher sometimes stops and conducts a cumulative review of the previously answered questions. In the final step of the format, the teacher summarizes by asking the four questions again. Following students' oral answers to the four questions, the teacher requires students to answer similar written comprehension questions or fill out a story map.

Advanced Story-Reading Comprehension Strategy

Story reading in the late primary and intermediate levels requires more inferential thinking as stories become more complex. As a result, the comprehension strategy for identifying and understanding story-grammar components needs to be more thorough than the strategy previously described. Students need to have more background knowledge to comprehend these stories. Similarly, stories are more likely to contain words critical to the meaning of sentences but not known by the student. Before presenting stories to the student, the teacher should preteach any critical information or vocabulary words students need to know.

This section presents teaching procedures for short-story comprehension based on the research by Gurney (1987) and Dimino (1988). The procedures provide a basic framework for teaching students to identify and interpret the wide range of characters, actions, events, and situations that take place in short stories.

The stories that appear in many basal reading texts often range from excerpts from well-known classics to contemporary children's literature. Although these stories are quite varied in their structure, story grammar, and storyline, the comprehension strategy we propose builds on the four core story-grammar questions taught for comprehending simple stories. We expand these four questions to categories as more complex stories are introduced. These categories, based on Dimino's (1988) analysis, are described as follows.

Category 1: Character Information. The teacher expands the first question, "Who is the story about?" by asking questions about the character. The teacher tries to have students anticipate what a character might do based on the information given. Questions can be asked about the following characteristics:

   a. *Actions:* What the characters do.
   b. *Dialogue:* What the characters say to themselves and each other.
   c. *Thoughts:* What the characters are thinking.
   d. *Physical attributes:* How the characters look.

Category 2: Conflict or Problem. The second question, "What are the characters trying to do?" is expanded to asking questions about the conflict or problem that exists. Some types of conflicts or problems the teacher may ask about are:

   a. *Disagreements:* A problem arises between two characters. For example, parents disagree with a son over using the car.
   b. *Tough decisions:* A character is faced with two difficult choices. For example, a character must choose between keeping quiet or revealing a friend's crime.
   c. *Struggle for survival:* A character tries to overcome the forces of nature. For example, a character tries to survive in the wilderness during the extreme cold.

Category 3: Attempts/Resolution/Twist.   The third question, "What happens when the characters try to do it?" expands to questions about how the characters attempt to solve the conflict or problem. The teacher asks questions about the following:

   a. *Attempts:* What the character does to resolve the conflict or solve the problem.
   b. *Resolution:* The final attempt that solves or fails to solve the problem.
   c. *Twist:* Any unexpected complication that occurs and causes an unexpected resolution of the problem.

Category 4: Reactions and Theme.   The final question, "What happens in the end?" is expanded in a different way. Instead of focusing just on what actually happens at the end of a story, the teacher requires students to focus on the meaning of the author's message. Questions are asked about the following:

   a. *Reactions:* What is the character's response to the events in the story?
   b. *Theme:* What is the underlying meaning of the story? What is the author of the story trying to tell the reader? What is the moral of the story?

Theme identification is likely to be the most difficult aspect of the instructional strategy. Students may have difficulty assimilating the events in the story and formulating a general statement that captures the underlying message. The teacher can model how to state a theme by reviewing themes from previous stories to illustrate how events in a story can be used to develop a theme.

Using Story Maps and Notesheets

Using graphic organizers such as story maps or notesheets can help students organize story information into meaningful relationships and facilitates retention of story information. Story maps and notesheets can help students summarize and clarify the story-grammar components during short-story reading. A story map appears in Table 19.2 and the outline notesheet appears in Table 19.2. As students read stories, they can be taught to fill out the story map notesheet.

Table 19.2
Story Map

Story Map

Title

Setting		Characters

Problem

Important Events

Outcome / Reaction

Theme

Table 19.3

Notesheet for Short-Story Comprehension Strategy

STUDENT NOTESHEET

Name _____ Date _____

Story _____

1. Name the problems or conflict. _____

_____

_____

_____

2. Identify the main characters and tell about them. _____

_____

_____

_____

3. Tell how the characters try to solve the problem. _____

_____

_____

_____

4. Tell how the problem is or is not solved. _____

_____

_____

_____

5. Is there an added twist or complication at the end of the story? _____

_____

_____

_____

6. What is the theme of the story? What is the author trying to say? ____

_____

_____

_____

Teaching Procedure.   When introducing story mapping, the teacher uses a think-aloud procedure to summarize and point out how to anticipate story-grammar questions to be asked.

The teacher begins the lesson by giving each student a notesheet. During story reading, students are stopped at designated points and asked the appropriate story-grammar question. The teacher records the information on a transparency of the notesheet while students record it on their individual notesheets. Students should be allowed to copy from the transparency but are encouraged to record the information in their own words. Students are advised that after a few stories, they will be responsible for determining and recording the components without the benefit of the transparency or class discussion.

During the first days of story reading, the teacher models asking questions and giving answers. After several lessons, the teacher calls on students to answer questions. For example, after the problem is stated in the story, the teacher asks, "Do we have a problem?"

After weeks of teacher-directed practice, students can work in cooperative groups to discuss story elements, fill out their notesheets, and review their answers.

As students become proficient at story mapping independent practice is given. In this independent-practice phase, identification and discussion of the story-grammar components does not take place until students have recorded the information on their notesheets. Students' responses on the notesheets are monitored, and time is allotted for students to correct their incorrect answers after each story-grammar component is discussed. Since answers are no longer being recorded on the transparency, the teacher must monitor students' written responses carefully.

Integrating Comprehension Instruction

As stated at the beginning of this chapter, comprehension is a complex cognitive process in which the reader employs multiple strategies to make sense of what is being read. Instruction in these various strategies must be explicit and systematic, and as students master various comprehension strategies, they also must be taught when and where to use the strategy. The challenge for the teacher is integrating multiple strategies on a daily basis as needed by students and as is appropriate for the text being read. This daily instruction must be active and transparent for the student. Teachers should never assume that students are understanding what is being read and are covertly utilizing comprehension strategies. The teacher needs to overtly guide students in the strategies and processes for building a rich understanding of the ideas, relationships, and themes the author is communicating to the reader.

Application to Your Curriculum

Evaluate Comprehension Instruction in Your Core Reading Program

1. Select three consecutive stories from the late first though third grade levels of your reading program. Determine what comprehension-related activities are taught before, during, and after story reading. Indicate if these activities are adequate in supporting students' understanding of the text. If not, indicate the modifications that are needed.

2. Identify a specific comprehension skill/strategy taught in your curriculum. Does the teacher's guide provide clear and explicit teaching procedures for this strategy? Is this instruction adequate and systematic enough that struggling readers and at-risk learners could acquire this strategy? Is there enough practice and review for students to master and continue to apply this strategy in future stories? Indicate the modifications needed.

3. Examine written comprehension exercises for three consecutive lessons. Indicate the relationships of these exercises to story-reading activities and other comprehension instruction. Determine if the written exercises provide appropriate practice and reinforce previously introduced comprehension skills. Indicate if the children have the necessary prerequisite skills to be successful. Indicate the modifications needed.

PART 3

Organizing the Classroom and School for Reading Instruction

CHAPTER 20

Overview

This chapter presents an overview of five important components of an overall schoolwide reading program: use of assessments, allotting time for instruction, grouping students for instruction, selecting materials, and creating a program for children significantly below grade level.

Assessment

The ongoing use of assessment is essential for maximizing student progress and for providing children with a successful learning experience.

Beginning-of-the-Year Assessments

Assessment is used at the beginning of the year to help the teacher determine a child's instructional level and to inform teachers and administrators of the numbers of children who are performing at, below, and above grade level. Beginning-of-the-year assessments generally are designed to take no longer than 5 to 10 minutes per child. These assessments can also be used during the school year when a new student enters a school. There are two types of assessments: curriculum-based assessments and program-specific placement assessments.

Curriculum-Based Assessments. The curriculum-based screening assessments are not tied to a particular commercial reading program, but to particular skills that have been identified as critical for that particular grade level. For example, a screening assessment for first grade might test the child on knowledge of letter-sound correspondences and the ability to blend isolated sounds to create a word. A test for third grade might include an oral reading fluency test. Teachers must be careful in selecting these assessments to ensure that the assessment is aligned with scientifically based reading research.

As part of the federal Reading First initiative, a group of assessment experts reviewed commonly used curriculum-based assessments to determine their overall technical adequacy, including their reliability and validity. The results of this review appear on the Institute for the Development of Educational Achievement (IDEA) website at the University of Oregon (**http://idea.uoregon.edu/**).

Program-Specific Placement Assessment. A program-specific placement assessment is designed to inform the teacher at what level and lesson of a particular commercial reading series to place a child for instruction. While some commercial reading materials have carefully designed placement tests that are clearly an integral part of the program, few of the comprehensive core reading programs (basals) have clear placement procedures. Suggestions for what to do in such cases for specific grade levels will be provided in the upcoming chapters.

Using Data from Beginning-of-the-Year Assessments.   Teachers must be careful in interpreting beginning-of-the-year assessment results. Some younger children may be shy or reluctant to respond to an adult they do not know well. Other children may perform poorly on a test given the first days of school; however, after several days of instruction, they can perform at a much higher level than their screening performance indicated. Teachers must remember that beginning-of-the-year assessments are just tools to help the teacher begin instruction at what appears to be the children's instructional level. Teachers should expect to make adjustments for children during the first weeks of the school year as the teacher receives more information on how the child performs. Teachers should watch for children who can perform above their current level, as well as those who are struggling.

Progress-Monitoring Assessments

There are two types of progress-monitoring assessments: curriculum-based assessments and program-specific assessments.

Curriculum-Based Progress-Monitoring Assessments.   Curriculum-based progress-monitoring assessments are not specifically related to what is taught in any particular commercial reading program, but is rather based on what a test developer has determined is essential content that students should have learned by particular points during the school year. Again, caution must be used in selecting these assessments to ensure use of a test that is aligned with scientific reading research and has validity and reliability. The assessment review on the Institute for the Development of Educational Achievement (IDEA) website (**http://idea.uoregon.edu/**) indicates the suitability of the various tests for use as progress-monitoring tools.

Program-Specific Progress-Monitoring Assessments.   A program-specific progress-monitoring assessment package includes a series of assessments designed to determine if children are in fact learning what is being taught in the specific reading program. Some publishers include a very carefully constructed package of progress-monitoring assessments accompanied by specific directions for what to do if students do not pass the assessment. Unfortunately, most comprehensive core reading programs do not have systematic progress-monitoring assessment and remediation procedures incorporated into their program. Suggestions for what to do in such cases will be provided in the upcoming chapters for specific grade levels.

Frequency of Administering Assessments.   The frequency of administering progress-monitoring assessments depends in part on the performance level of the students. Teachers working with students who are performing below grade level should administer progress-monitoring assessments more frequently, administering assessments weekly to children performing significantly below grade level, every 2 weeks to children slightly below grade level, and every 4 to 6 weeks for children performing at or above grade level.

Oral Reading Fluency Measures.   Oral reading fluency has been identified as a very powerful indicator of student success in reading, particularly in the elementary grades. We recommend that from the point in a reading program where children begin reading connected text (usually a third of the way through first grade) progress-monitoring assessments include a section in which children orally read a passage. The tester records the number of errors and the number of words read correctly within a specific time period.

Using Information from Progress-Monitoring Assessments.   The data from progress-monitoring assessments should be examined shortly after the assessments are administered. Ideally, the data will be examined in a grade-level meeting held the day after assessments are administered. The principal and all teachers who are working with the students should attend. Information from progress-monitoring assessments can be used in three ways.

First, the results of progress-monitoring assessments can be used to plan lessons to remedy specific skill deficits that are common to several children in a group. If more than one-third of the children in a group make errors on a particular skill(s), the teacher should repeat several lessons and concentrate on those particular skill(s). Note that if progress-monitoring data shows a number of children having difficulty, their poor performance indicates that the teacher must improve his or her teaching presentation, making instruction more explicit and carefully monitoring and correcting to ensure that students are receiving enough practice to master important skills.

Second, the results of informal progress-monitoring assessments can be used to identify individual students in need of extra instruction. Children who perform poorly on a progress-monitoring assessment should receive extra instruction on particular tasks presented earlier in the program that teach the specific skills tested. If, after the teacher presents remediation exercises, the student still performs poorly, a teacher should administer a more in-depth assessment to determine more specific problem areas. For example, if a student makes errors on two of five sounds and two of five words in a first-grade progress-monitoring assessment, the teacher would first work on recent tasks that presented sounds and word reading. If students still had difficulty, the teacher would test the child on all letter-sound correspondences and all word types that had been previously introduced. The teacher then reteaches all previously introduced material that the student did not know. If this reteaching does not prove successful, the teacher might place the student in a lower-performing group. Conversely, a student who is noticeably more fluent than other students in the group might be placed in a higher-performing group.

Third, the progress-monitoring data can be used to determine if the group as a whole needs to repeat lessons or can be accelerated.

Dynamic Indicators of Basic Early Literacy Skills (DIBELS). The Dynamic Indicators of Basic Early Literacy Skills (DIBELS) is a curriculum-based assessment that at the time of this book's writing is the most frequently used assessment tool in kindergarten through third grade in the Reading First project. DIBELS can serve as a screening assessment to identify children at risk of reading failure because of literacy-related deficit and as a progress-monitoring tool. DIBELS is available at no cost on the University of Oregon website (**http://dibels.uoregon.edu**). DIBELS classifies student performance based on data that shows a relationship between student performance levels and future success in later grades. DIBELS can be an effective indicator to determine if a child's current level is at or below grade level and can be used to determine if the student is making sufficient progress to reach grade-level standards.

Scheduling Instructional Time

In scheduling minutes for daily reading instruction, a prime consideration should be how much students need to learn in order to reach grade-level performance standards. If a child is performing significantly below the norm for that child's grade level at the beginning of the school year, significantly more time needs to be scheduled for reading instruction if the child is to reach grade-level performance. We recommend that schools place a priority on providing this extra time for reading because reading is a gateway for learning in all academic areas. A child who is not reading well is likely to struggle throughout the school day. By focusing on the essentials of reading until the child is at grade level, the teacher is preparing the child for later success. The earlier this happens the better for the child.

Children who are at risk of reading failure need to be identified at the beginning of kindergarten (or ideally preschool). An intensive program of instruction that begins in preschool or kindergarten can have a powerful effect on a student's academic career.

Specific recommendations will be made in the specific grade-level chapters that follow.

Grouping and Placement

Efficiency is a critical factor for children who are at risk. If struggling readers and at-risk children are to progress at an accelerated rate, all the instruction provided to the students needs to be taught very efficiently. This efficiency occurs best when a child is placed at his or her instructional level. When a student is at his or her instructional level, the student has sufficient knowledge of earlier content so that the student can reasonably be brought to mastery on new content while still maintaining a reasonable success rate during the lessons. A student is usually at his or her instructional level when the student can respond with about an 85% success rate to all the tasks in the lesson and can readily be brought to 100% accuracy on all tasks by the end of the lesson.

In addition to placing students at their instructional level, we strongly recommend that children who are at risk be placed in an instructional group with children at the same instructional level. Creating such groups is referred to as homogeneous grouping for instruction. The issue of homogeneous grouping has been one of great controversy. If misused, homogeneous grouping can lead to tracking in which lower-performing students are placed and maintained in settings that do not bring out their full potential to learn. If used well, homogeneous grouping can lead to acceleration of student progress and higher student success levels. Acceleration is possible because during the lesson, the teacher does not have to make significant compromises between meeting the needs of higher performers and lower performers.

A critical condition that must be in place for effective homogenous grouping is that placement in groups must be flexible. That means that during the school year a child's placement in a group is not fixed, but can and will be changed based on the child's performance. If a child's performance indicates that the child is able to perform at a higher level, the child is moved to a group that is further ahead in the program and vice versa. In order to facilitate this flexibility, school schedules need to be coordinated in order to allow children to be moved from one group to another. Meeting the academic needs of students must be the first priority in establishing school schedules.

The number of children in an instructional group should depend on the instructional sophistication of the students. Children who are instructionally sophisticated, attentive to teacher's instruction, and not likely to become confused easily can be taught in instructional groups with more children. Children who are less attentive to teacher instruction, more likely to be easily distracted, and likely to need more practice to master content should be in instructional groups composed of fewer children. When children are in the beginning stages of reading instruction, small-group instruction is called for as teachers must be able to provide immediate feedback to students. As children move up in their skill level, the number of children in instructional groups can increase.

Efficient grouping is critical in all aspects of the reading program. Sometimes schools will send all children in a particular grade who are behind to a special reading teacher for instruction. This arrangement is not efficient because there is likely to be great disparity among the children's instructional levels. We recommend arranging the scheduling and grouping of students so that children at the same level receive instruction together. If children are sent to a reading specialist, the school schedule should be arranged so that children at the same instructional level from several classes go to the reading specialist at the same time.

Selecting Instructional Materials

In selecting commercial reading instructional materials, teachers must be careful and informed consumers. A publisher's claims that a program is research-based and effective must be treated with suspicion. Instructional materials must be examined to ensure that the materials are in fact consistent with the scientific reading research. Equally important, instructional materials must be examined to determine how well constructed the reading program is to meet the needs of the struggling reader and at-risk student.

Determining if a Program Is Research-Based

The major differences between beginning reading programs that are aligned with scientific reading research findings and those not aligned with those findings involve how phonemic awareness and phonic instruction are presented in the beginning reading stage.

In a research-based program, there is direct teaching of a set of letter-sound relationships in a clearly defined sequence. The set includes the major sound/spelling relationships of both consonants and vowels. Materials provide for substantial practice in applying knowledge of these relationships to read words, both in isolation and in text. Phonemic awareness instruction is aligned with phonic instruction.

A teacher can determine if a beginning-reading program is research-based by examining and evaluating the first 15 to 30 lessons of the program, which deal with teaching reading words. If the program is research-based, all of the following questions will be answered affirmatively:

1. Are the letter-sound correspondences taught explicitly? Is sufficient practice provided to ensure mastery? Are both vowel and consonants introduced, and do vowels receive equal emphasis?

2. Are students taught to use a word-reading strategy in which sounds for all the letters in a word are combined (e.g., a blending strategy) as their primary strategy to read words? Does the program avoid reliance on context or picture cues as a strategy to read unknown words?

3. Is ample practice in applying the word-reading strategy to read word lists and stories provided?

4. Are the stories that students read written so that a high percentage of words are decodable (decodable words contain only letters for which students have been taught the letter-sound correspondences)? In a non-research-based approach, words in stories are not selected on the basis of regularity of letter-sound correspondences. Instead, words are selected because they frequently appear in print. Many frequently occurring words are irregular. Therefore, it is common, for example, to see the words *done, to, not,* and *book* among the first 50 words introduced

in a meaning-emphasis program. Note that in each word, the letter *o* represents a different sound.

Determining Potential Effectiveness with Struggling Readers and At-Risk Students

Beginning in the early years of the new millennium, significant changes in published beginning-reading programs became evident. The publication of the National Reading Panel report in 2000, the incorporation of these findings in the No Child Left Behind legislation, the pressure of the accountability movement, and new adoption requirements by California, Texas, and Florida seem to have led many publishers to produce materials more congruent with the research findings. Since 2002, all the major publishers of comprehensive reading programs have published new core programs that are significantly more aligned with the research findings. However, there are still significant differences in levels of explicitness, emphasis, and extent to which skills are taught explicitly and systematically. Educators must be aware of these differences so that they can select programs that will be of most benefit to their students. The following list contains characteristics that contribute to a program's ability to be effective with the struggling reader and at-risk child.

Phonemic awareness instruction includes:

■ Clear demonstrations of how to model segmenting and blending of spoken words and sounds.

■ Highly interactive teaching in which the teacher models segmenting and blending of sounds in spoken words, leads the students through segmenting and blending exercises, and tests the students by asking individual students to perform the tasks independently.

■ Sufficient practice in blending and segmenting spoken words.

■ Phonemic awareness exercises that are aligned with phonic instruction such that blending and segmenting sounds in spoken words precedes sounding out written words composed of those same sounds.

■ Lesson construction that avoids too many different types of phonemic awareness skills being taught simultaneously.

Letter-sound correspondence instruction includes:

■ Simple non-language-ladened modeling of letter-sound correspondences.

■ Highly interactive teaching in which the teacher models sounds, monitors students as they pronounce the sounds, and asks students to pronounce the sounds to evaluate their performance.

■ Sequence of letter-sound correspondences that avoids confusion of similar letters.

■ Realistic rate of introducing new letter-sound correspondences: The introduction of a new sound is separated by 3 to 4 days before another new sound is taught, assuming students do not know letter names. The introduction of a new sound is separated by 2 to 3 days before another new sound is taught, assuming students do know letter names.

■ Daily practice with cumulative review of previously introduced letter-sound correspondences.

Word-reading instruction includes:

■ Specific directions to teachers on how to clearly model blending sounds to read regular words.

■ Highly interactive teaching in which students blend sounds for all letters, and the teacher provides immediate feedback.

■ Sufficient daily practice in applying the sounding-out strategy to read words in isolation and in connected text.

■ Logical sequence from easier to more difficult words. Sufficient practice with easier types before introducing more difficult word types.

■ Carefully controlled introduction and review of irregular words.

Story-reading instruction includes:

■ Initial stories have a very high percentage of regular words in which students know all letter-sound correspondences.

■ Guided practice in using a strategy that focuses on examining all letters in a word.

■ Teaching procedure that keeps all children actively involved.

■ Highly interactive teaching in which teacher provides immediate feedback.

■ Daily practice in story reading.

Spelling includes:

■ Ample opportunities for students to apply phonics to spell words.

■ Careful coordination of phonics and spelling instruction to ensure that students have learned the letter-sound correspondences needed to spell the words that appear in spelling exercises.

Relying on Data

No specific scientific formula has yet been developed to evaluate the potential effectiveness of a beginning reading program. For a school staff, the most reliable evidence regarding a reading program's potential to serve as an effective instructional tool is documented evidence that schools using the program with similar students and teachers have had success. Programs that have consistently produced high levels of achievement in similar schools should be carefully considered for adoption. Schools serving lower-income student populations, in particular, should select a program that has been demonstrated to be highly effective in schools serving comparable students. Sometimes schools may locate a reading program that has produced high levels of student performance in schools serving similar student populations, but the program may not include coverage of every topic included in state standards. We suggest that, in such instances, the school seriously consider adopting the program that has produced good results, and then obtain or construct supplementary materials to teach the content for the other standards.

Guidelines for Establishing a Comprehensive Program for Children Who Are Behind

The following guidelines are for establishing a program for children who begin any grade level not performing at the norm for children of that particular grade level. Children who perform below the 40th percentile on any standardized test are likely to have difficulty with grade level material. Children performing below the 25th percentile are performing significantly below grade level and need the most systematic and explicit instruction, the most instructional time, and an overall carefully planned-out program. Unfortunately, more often than not, children performing below grade level receive disjointed instruction and little instruction at their instructional level. A schoolwide effort is needed in planning instruction for these children. Elements of this planning are discussed in the following text.

Intervene Early

Ideally, an intensive comprehensive program for children who are at risk will start in preschool or kindergarten. However, at any grade, an intensive comprehensive program should begin as soon as possible, ideally during the first week of school, for children functioning below grade level.

Provide Extra Instructional Time

The amount of instructional time for children reading below grade level should be adequate for children to make significantly more than a year's progress during a school year. Children who are functioning significantly below grade level should receive at least two full reading lessons a day and 1 also a full oral language lesson if they also have language deficits. In some cases, a daily after-school period may be needed in addition to the instruction provided during the school day.

Utilize Small-Group Instruction

Arrange instructional groups so that all children are at the same instructional level. Teachers can be most efficient in accelerating the performance of a group of children when all the children in the instructional group are at the same instructional level. Make grouping flexible, meaning children can be moved to higher- or lower-performing groups when the student's performance indicates a need for a change. In order to facilitate this flexibility, school schedules need to be coordinated. Meeting the academic needs of students must be a first priority in establishing school schedules.

Use Effective Instructional Materials

Select focused materials that are specifically designed to accelerate the reading performance of children performing below grade level. These programs should (a) be highly explicit and systematic; (b) provide for highly focused instruction on essential reading skills rather than on providing cursory coverage of many topics; and (c) include placement testing and progress-monitoring assessment to ensure that students are properly placed and can proceed at an accelerated level.

Rather than using a number of programs that work on individual skills, try to find a comprehensive program that carefully integrates instruction in all areas of reading.

Most importantly, ensure that the materials have proved effective with similar children.

One specific caution: Publishers of comprehensive core reading programs will have components that are designated as intervention materials for children who are behind. Unfortunately, as of this book's writing, none of these intervention materials provide for systematic instruction for children who are significantly below grade level. The core publisher's intervention materials provide some extra practice in a slightly simpler manner than the regular core lessons. For children who are significantly behind, these materials are not sufficient.

Several university centers that were funded by the federal Reading First initiative to provide technical assistance to states have examined commercial programs and prepared reports on their instructional design and potential effectiveness as intervention programs. See the information on intervention programs on the University of Oregon website for Oregon Reading First (**http://oregonreadingfirst.uoregon.edu/SIreport.php**).

Create a Comprehensive Aligned Program

All persons who are providing instruction to the children should be using the same instructional strategies as well as materials that introduce content in the same sequence. All staff working with the same children should meet frequently to examine progress-monitoring data.

Administer Progress-Monitoring Assessments Frequently

Progress-monitoring assessments should be administered frequently to ensure that students are progressing adequately and learning what is being taught. The information from these assessments should be used to make timely adjustments in instruction, providing reteaching of skills not mastered, and, if needed, making adjustments in grouping.

Ensure Well-Trained Teaching Personnel

In the past, struggling students were often sent to volunteers or other untrained personnel who, with little guidance, were asked to teach the students. Volunteers and paraprofessionals can perform very useful functions such as listening to the students read and presenting structured small-group and one-on-one tutoring programs from highly prescriptive reading programs. However, careful guidance and direction for the paraprofessional or volunteer are required along with careful ongoing monitoring of student performance. Professional development should be provided for the paraprofessionals and volunteers prior to them using a program. The initial training should be followed up by observations and coaching while they work with students. Students with the most intensive reading needs should generally not be assigned to volunteers.

CHAPTER 21

Classroom Instruction in Kindergarten

The questions of how much and what kind of reading instruction to provide in kindergarten are important, particularly in schools with high percentages of children who are at risk because of deficits in literacy-related skills and/or language skills.

Most state standards require that in kindergarten, children learn letter names, letter-sound correspondences, and phonemic awareness skills. Few states require children to do extensive reading of words and sentences in kindergarten. However, there is research to indicate the powerful benefits of beginning structured reading instruction in kindergarten, particularly for struggling readers and at-risk children.

In a multi-school implementation of a highly systematic and explicit reading program, *Reading Mastery,* in high-poverty schools in Baltimore and Houston, children who began in kindergarten performing significantly below grade level were by the end of first grade scoring at and above grade level (Berkeley, 2002; Carlson & Francis, 2002).

Providing effective and efficient academic instruction in kindergarten is essential if the achievement gap between at-risk students and more advantaged students is to be closed. Students who learn to read early can use reading as a means of learning new information and vocabulary.

Instructional Material in Kindergarten

The kindergarten level of most recent core reading programs includes instruction in phonemic awareness, letter-sound correspondences, and word attack. However, many of these programs have serious instructional-design flaws that detract from their potential to accelerate the progress of the struggling reader and at-risk child. Among the problems commonly detected in the kindergarten core reading programs are:

- *Too much information is presented at once.* Programs will present a number of concepts or pieces of information in a single lesson. For example, letter names and letter-sound correspondences, as well as upper- and lowercase letters, are often introduced simultaneously.

- *Sequences that can cause confusion.* Programs will introduce concepts or information in an order that can lead to student confusion. For example, one program introduced letter-sound correspondences in alphabetical order, resulting in the letters *b* and *d,* as well as *m* and *n,* being introduced in near consecutive order.

- *Too little practice and review.* Sufficient practice is not provided to enable students to develop skill mastery as well as sufficient automaticity in its use. For example, a particular language concept or letter-sound correspondence might be taught for a couple of lessons and then not appear again for weeks.

- *Confusing language in teaching demonstrations.* Many of the teacher explanations are too wordy and potentially confusing for students with limited knowledge of language. For example, words like *same* and *different* might appear early in the program. In one program that we reviewed, this was a typical task: "Listen as I say two words. If both words end with the same sound as *pig,* raise your hand. Bug, dog." In low-income schools, many entering kindergartners do not know the terms *end* and *same.*

- *Lack of explicit teaching.* Programs may not explicitly model a strategy. Students will be asked to do tasks independently without the teacher modeling how to perform the task.

Though few in number, some commercial programs are designed to provide explicit and systematic instruction to kindergarten children. We strongly recommend that teachers who work with children entering school with limited literacy-related skills obtain such a program. The program that, from our perspective, is the most systematic and explicit is *Reading Mastery.* The manner in which *Reading Mastery* controls the language of instruction, clarity of presentations, rate of introduction of skills, and provisions for adequate practice make it the most supportive of the child who has limited language and literacy development upon entering kindergarten. A great deal of research exists validating the use of *Reading Mastery* to produce success in high-poverty urban and rural kindergartens (Engelmann & Adams, 1998). However, in order to produce this success, the program must be implemented with great care, utilizing all the mastery-teaching techniques discussed throughout the first parts of this book. A good deal of inservice training (2-4 days) is needed prior to its use, as well as in-class coaching from a program expert. A series of 12 videotapes, titled "Reading Mastery Training Series," presents the rationale of the *Reading Mastery* program and demonstrates teaching techniques. This video series is available from the publisher, Science Research Associates (ISBN: 0-07-584122-3). The need for intensive, systematic inservice and coaching applies to any program designed for use with at-risk students.

Another program, *Early Reading Intervention,* was developed at the University of Oregon's Institute for the Development of Educational Achievement (IDEA) in the College of Education (**http://idea.uoregon.edu/**) to better prepare kindergarten children for first grade. The *Early Reading Intervention*

Program, now published by Scott Foresman, provides intensive intervention in phonological awareness, letter names, letter sounds, word reading, spelling, and simple-sentence reading. The program consists of 126 lessons that emphasize the strategic and systematic instruction of phonemic awareness and alphabetic understanding. Each lesson consists of two 15-minute components that can be delivered consecutively in daily, 30-minute lessons or in two separate 15-minute lessons. In the first 15 minutes, instruction establishes and reinforces the phonologic skills of (a) first and last sound isolation, (b) sound blending, and (c) sound segmentation. In addition, the intervention emphasizes the acquisition and application of the fundamental alphabetic skills and strategies of (a) letter-name identification, (b) letter-sound identification, (c) letter-sound blending to read consonant-vowel-consonant (CVC) words, (d) selected irregular word reading, and (e) sentence reading of controlled text. The second 15 minutes reinforce previously taught phonological awareness and alphabetic skills and extend these skills through instruction in handwriting (e.g., letter dictation and formation), integrated phonologic and alphabetic tasks, and spelling. The spelling component begins with tracing and writing previously taught letters and progresses to writing initial and final sounds in words, and then to the systematic sequential analysis and synthesis of all sounds and letters in CVC and CVCC (consonant-vowel-consonant-consonant) words.

Kindergarten teachers must teach receptive and expressive language concepts and skills as well as reading skills. Selecting a well-designed language program is as critical as selecting a well-designed reading program, particularly for children at risk because of limited knowledge of foundational language skills.

Major modifications are necessary to make most commercial kindergarten materials suitable for teaching students with significant language needs. Modifying a program's vocabulary and language component is much more difficult than modifying a reading program's decoding component because illustrations and/or objects may be required to teach the meaning of a new word or concept. Our suggestion is not to attempt to modify the language and vocabulary components of inadequate programs, but rather to obtain a highly explicit and systematic program with research to document its effectiveness such as SRA's *Language for Learning.*

Use of Assessments in Kindergarten

Beginning-of-the-Year Screening Assessment

At the beginning of the school year, ideally during the first week, the teacher should assess each child's language and literacy level in order to identify kindergarten children who are at risk because of literacy-related deficits and/or language-related deficits.

Literacy-Related Skills.   We present two options that teachers can use to asses literacy-related skill. The teacher can administer the DIBELS screening assessment for kindergarten. The DIBELS screener takes about 5 minutes and will identify children who are at risk.

Teachers may also create a simple teacher-made test. In this informal screening, the teacher asks the child to say the name and the sound of five common consonants (*m, s, r, d, f*), five vowels (*a, i, o, u, e*), and then to read three simple CVC words (*sad, rug, fit*). The teacher prepares for the testing by writing the letters and words on a piece of paper, and then assesses the child by asking the name of each letter, the sound of each letter, and then asks the child to read the three words.

Language-Related Skills.   There are not as many language-related screening assessments as literacy-related assessments. Reviews of the more commonly used language assessments also appear on the Institute for the Development of Educational Achievement (IDEA) website. The screening assessments tend to be too lengthy to be practical for classroom teachers, as most take 15 or more minutes.

We have constructed an informal screening assessment (see Appendix B) for identifying kindergarten children with limited oral language-related knowledge. The test includes 10 tasks, each testing an early language concept, that is administered orally to individual students.

Using Data from the Screening Assessments.   Data from the screening assessments will indicate children who are at risk because of entering school with literacy and/or language-related deficits and who should be placed in highly explicit programs. Students who know fewer than seven letter names or sounds can be considered at risk and should be placed in a highly systematic and explicit program. Students who miss four or more items on the informal language assessment will need intensive language instruction and should be placed in a reading program that carefully controls the language used in teacher presentations.

Progress-Monitoring in Kindergarten

Curriculum-Based Progress-Monitoring Assessments.   The DIBELS assessment mentioned earlier as a screening assessment can also be used as a progress-monitoring assessment for all students in kindergarten. It tests oral segmenting, letter-name knowledge, and reading of simple regular short nonsense words. The test results will tell how the student is performing in regard to reaching performance levels that predict success in future grades. We recommend administering DIBELS at least two times during the school year in addition to the begining-of-year screening.

Program-Specific Progress-Monitoring Assessments.   We also recommend that teachers use progress-monitoring assessments that are aligned with the sequence in which important content is introduced in their core reading program.

Programs such as *Reading Mastery* and *Early Reading Intervention* have carefully constructed, ongoing progress-monitoring assessments. Unfortunately, most core reading programs do not have carefully constructed progress-monitoring assessments.

If the kindergarten reading program does not have an adequate progress-monitoring assessment system, teachers should construct informal progress-monitoring measures to test students' progress in learning literacy skills. Student performance would be assessed every 2 weeks. Each progress-monitoring assessment might include: (a) asking students to produce the sound for approximately five of the most recently introduced letter-sound correspondences including at least two vowels; (b) oral blending and segmenting of several words; and (c) once reading words is introduced, reading several regular words and irregular words. The words and letters tested should come from recently presented lessons.

Children who do poorly on the informal progress-monitoring assessments would be tested on all letter-sound correspondences introduced and all word types introduced to date. Extra instruction would be provided on specific skills with which a student has difficulty. If more than one-third of the group has difficulty with a particular skill, the teacher might reteach previous lessons, concentrating on the particular skill.

Developing a language progress-monitoring assessment is much more difficult than developing a literacy assessment because pictures will often be needed for the language assessments. An example of a progress-monitoring assessment for language can be found in the *Language for Learning* program that was described in the beginning vocabulary chapter.

Time Allocation

The authors of this text, through working extensively with low-income schools, have been privileged to visit schools where bringing struggling readers and at-risk children to grade-level performance is the norm rather than the exception. In these schools, children who entered school with little literacy-related knowledge would receive 30-minute small-group reading instruction and 30-minute small-group language instruction, both in the morning and in the afternoon in kindergarten. This amount of instruction (2 hours of small-group instruction) combined with a strong reading program and well-trained teachers resulted in high degrees of success, with the children scoring on a par with their more privileged peers (Berkeley, 2002). In order for classroom teachers to be able to provide this amount of instruction, a schoolwide focus and priority on reading achievement needs to be present. The use of instructional assistants who teach a second lesson or who teach a language group can play an important part in establishing an intensive program.

At a minimum, we recommend that all struggling readers and at-risk children receive at least 30 minutes a day of small-group instruction in reading-related skills and 30 minutes a day in language-related skills. In addition, afternoon sessions of 15 to 30 minutes should be provided daily to children who need more practice to reach the desired levels of performance.

Grouping and Scheduling in Kindergarten

For struggling readers and at-risk children in kindergarten, we recommend small-group instruction for reading and language. In a class with a high percentage of struggling readers and at-risk children, the teacher should try to form three groups—a higher-performing group, a middle-performing group, and a lower-performing group. In a class of 20 students, for example, the groupings might be something like this: high-performing group of 8 to 10 students, middle-performing group of 6 to 8 students, and lower-performing group of 4 to 6 students. Screening test results can be used to initially group students. As the year progresses, teachers should be prepared to switch children as some children who enter school with little information may prove able to learn at a faster rate than other children in their initial group.

Using the Kindergarten Level of a Core Reading Program

Kindergarten teachers may find themselves in a situation where they have a reading program that is not highly explicit and systematic enough for the students in their class. In such instances, we recommend that the program be modified by adding tasks to provide more practice and incorporating effective instructional principles to teacher presentation exercises. In the following paragraphs, we offer suggestions for making modifications.

Phonemic awareness instruction can be modified to make it more explicit and systematic through incorporating the procedures presented in Chapter 5. Oral blending and segmenting should be prioritized since these skills directly prepare children to read words. In addition, research indicates that these are the most critical phonemic awareness skills. The formats in Tables 5.1, 5.2, and 5.3 can be used to teach blending and segmenting. If a program simultaneously includes a number of other phonemic awareness tasks with blending and segmenting, the teacher should delay the introduction so there are not too many different types of phonemic awareness tasks presented simultaneously and that blending and segmenting are prioritized. The format in Table 5.4 can be used for teaching rhyming when students have mastered blending and segmenting.

Letter-sound correspondences can be taught using the principles specified in Chapter 7. Preparing letter-sound correspondence exercises is not very time-consuming; the teacher simply writes the letters on the board or an overhead and presents the formats. Letter-sound correspondences should be practiced daily. A lesson would include two letter-sound correspondence exercises, one early in the lesson and one later in the lesson. The format in Table 7.3 can be used to introduce a new letter-sound correspondence. The format in Table 7.4 can be used to provide practice on letter-sound correspondences.

The teacher can follow the sequence in the basal program for introducing letter-sound correspondences unless there are serious violations of sequencing principles (e.g., *b* and *d* or similarly sounding vowel letters are introduced too close together in the sequence). Serious sequencing violations should be remedied by delaying the introduction of one of the similar letters. If upper- and lowercase letters are introduced simultaneously, the teacher can delay the introduction of the uppercase letters if it appears that students are having difficulty.

Word reading. Begin teaching students to read regular words after the children have learned about six to eight letter-sound correspondences. Explicitly teach children the strategy for sounding out words, first in word lists, then on worksheets. Use the procedures in Chapter 9 to teach sounding out in word lists and to make the transition to sight-reading. Include daily exercises in word reading. Carefully select words in which each letter is representing its most common sound and all the letter-sound correspondences have been taught.

Irregular words. Many core reading programs introduce quite a few (20–30) irregular words in kindergarten. As you teach early phonic skills, it is important not to overwhelm children with too rapid an introduction of irregular words. If possible, delay the introduction of irregulars until children have become facile in sounding out regular words. Use the procedures in Chapter 9 to introduce irregular words. Do not introduce new irregulars when children have not mastered earlier irregulars. Once an irregular word is taught, provide daily review.

Story reading. Core reading programs will include sets of stories for children to read. These stories are often referred to as decodables and will be controlled to include regular words that students can read and irregular words that have been previously taught. There are two major problems: First, the programs do not generally include sufficient numbers of stories to facilitate daily story reading in decodable tests. Second, a number of the basal core programs have stories appearing early in kindergarten in which a high proportion of the words are irregular. If teachers have a program in which early stories have a high proportion of irregular words, we recommend that teachers initially replace these stories, making up worksheets with sentences or short stories composed of regular words use to provide the children with practice in using their sounding-out strategy in reading text. When introducing stories from the program, do not expect students to read all the irregular words; rather, prioritize the most useful words. When coming to a word in the story that has not been taught, the teacher reads the word. Use the procedures in Chapter 12 for presenting stories and making the transition from sounding out to sight-reading.

Vocabulary and language. Vocabulary and language development should be a major part of the kindergarten curriculum. Teachers working with children who have limited vocabulary and language skills should use a systematic and explicit program such as *Language for Learning* daily for at least 30 minutes a day throughout the school year, ideally with groups of 4 to 10 children.

Comprehension. Since children will not have the decoding skills to read longer stories, story-related comprehension teaching in kindergarten focuses on stories that the teacher reads aloud to the children. We suggest following the procedures in Chapter 18 to incorporate early comprehension skills of answering simple questions, sequencing, and basic story grammar into shared reading time.

Embedding Explicit Instruction into Daily Lesson

A 30-minute kindergarten lesson on early literacy-related skills incorporating the recommendations in this chapter might include the following tasks:

Task 1	letter-sound correspondence	Table 7.4	3–4 minutes
Task 2	segmenting and blending	Table 5.3	2–3 minutes
Task 3	letter-sound correspondences	Table 7.4	2–3 minutes
Task 4	rhyming	Table 5.4	3–4 minutes
Task 5	sounding out words—word list	Table 9.2	5–7 minutes
Task 6	sounding out words—worksheet	Table 12.1	5–7 minutes
Task 7	writing letters for sounds		3–4 minutes

An additional 30-minute period should be provided for language instruction. Comprehension activities should be presented during the time the teacher reads to the children.

## CHAPTER 22

Classroom Instruction in First Grade

It is very important that children learn enough reading skills to become fluent and accurate readers by the end of first grade. For struggling readers and at-risk children, especially, learning to read well by the end of first grade is a critical first step toward enabling them to reach high levels of performance in the upper grades. Many struggling readers and at-risk children have smaller vocabularies and much less background knowledge than their more privileged peers when entering school. The child who is a fluent reader at the end of first grade has a tool (reading) to learn new information and vocabulary independently as well as through teacher-directed instruction.

The goal of having nearly all children read at grade level by the end of first grade is reachable, even in schools serving children from the highest poverty areas, if (a) the teacher uses a well-designed, research-based instructional program; (b) the teacher has received adequate training and professional development; (c) there is strong administrative support at the building level (e.g., allocated time, personnel resources, budgetary); (d) the teacher uses student assessment data to guide instruction; and (e) instructional time is sufficient. Reaching this goal is made more possible by beginning reading instruction in kindergarten.

By the end of first grade, children should be able to read late-first-grade materials with accuracy, fluency, and comprehension. They should read at a rate of at least about 50 to 60 words per minute with expression. Children should know all letter-sound correspondences for single letters and for common letter combinations. They should know common prefixes and suffixes, and be readily able to apply this knowledge to read words.

A successful experience in learning to read in first grade not only is important academically but can make a very important contribution to a child's self-esteem.

In this chapter, we describe assessment and teaching practices that will enable students to reach the goal of grade-level reading by the end of first grade.

Use of Assessments in First Grade

Beginning-of-the-Year Screening Assessment

Literacy-Related Skills.   The teacher needs to find out during the first days of the school year how well prepared a child is to be successful in the reading program used in the classroom. In most of the widely distributed core reading programs, new phonic elements and irregular words are introduced at a very fast rate. The speed at which new skills are introduced implies an unwritten assumption that children know most letter-sound correspondences and are able to readily sound out words on entering first grade. A child who does not have these skills at the beginning of the school year will be at risk of failure in many reading programs without extensive intervention.

The beginning-of-the-year literacy-related assessment should identify children who do not know letter-sound correspondences and who cannot sound out regular words. Unfortunately, few of the core reading programs have beginning-of-the-year assessments that test these skills.

We present two options that teachers can use. The teacher can administer the beginning of first-grade DIBELS assessment. The DIBELS assessment tests phoneme segmentation, reading of phonetically regular nonsense words, and knowledge of letter names. We have also developed an informal screening assessment that teachers can use to test students' knowledge of letter-sound correspondences and their ability to read regular words. This assessment, titled "Beginning Phonics Assessment," appears in Appendix C. Instructions for administering the assessment appear first followed by display pages for the students and both individual and class record forms.

Language-Related Skills.   Teachers also need to identify children who need additional instruction in language skills. We have prepared an informal screening assessment (see Appendix B) that can be used for identifying children with limited language-related knowledge. The assessment includes 10 items. First-grade children who answer fewer than seven questions correctly should be considered for placement in a structured language and vocabulary program such as *Language for Learning.*

Using Data from the Screening Assessments.   Information based on the results of these assessments should be used for determining instructional time allocation, forming instructional groups, and selecting appropriate curriculum materials. More details on using these assessment results will appear later in this chapter.

Progress-Monitoring in First Grade

Literacy-Related Skills.   Teachers should assess frequently during the school year to determine if students are learning what is being taught in the reading program. The progress-monitoring assessments should be aligned with the sequence in which important content is introduced in their reading program, specifically letter-sound correspondences and word reading, both regular and irregular words. Student performance should be assessed every 2 weeks during the beginning months of first grade. After that time, students who are progressing with few errors can be tested less frequently.

During the first 2 to 3 months of first grade, each progress-monitoring assessment might include: (a) producing the sound for about 10 of the latest letter-sound correspondences including all the vowels introduced to date, (b) reading several of the latest regular word types introduced (e.g., CCVC and CVCC words), and (c) reading several irregular words. Oral story reading should also be added to the progress-monitoring assessment once students begin story reading. When students can read stories, their reading rate and accuracy should be recorded regularly.

During the school year, the criteria for how fast a student reads should gradually be increased so that by the end of the year the student will be reading at least 60 words per minute. By the beginning of the third month of school students should be reading about 20 words a minute. The rate should grow about five words per minute each month. Accuracy should always be high; students should be reading with at least 95% accuracy.

Once students can read text, the progress-monitoring assessment should also include some written comprehension items similar to those students have been working on during the preceding weeks.

Some commercial programs, generally the more highly systematic and explicit programs such as *Reading Mastery, Horizons*, and *Read Well*, have carefully constructed progress-monitoring measures built into the program. Unfortunately, the more widely distributed core reading programs generally do not have assessment measures that have children orally identify sounds and read words. Teachers should examine the assessments in their program. If the program does not have frequent testing of letter-sound correspondences and words introduced to date and/or does not have periodic oral reading fluency assessments, teachers will need to construct informal progress-monitoring assessments. The DIBELS Assessment package can also be used to monitor student progress during first grade.

Classroom Practices

The classroom practices include allocating time for instruction, grouping and placing students for instruction, and using the instructional materials for children at and below grade level.

Time Allocation

Sufficient time should be allocated for reading instruction to enable all children to read at grade level by the end of first grade. For teachers working with children who enter first grade behind the norms in literacy and language skills for children their age, significant extra time will need to be allocated for reading instruction.

For children who enter first grade with few literacy skills, two full 30- to 45-minute small-group reading periods should be provided each day along with at least one small-group 30-minute language period. In addition, more time after school and during the summer should be scheduled for children who are not making the necessary progress during the regular school day or year.

For children who enter first grade with slightly below average skills, an extra 30-minute small-group period should be scheduled daily in addition to the regular scheduled period for each group of children who are behind. During this time, the teacher would focus on teaching critical skills (letter-sound corre-spondences, word-list reading, and story reading) from the core lessons.

Grouping and Placement

Children should be placed in groups with other children who are at the same in-structional level for reading instruction as indicated by the beginning-of-the-year assessments. Grouping should be very flexible, so that children can be moved to a higher- or lower-performing group when the child's performance indicates the current placement is not appropriate. (The child makes many more or many fewer errors than other children in the group or takes a signifi-cantly longer or shorter time to read words.)

The number of students in a group should depend on the skill level and at-tentiveness levels of the students. In the beginning stage of reading instruction, small-group instruction is preferred because teacher monitoring of oral responses and immediate corrective feedback are such important features of instruction. Once children have mastered most letter-sound relationships and are able to ac-curately and fluently apply this knowledge to read passages orally, group size can be increased. For a first-grade classroom in which the children had reading in-struction in kindergarten, we recommend groups of 8 to 12 children. Children who enter first grade with little knowledge of letter-sound correspondences and little ability to read words would be placed in groups with fewer children.

At the beginning of first grade, the number of letter-sound correspon-dences known and the number of words the student is able to read should be considered when forming groups. The teacher should try to form groups in which the number of letter-sound correspondences the students know are within four or five letters of each other.

Some reading programs require whole-class instruction, with follow-up instruction in small groups for students struggling with particular skills. In such cases, we highly recommend grade-wide homogeneous grouping for a 150-minute block, with one class having the high performers, another the middle performers, and another the lower performers. The class with the lower per-formers should have the fewest students and should receive extra assistance from a teacher aide or extra teacher. The 150-minute period will provide time for the activities to be taught to the whole class and time for small-group in-struction for the children on high-priority skills that they have not mastered dur-ing large-group instruction.

Instructional Materials for First Grade

We strongly recommend the use of a core reading program that is aligned with the reading research and is highly explicit and systematic. Most widely distrib-uted core reading programs published in 2002 or later are aligned with the re-search findings, but vary in their degree of explicitness. Editions of some programs published before 2002 (*Reading Mastery, Horizons, Read Well, Open Court*) also were aligned with the research findings.

Pages 244–247 of Chapter 20 present criteria to use in determining if a program is aligned with the research and is highly explicit and systematic. Above all, the main criteria for program selection should be its proven effectiveness in producing high levels of achievement with similar student populations.

Material for Children with Little Literacy Knowledge

Ideally, a teacher working with children who have little literacy knowledge upon entering first grade (know less than 10 letter-sound correspondences and read fewer than 10 regular words) will have available a core program constructed with the assumption that the children being taught with that program have little knowledge of literacy-related skills. The program should introduce new skills in a realistic manner for such children. Unfortunately, most widely distributed core reading programs introduce letter-sound correspondence, and reading of regular and irregular words very quickly at the beginning of first grade. Some programs include a section reviewing kindergarten skills. Unfortunately, upon examining these review sections, we noted that none provided the kind of systematic and explicit instruction needed to thoroughly teach the beginning skills.

If the main reading program introduces new skills too quickly, we recommend that for children with few literacy skills, the teacher try to obtain a focused core program that is highly systematic and explicit and realistically designed for children with few literacy skills to serve as a replacement core program. The focused programs we recommend—*Reading Mastery, Horizons*, and *Read Well*—teach all the critical elements of reading at a rate that is realistic for the child entering first grade with few skills.

If it is not possible to use a focused core program instead of the core program, we recommend using the focused program during an extra reading period for the children who are highly at risk. This situation is not ideal since the children will essentially be in two reading programs that don't have the same sequence, but is better than allowing the children to flounder. The focused core program will provide the systematic instruction the children need on beginning skills.

If it is not possible to obtain one of these focused core programs, the teacher can try to obtain an intervention or supplementary program that teaches beginning phonics and phonemic awareness skills. This program should include (a) oral blending and segmenting, (b) letter-sound correspondence, (c) how to read regular and irregular words, and (d) decodable stories coordinated with the sequence of letter-sound correspondences and word introduction. The same criteria that were listed earlier for evaluating comprehensive core reading programs should be used to evaluate these intervention and supplementary programs. The teacher would use the intervention or supplementary program at the beginning of the school year before beginning instruction in the core reading program. When the students have mastered about 15 to 20 letter-sound correspondences and can read regular words composed of those letter-sound correspondences, the teacher can begin use of the core program. The teacher would continue the use of the supplemental or intervention program in an extra period each day in addition to the core program.

Information on intervention and supplementary programs is available on the Oregon Reading First website (**http://oregonreadingfirst.uoregon.edu/SIreport.php**) and the Florida Center for Reading Research website. (**www.fcrr.org**). In selecting one of these intervention or supplementary programs, the teacher should look for a program that has been used successfully with similar children and a program for which the publisher will provide professional development and support.

Instruction in the Core Reading Program

Teachers who are required to use the school's core reading program with all their students should be prepared to make modifications to make the program more systematic and explicit as well as provide extra 30-minute small-group periods daily for children who have difficulty.

Presenting Daily Lessons

Many teachers will be in schools using a core program that, although incorporating research-based elements, may have instructional-design problems. We have identified characteristics of basal programs that can be particularly troublesome in first grade:

- The program contains more activities than it is possible to present in a single day. In many cases, what is to be presented on any day is unclear as well as how to present the skills.
- The teaching explanations incorporate too many language concepts the students do not know. The teaching demonstrations are not clear.
- There are not sufficient decodable text stories for the children to read. There is not a sufficient number of stories with carefully controlled text for conducting story reading daily.
- The rate at which irregular words are introduced is very fast, leading to early stories in which up to half the words in the story are irregular.
- There is not daily cumulative review of letter-sound correspondences or word reading.
- The teaching procedures may not be highly interactive. Students do not make a sufficient number of responses to enable the teacher to determine if students have mastered the skill.

Teachers should be prepared to modify a program in response to their students' performance. There are three major types of modifications: (a) structuring the daily lessons so that critical skills are taught daily and systematically,

(b) modifying teaching presentations to make them more explicit, and (c) making changes in the sequence in which skills are introduced to avoid likely confusions. The following list presents specific suggestions for modifying reading components:

Phonemic awareness skills. Ensure that blending and segmenting are taught adequately. Present the segmenting and blending exercises at the beginning of the school year. Use the procedures described in Chapter 5.

Letter-sound correspondence. Daily practice in letter-sound correspondences needs to be provided beginning with individual letters and progressing to letter combinations. New letter-sound correspondences are introduced in the same sequence the program uses unless there are serious problems such as very similar letters being introduced too near each other in the sequence. In such cases one of the pair should be delayed. The formats in Chapters 7 and 8 can be used for introducing and practicing letter-sound correspondences.

Regular word reading in lists. Provide daily exercises in which students practice word reading. Follow the sequence in the program. If a particular word type does not receive enough practice, create extra practice exercises on that word type. A common problem is that words beginning with a stop sound are introduced before students have had adequate practice with words beginning with continuous sounds. If this problem occurs, delay the introduction of words with a stop sound until students can read words that begin with a continuous sound with little effort. Use the procedures in Chapters 9 and 10.

Irregular words. Introduce irregular words several lessons before they appear in stories. Provide daily practice on the irregular word in list exercises for several days before it appears in stories. If the program contains too many irregular words, prioritize the teaching of the most useful words. Delay the introduction of other words. Use the procedures for teaching irregulars given in Chapters 9 and 10.

Story reading. Provide for daily oral reading of story text that is carefully controlled to contain only words that the students have the skills to read. In the more widely distributed core reading programs, there are booklets and black-line masters identified as "decodables" or "phonics stories" that are controlled to include only regular and irregular words that have already been taught. It is important that a school purchase these booklets so that teachers will have sufficient stories for children to read. Story reading in decodable text should be done daily. If a program does not have sufficient number of decodables, teachers may have to make up extras or repeat earlier stories. If a story contains too many unknown irregular words, the teacher can simply tell the students the unknown words when they come up in the story. The programs rarely provide guidance for how to conduct the story reading. Teachers can incorporate the procedures in Chapters 12 and 13. Teachers should maintain a major focus on accurate reading throughout the year.

Fluency. When students begin reading stories that contain 30 or more words, begin rereading exercises to develop fluency. Continue rereading exercises daily throughout first grade, providing more or less rereading practice based on the students' performance on oral reading fluency assessments. Students whose rate is not developing at desired levels should receive extra practice. Include exercises to teach students to read with expression. Use the procedures presented in Chapter 13.

Comprehension activities. As students read stories teachers should ask comprehension questions beginning with literal questions. Questions related to story-grammar elements should be incorporated later. Teaching other comprehension skills such as sequencing, summarizing, and comprehension monitoring should also be addressed as students begin to read longer stories.

Non-Research-Based Programs

Before 2002, most major publishers produced reading programs that were not aligned with the research. These programs, often referred to as meaning or literature based, did not teach letter-sound correspondences systematically; students were taught to rely heavily on the use of pictures and context. Words in stories were not controlled according to the relation between letters and sounds.

Children who enter school with a good deal of literacy and language-related knowledge and who receive a great deal of continuing support from their home environment may survive what is potentially very confusing initial instruction in these meaning-emphasis and/or literature-based programs. However, it is not unusual to see a significant percent of students from middle- and high-income homes struggle in these kinds of programs that are not supported by research. A disproportionately larger percentage of students from low-income homes struggle in such programs. Any student who enters first grade without knowledge of many individual letter-sound relationships, without highly developed oral language, and without the ability to readily blend sounds represented by letters in phonetically regular words is at significant risk of failure if placed in a meaning-emphasis program.

We strongly recommend the use of a program that is aligned with the research findings and that is highly explicit and systematic. Below are some suggestions for teachers working in a school in which a non-research-based program is being used.

As a first step, we recommend that teachers try to convince the school principal of the importance of using a research-based beginning program, particularly with the struggling readers and at-risk students. Before approaching the principal, administer the DIBELS assessment to your first graders. Remember DIBELS can be downloaded at no cost (**http://dibels.uoregon.edu**). Present the

DIBELS results to the principal, pointing out the children whose scores show them to be highly likely to struggle in the current non-research-based program. There are several articles on the Florida Center for Reading Research website **www.fcrr.org/science/publications.htm** that teachers can share with the principal that point out the need for children who score at risk on DIBELS to be placed in highly systematic and explicit research-based reading programs.

If it is not possible to obtain a highly explicit and systematic core program to replace the non-research based core program we recommend that the teacher obtain one of the focused-core or intervention programs mentioned earlier in this chapter. The teacher can use this program for several months before beginning the core basal and continue using the intervention program throughout the year during an extra daily 30-minute reading period. This option, while not ideal, can produce modest gains in student reading achievement.

CHAPTER 23

Classroom Instruction in Second and Third Grade

A school must organize instruction to meet the needs of a wide range of second- and third-grade students: children who are well prepared for their current grade, having mastered all the content from previous grades, as well as children who have not mastered the content from previous grades. Children who are behind in second and third grades are greatly at risk for future failure in their school career. With an intensive well-planned school-wide program, the needs of all children can be met.

This chapter addresses the use of assessments, organizational issues such as time allocation and grouping, how to establish and implement programs for children at grade level, and how to establish and implement programs for children who are significantly below grade level.

Use of Assessments in Second and Third Grade

Beginning-of-the-Year Screening Assessment

The purpose of beginning-of-the-year assessment is to determine each student's instructional level. Some of the more explicit and systematic core and intervention programs will have a placement test that can be used to determine a student's instructional level in the particular program. Unfortunately, most core reading programs will not have this level of specificity in their placement procedures.

If the program being used does not have a placement test procedure for the beginning of the year, we recommend that the teacher administer DIBELS, which is available for free on the University of Oregon website (**http://dibels.uoregon.edu**). In second and third grade, DIBELS focuses on oral reading fluency and measures the correct words read in a minute and the number of words missed.

DIBELS classifies students based on their performance as *benchmark* students (able to function in grade-level materials), *strategic* students (able to function in grade-level materials with extra instruction), and *at-risk* students (not able to function in grade-level materials).

Using Data from the Screening Assessments

At the beginning of second grade:

- *Benchmark.* Children who can read second-grade-level text material at a rate of at least 44 words a minute with an accuracy rate of about 95% can be placed in grade-level materials.

- *Strategic.* Children who can read second-grade-level text material at a rate of 26 to 43 words a minute with an accuracy rate of about 95% will need some firming up with late first-grade materials, then can be placed in grade-level materials.

- *At-risk.* Children who read second-grade-level text material at a rate of less than 26 words a minute or with an accuracy rate of less than 90% are likely to not have mastered many important first-grade skills and should be considered for placement in a reading program that is highly explicit, systematic, and designed to accelerate the reading performance of the child who is significantly behind.

At the beginning of third grade:

- *Benchmark.* Children who can read third-grade-level material at a rate of at least 77 words a minute with an accuracy rate of about 95% can perform comfortably in grade-level materials.

- *Strategic.* Children who can read third-grade-level material at a rate of 53 to 76 words a minute with an accuracy rate of about 95% will need some firming up with second-grade materials, then can be placed in grade-level materials.

- *At-risk.* Children who read third-grade-level material at a rate of less than 53 words a minute or with an accuracy rate of less than 90% are likely to not have mastered many important first- and second-grade skills and should be considered for placement in a reading program that is highly explicit, systematic, and designed to accelerate the progress of the child who is significantly behind.

More comprehensive assessment should be done with children who are functioning below grade level. Children who are near grade level should be tested on phonic elements introduced in the previous grades. Later in this chapter, information on an assessment that can be used for this purpose will be presented. Children who are significantly behind should be given the placement tests for the specific materials that will be used.

Many students, after a week or two of instruction, will perform significantly better than they did when the school year started.

After a week or two of instruction, the teacher should assess the performance of students who seem to be misplaced to see if they might be able to perform at a higher level. The teacher can readminister a different version of the DIBELS test or have the students read a passage from the program. Reviewing grouping and placement after 1 to 2 weeks of instruction is critical.

Progress-Monitoring in Second and Third Grade

In second and third grade, teachers should administer periodic progress-monitoring assessments to ensure that children are learning what is being taught in the programs and that what is being taught in the programs is preparing them for what they are expected to know at the end of the school year.

The progress-monitoring assessments in second and third grade should include two parts: oral reading fluency and comprehension.

Some highly explicit and systematic reading programs include oral reading fluency progress-monitoring assessments. Most do not. If a program does not include oral reading fluency assessments, DIBELS assessments can be used.

Oral reading fluency should be assessed until children are able to read with 97% accuracy and at a rate of at least 135 words per minute in material for the grade level.

The frequency of oral reading fluency assessment in second and third grade should depend on the child's beginning-of-the-year performance.

- Children who begin the school year at grade-level benchmarks for accuracy and rate can be tested every 2 to 3 months to ensure that they are maintaining their grade-level performance. (The second-grade beginning-of-the-year benchmark is at least 44 words per minute and 95% accuracy. The third-grade beginning-of-the-year benchmark is at least 77 words per minute and 95% accuracy.)

- Children who begin the school year at lower-than-desired but moderately developed levels for accuracy and rate should be tested at least monthly to ensure that they are gaining at the desired rate toward grade-level performance. (The second-grade beginning-of-the-year performance is between 26 and 43 words per minute with 95% accuracy on DIBELS assessments. The third-grade beginning-of-the-year benchmark is at least 53 to 76 words per minute with 95% accuracy.)

- Children who begin the school year at fluency levels for accuracy and rate that are significantly below grade-level performance should be tested at least each second week. (The second-grade beginning-of-the-year performance is below 26 words per minute or 90% accuracy. The third-grade beginning-of-the-year performance is below 53 words per minute or 90% accuracy.)

Comprehension progress-monitoring assessments should test the specific skills taught in the program. These assessments can consist of written items similar to the types students do in the specific reading program and periodically on assessments similar to those in state exams.

Determining if Students Are Making Desired Progress

Students should be gaining sufficient fluency and accuracy during the school year to reach grade-level benchmark standards by the end of the school year. DIBELS calls for children to be reading at 90 words per minute in grade-level passages at the end of second grade and at 110 words per minute in grade-level passages at the end of third grade.

Teachers should monitor fluency to ensure that children are making steady progress toward benchmark performance. The teacher can establish a weekly progress goal by subtracting the student's beginning-of-the-year fluency rate from the end-of-the-year benchmark goal for fluency and dividing this by the number of weeks in the school year. For example, a second grader begins the year reading at 30 words per minute. The benchmark fluency goal for the end of second grade is 90 words per minute. There are 32 weeks available for instruction. We subtract 30 from 90 to end up with the fluency gains to be made during the school year and then divide by 32, the number of weeks, to determine the weekly target (90–30 = 60/32 = 1.875 words per week gain in fluency). This means that the child should be gaining about seven to eight words a month in fluency.

Classroom Practices

The classroom practices include allocating time for instruction, grouping and placing students for instruction, and differentiating instruction based on student needs.

Time Allocation

Teachers working with children who come from social and home environments that provide little instruction outside of school need to take the responsibility for ensuring that students receive sufficient instruction during the school day to learn all needed information to be at grade level by the end of the school year. For classroom teachers working with large numbers of struggling readers and at-risk students, we recommend at least 150 minutes daily be devoted to reading/language arts instruction in second and third grade, with most of this time devoted to direct teaching of critical reading skills.

Children at a strategic level (able to function in grade-level materials, but who are not reading at the benchmark fluency level) will need extra instruction daily in addition to that provided in the core program. Ideally, a 30-minute extra period would be provided daily for these students during which the teacher would review any phonic elements the students are having difficulty with and work on developing fluency and accuracy in story reading. Once these children are at desired levels for fluency, the extra time can be devoted to comprehension activities.

The amount of instructional time for children reading significantly below grade level should be adequate for children to make significantly more than a year's progress during a school year. Children who are functioning at beginning reading levels should receive at least two 30- to 45-minute small-group periods daily in reading materials that are highly explicit and systematic and at the students' instructional level, and also a 30-minute oral language group instruction if they also have low language skills. In some cases, a daily after-school period may be needed in addition to the instruction provided during the school day. Summer school also should be provided.

To provide this amount of instruction, a schoolwide plan will have to be made, with the principal and teachers working together to use available resources most efficiently to meet the needs of all students.

Grouping and Placement

When students are first learning to read, we recommend that instruction be provided in small groups since teachers must be able to hear responses and provide immediate feedback. As students become more knowledgeable about phonics and can read with increasing fluency and accuracy, the number of children in groups can increase.

Children whose instructional level is still at a beginning reading level should be taught in small groups of 4 to 10 students. Note that if the children also have language deficits, the number of children in groups should be less.

Second graders and third graders who can read grade-level material with high accuracy (97%) and fluency of at least 50 to 60 words per minute can be instructed in larger group settings. For children who do not have serious language and comprehension difficulties and can read grade-level material accurately, groups can be class size. For children with serious language or comprehension problems, groups size should be limited to 10 to 15 students so that the teacher can monitor oral answers and provide more immediate feedback.

Instructional efficiency can best be achieved when the children in an instructional group are all at or near their instructional level. In schools where classrooms are formed by other criteria than students' academic level, teachers may find that they have a large range of skill levels in their classroom. In such cases, we recommend that a 150-minute language arts period be established where children regroup within or across grade levels for instruction. Teachers working with the higher-performing children would have the most children for reading instruction. Teachers working with the lower-performing children would have the fewest students in their class during reading instruction or be provided with additional teacher support.

As group size gets larger, teachers should be prepared to provide daily extra instruction in a small-group setting for children in the larger group who are struggling with any particular skill. The small-group session might last just 10 to 15 minutes while the rest of the class works independently.

Teaching the Program—Differentiating Instruction

Problems with Core Programs

As previously mentioned, most core reading programs are designed in a manner that can be described as "too little of too much." This program construction creates problems for many students, particularly struggling readers and at-risk students, because they receive neither enough initial instruction to develop mastery nor enough practice and review to facilitate retention. A second related problem is that too much is introduced at one time. The fast introduction can result in student and teacher frustration. A third problem is the lack of guidance provided for the teacher regarding how to explicitly teach particular skills. A fourth problem is the lack of guidance provided for the teacher in how to make instruction highly interactive.

Program Enhancements for Children at or Near Grade Level

Teachers can enhance their programs by incorporating the procedures presented in this book. The extent of the modifications needed will depend on (a) how explicitly and systematically the skill and strategies are taught in their program, and (b) the needs of the particular students with whom the teacher is working. Teachers working with more instructionally sophisticated students may find a particular program to be adequate, while teachers working with more instructionally naive students might find the program problematic. Teachers must be prepared to make needed modifications if students struggle.

The major steps in making enhancements in second- and third-grade materials are (a) determining what to teach on a daily basis, (b) providing more explicit and clearer teaching demonstrations, (c) providing guided practice with feedback to help students apply the strategies, and (d) providing extra practice to enable students to develop mastery and retain information.

The following text includes specific suggestions to enhance instruction for each component of reading instruction.

Phonic Instruction.   The teacher examines upcoming lessons to determine if phonic elements are clearly taught and if there is sufficient practice. The teacher can use the formats and procedures in Chapter 10 for teaching phonic elements and their application to word reading.

Appendix A includes a list of words the teacher can select in teaching the various phonic elements. When preparing word-list exercises, the teacher should include adequate discrimination practice in which words with previously introduced similar phonic elements are included in the word list along with words that contain the new phonic element. The teacher focuses on a new phonic element until students can read words with that new element without error in a discrimination list. The new element should be periodically reviewed.

Irregular words should be introduced at a realistic rate. Words that will be appearing in upcoming stories should be presented in irregular word-list exercises. If too many irregular words appear in upcoming stories, the teacher should prioritize, teaching the words that are likely to appear more in future reading.

Oral Passage-Reading and Fluency Instruction. Oral story reading should be incorporated into daily lessons. The story-reading procedure discussed in Chapter 13 can be used for presenting story-reading exercises. Teachers should ensure that the stories students are to read do not have words the students don't have the skills to read.

Fluency should also be worked on daily with the amount of time provided for fluency based on the students' reading rate. Students reading below the desired reading rate should receive extra rereading fluency practice. The procedures for fluency building are presented in Chapter 13. In second grade, students should be progressing at a rate to read grade-level materials at 110 words per minute by the end of the school year. In third grade, students should be progressing at a rate to be reading grade-level materials at a rate of 135 words per minute by the end of the school year. Note that this rate is higher than the DIBELS goal. We recommend this higher rate to enable at-risk children to be able to put more focus on understanding.

Vocabulary and Background Knowledge. Struggling readers and at-risk children often have difficulty with comprehension exercises because programs do not adequately preteach critical vocabulary and background knowledge, and the children do not have this knowledge in place.

Teachers should examine passages at least several days prior to having students read them. The teacher notes the words that students are not likely to know the meaning of that are critical to understanding the text. The teacher compares these words with the words the program presents in vocabulary exercises. If the program does not provide for teaching of the important unknown words, the teacher supplements the vocabulary teaching in the program using the procedures specified in Chapter 16. The teacher would do the same procedure with critical background information, determining what knowledge students will need in upcoming comprehension exercises and creating and implementing exercises to teach this knowledge if the program does not.

Comprehension. Many basal reading programs at the second and third grade level do not provide systematic introduction and integration of comprehension skills and strategies for students to learn and use over time. Teachers should review suggested strategies and determine which are appropriate for the students' level of comprehension skill. If strategies (such as summarization) are not explicitly taught, the teacher can refer to Chapter 19 for procedures to teach these strategies.

In second and third grade, teachers should require students to do written comprehension exercises aligned with story reading so that the teachers can determine if children are able to apply their comprehension skills. Student work should be corrected in a timely manner and students who have difficulty on the written comprehension should receive extra teaching to help them correct missed items.

Strategic Students

Strategic students are students who are not at benchmark levels on oral reading fluency, but who learned enough in the previous grades to be able to function in grade-level materials with some extra support.

During the first weeks of the school year, the teacher can work in materials from the previous grade to firm up the phonic and fluency skills on which the students need more work.

In order to determine which phonic skills to work on, we have prepared an informal diagnostic assessment to help teachers determine which phonic elements a student knows and does not know. The "Primary Phonics Assessment" (see Appendix D) is designed to serve as a preliminary indicator of what phonic elements a student does and does not know. Note that we use the word *indicator* because no one test is definitive. Correctly identifying a word with a phonic element does not necessarily mean that the student could identify the same phonic elements in other words. For example, the student may read the word *hawk* correctly but not be able to generalize to another *aw* word such as *claw.*

The Primary Phonics Assessment is an individually administered oral test in which students read words in a list. The words are ordered according to the sequences we recommended for introducing phonic elements. Each word is designed to test a specific phonic element. The element tested is written in front of the word on the class record forms. The teacher records each individual's performance on a student record form and then summarizes the data for the class on the class record form. Both these record forms as well as instructions for administering the assessment are in Appendix D.

The teacher can use the data on the class record form to plan firm-up instruction. The teacher begins instruction with the first phonic or structural element that one or more students missed on the Primary Phonics Assessment. Before spending significant time reteaching an element, the teacher might retest the students who missed the word containing that element. The retest is to verify that the student does not know the element. The teacher retests by writing the phonic element in isolation and asking the students, "What do these letters usually say?" and then selecting two to three additional words containing that element and having the student read those words.

Appendix A includes a list of words the teacher can use in selecting words for teaching the various elements. When preparing word-list exercises, the teacher first presents words with the element being taught, then provides a discrimination list that includes words with the target element and words with the other similar elements that the students have already mastered. The formats for presenting these skills appear in Chapter 10.

The teacher focuses on a new phonic element for several days. When the students are able to read words with these new skills in a discrimination list for several days, the teacher looks at the chart and determines the next phonic element a student did not know and teaches that element.

In addition to working on the phonic skills, the teacher would also work on developing fluency using passages from the previous grade-level material. The teacher should find stories at the student's instructional level, a level at which the child can read with about 95% accuracy before instruction.

When the teacher has firmed up phonic skills taught in earlier grade levels, the teacher can begin the children in the grade-level materials. An extra half hour of small-group instruction should be provided daily for extra work on fluency and any other skills on which the students may need extra help.

Teachers may find it useful to use supplementary commercial materials. There are some programs that focus just on teaching phonic elements and using those elements to read words. These phonic programs may be useful if there is great variance among students in their phonic knowledge. One such program is *Phonics for Reading* by Anita Archer. There are several sources of materials that provide passages and procedures to use to develop fluency. A company named Read Naturally has prepared a wide variety of materials for work on fluency. (See **http://www.readnaturally.com**)

Several university centers that were funded by the federal Reading First Initiative to provide technical assistance to states have examined commercial programs and prepared reports on their instructional design and potential effectiveness as supplementary programs for phonics and fluency. Reports on these programs can be found on the website for the Florida Center for Reading Research (**www.fcrr.org**) and the University of Oregon (**http://oregonreadingfirst. uoregon.edu/SIreport.php**).

Children Significantly Below Grade Level

The reading program for second and third graders performing significantly below grade level should be designed to provide the level of intensiveness needed to enable children to make more than a year's progress during the school year.

Children who are functioning at beginning reading levels should receive at least two 30- to 45-minute small-group periods daily in reading instruction and also a 30-minute oral language instructional period if they also have language needs. In some cases, a daily after-school period may be needed in addition to the instruction provided during the school day. The comprehensive program should begin immediately at the beginning of the school year.

The instructional materials used with the child performing significantly below grade level should be highly systematic and explicit. The overall program should be designed to accelerate performance of students who are behind by focusing on critical skills. Unfortunately the overall program for children who are significantly behind is often disjointed with different materials used concurrently to teach the same skills, resulting in the most vulnerable children receiving the least coordinated program. Rather than selecting a variety of materials to use with these students, we recommend finding an intervention or focused core program that teaches all components in an aligned manner. Unfortunately, many programs marketed as being appropriate for at-risk students prove, on close examination, not to be instructionally sound. Reports on intervention programs can also be found on the website for the Florida Center for Reading Research and the University of Oregon.

Among the intervention programs we examined, the Direct Instruction programs developed by Sigfried Engelmann are the most instructionally potent. Engelmann developed several programs that can be used to accelerate the performance of second and third graders who are significantly behind. The first program is the *Reading Mastery Fast Cycle* program. This program covers the first two levels of the *Reading Mastery* program in just one year of reading instruction. *Reading Mastery* is particularly powerful for the child with significant language as well as literacy deficits. *Reading Mastery Fast Cycle* can be used to bring a child from a nonreader stage to an mid-second-grade level in a school year. The second comprehensive program developed by Engelmann is the *Horizons A/B* program, which also covers two years of content in one year. *Horizons A* and *Horizons B* are both year-long programs, which are very explicit and systematic. Unlike *Reading Mastery,* which utilizes a modified orthography in the first level. *Horizons* uses a traditional orthography throughout both levels. *Horizons* requires slightly more sophistication for the beginning learner than *Reading Mastery*. A computer program, *Funnix,* has been developed to deliver the lessons from *Horizons. Funnix* is very unique. Unlike most computer programs that just deal with one or two components of reading, *Funnix* is basically a focused core reading program that includes over 200 comprehensive lessons including aligned teaching of all five elements of reading instruction: phonemic awareness, phonics, fluency, vocabulary and comprehension. *Funnix* can serve as an independent program or be used to supplement *Horizons*. See **www.funnix.com** for information on *Funnix*.

Appendix A

Word Lists*

Contents

- CVC Words Beginning with a Continuous Sound
- CVC Words Beginning with a Stop Sound
- CVCC Words Ending with a Consonant Blend or Double Consonants
- CCVC Words Beginning with a Consonant Blend
- CCVCC, CCCVC, and CCCVCC Words
- VCe Pattern Words in Which the Vowel Is Long
- Letter Combinations
- Suffixes (Listed Alphabetically)
- Prefixes (Listed Alphabetically)
- CVCe Derivative Words
- Two-Syllable Words with a Single Consonant or Consonant Blend in the Middle

---

*Parentheses in Appendix A indicate a minimally different word that can be used in discrimination exercises.

CVC Words Beginning with a Continuous Sound (Chapter 9)

a	i	o	u	e
fad				fed
fan	fin		fun	
fat	fit			
lad	lid			led
lag		log		leg
lap	lip			
	lit	lot		let
mad	mid		mud	
		mom	mum	
man				men
map		mop		
mat	mit			met
		nod		Ned
Nat	nit	not	nut	net
nap	nip			
	rid	rod		red
rag	rig		rug	
ram	rim		rum	
ran		Ron	run	
rap	rip			
rat		rot	rut	
sad	Sid	sod		
Sam			sum	
	sin		sun	
sat	sit			set
sap	sip			

CVC Words Beginning with a Stop Sound (Chapter 9)

a	*i*	*o*	*u*	*e*
bag	big		bug	beg
bad	bid		bud	bed
bam			bum	
bat	bit		but	bet
cap		cop	cup	
cab			cub	
can		con		
cat			cut	
dad	did		dud	
Dan		Don		den
	dig	dog	dug	
	dip			
gas			Gus	
gag				
			gun	
had	hid			
ham	him		hum	
has	his			
hat	hit	hot	hut	
	hip	hop		
		hog	hug	
				hen
jab		job		
jam	Jim			jet
	jig	jog	jug	
	kin			Ken
	kid			
pan	pin			pen
pat	pit	pot		pet
	pig			peg
		pop	pup	pep

(continued)

CVC Words Beginning with a Stop Sound (Chapter 9)

a	i	o	u	e
tab			tub	
tag			tug	
tan	tin			ten
tap	tip	top		
	Tim	Tom		

CVCC Words Ending with a Consonant Blend or Double Consonants (Chapter 9)

a		i		u		e		o
act	(at)	fill		bump	(bum)	belt	(bell)	golf
and	(add)	film		bunt	(bun)	bend	(Ben)	honk
ant	(an)	fist	(fit)	bust	(but)	bent	(Ben)	lock
band	(bad)	hint	(hit)	dump		best	(Bess)	pomp
bank		ink		dust				pond
camp	(cap)	lick		gulp		dent	(den)	rock
can't	(can)	lift		gust	(gut)	end	(Ed)	romp
cast	(cat)	limp	(lip)	hunt	(hut)	felt	(fell)	sock
damp	(dam)	milk		hung	(hug)	held	(help)	soft
fact	(fat)	mint	(mit)	jump		left	(let)	
fast	(fat)	mist	(miss)	junk		kept		
gasp	(gas)	sick		luck		melt	(mell)	
hand	(had)	tilt	(till)	lump		mend	(men)	
lamp	(lap)	wind	(win)	must		neck		
land	(lad)			punk		nest	(net)	
last				runt	(run)	pest	(pet)	
mask				rust	(Russ)	self	(sell)	
mast	(mass)			suck		send		
pant	(pan)			sung		sent		
past	(pass)					test		

(continued)

CVCC Words Ending with a Consonant Blend or Double Consonants (Chapter 9)

a		i	u	e		o
raft	(rat)			tent	(ten)	
sack				weld	(well)	
sand	(sad)			went	(wet)	
sank						

CCVC Words Beginning with a Consonant Blend (Chapter 9)

bl—bled (bed), blot
br—brag (bag), brat (bat), bred (bed), brig (big), brim
cl—clad, clam, clan (can), clap, clip, clot, club (cub)
cr—crab (cab), cram, crib, crop (cop)
dr—drag, drip (dip), drop, drug (dug), drum
fl—flag, flap, flat (fat), fled (fed), flip, flop
fr—frog (fog), from
gl—glad, glum (gum)
gr—grab, gram, grim, grin, grip
pl—plan (pan), plop (pop), plot (pot), plug, plum, plus
pr—prop (pop)
sc—scan, scat (sat), scab
sk—skid, skim, skin, skip, skit
sl—slam (Sam), slap (sap), slat, sled, slim, slip (sip), slob (sob), slot, slug, slum (sum)
sm—smog, smug
sn—snag, snap (sap), snip, snub, snug
sp—span, spat (sat), sped, spin, spit (sit), spot, spun (sun)
st—stab, stem, step, stop, stun (sun)
sw—swam (Sam), swim
tr—trap (tap), trim (Tim), trip (tip), trot (tot)
tw—twig, twin (tin)

CCVCC, CCCVC, and CCCVCC Words (Chapter 9)

bl—blast, blimp, blunt (bunt), blond, blend (bend), blink, bliss, black (back), block, bluff
br—bring, brunt, brand (band), brass (bass)

cl—clamp (camp), clasp, cling, clump, clung, clink, class, cliff

cr—cramp, crust, craft, crisp

dr—drink, drank, drift, draft, dress, drill

fl—fling, flung, flunk

fr—frost, frank, frisk, frill (fill)

gl—gland, glint, glass (gas)

gr—gramp, grand, grump, grant, grasp, grunt, grass (gas), grill

pl—plant (pant), plump (pump), plank

pr—print, prank, press

sc—scalp

sk—skunk, skill

sl—slang, slant, slump, slept, sling

sm—smack (sack), smell (sell)

sn—snack (sack), sniff

sp—spend (send), spent (sent), spank (sank), spunk (sunk), spell (sell), spill

st—stand (sand), stamp, stump, sting (sing), stink (sink), stomp, still, stiff, stack (sack), stuck (suck)

sw—swift, swang (sang), swung (sung), swing (sing), swell (sell)

tr—tramp, trunk, trust, trend, trick (tick)

tw—twang, twist

spl—split (spit), splint, splat

str—strip, strap, strung, strand, struck

scr—scrap, scram, script

VCe Pattern Words in Which the Vowels Is Long (Chapter 9)

1. Words Beginning with a Single Consonant (CVCe)

a		i		o		u		e	
vane	(van)	time	(Tim)	hope	(hop)	cute	(cut)	Pete	(pet)
fade	(fad)	like	(lick)	note	(not)	use	(us)	eve	
made	(mad)	site	(sit)	robe	(rob)	mule			
bake	(back)	Mike	(Mick)	home		cure			
cane	(can)	mile	(mill)	joke		pure	(purr)		
tape	(tap)	ripe	(rip)	hole		fume			
mate	(mat)	file	(fill)	nose		mute			
hate	(hat)	tile	(till)	rope					

(continued)

VCe Pattern Words in Which the Vowels Is Long (Chapter 9)

1. Words Beginning with a Single Consonant (CVCe)

a		*i*		*o*		*u*	*e*
sake	(sack)	pile	(pill)	mope	(mop)		
Jane	(Jan)	ride	(rid)	pope	(pop)		
pane	(pan)	mite	(mit)	bone			
same	(Sam)	fine	(fin)	cone	(con)		
cape	(cap)	wine	(win)	dope			
wave		pike	(pick)	hose			
tame	(tam)	bite	(bit)	note			
take	(tack)	kite	(kit)	yoke			
save		dime	(dim)	poke			
make	(Mack)	hide	(hid)	pole			
gaze		pine	(pin)	rose			
		tide		rode	(rod)		
		side	(Sid)				
		hire					
		fire					
		wire					
		dine					
		dire					
		line					
		like					
		dive					
		five					
		lime					
		bike					
		nine					
		size					

2. Words Beginning with a Consonant Blend (CCVCe)

a		i		o		u
skate		slide	(slid)	spoke		brute
state		snipe	(snip)	broke		
trade		gripe	(grip)	close		
stale	(stall)	prime	(prim)	drove		
scale		spine	(spin)	globe		
snake	(snack)	spite	(spit)	froze		
slave		bride		scope		
slate	(slat)	crime		smoke		
scare		pride		stone		
plate		prize		stove		
plane	(plan)	smile		slope	(slop)	
grape		stripe	(strip)			
grade						
frame						

3. Multisyllabic Words with a VCe Syllable

a	i	o	u	e
careless	perspire	hopeless	excuse	complete
escape	dislike	explode	confuse	stampede
inhale	likely	backbone	reuse	
take-off	umpire	pinhole	costume	
handmade	entire			
grateful	lifetime			
pancake	ninety			
	timeless			

Letter Combinations (Chapter 10)

ai   aid, aim, bail, bait, claim, fail, fair, laid, maid, mail, main, pail, paid, pain, paint, plain, rain, tail, stair, trait, afraid, complain, remain, explain, tailor, daily, ailment, maintain, obtain, aimed, failing, mailing, painter, raining, aid (add), aim (am), bait (bat), fair (far), maid (mad)

al   fall, call, tall, ball, small, wall, mall, salt, false, bald, waltz, also, always, almost, salty, all right, walnut, hallway, walrus, alter

ar   arm, bark, barn, card, cart, farm, far, star, hard, harm, mark, park, part, art, car, dark, mars, smart, start, yard, starve, shark, artist, darling, barber, target, party, carpet, partner, harvest, barking, starring, parked, smarter, started, bark (back), hard (hand), art (at), car (care), star (stare), bar (bare)

au   fault, vault, sauce, cause, taught, haunt, laundry, author, autumn, August, daughter, applaud, because, auto

aw   bawl, brawn, claw, dawn, hawk, jaw, law, lawn, paw, pawn, raw, saw, straw, crawl, shawl, yawn, awful, drawing, lawful, sawmill, lawyer, seesaw, outlaw, strawberry, awkward, awning

ay   day, gay, may, ray, say, clay, gray, play, pray, spray, tray, payment, today, played, saying, player, playing, prayed, praying, away, Sunday

ch   chap, chat, chip, chop, cheek, chug, charm, chimp, chain, cheap, chest, chill, chair, champ, catch; match, patch, pitch, switch, ditch, much, march, starch, crunch, arch, pinch, teach, touch, rich, hunch, chip (ship), chop (shop), chap (clap), ditch (dish), catch (cash), catcher, pitcher, pitching, chopped, teacher, touched, rancher, chuckle, chilly, marching

ea   bead, bean, beast, dean, deal, fear, hear, heal, heat, Jean, lead, meal, least, mean, meat, neat, read, sea, seal, seat, speak, steam, east, eat, freak, leave, please, sneak, wheat, treat, bean (Ben), beat (bet), beast (best), meat (met), speak (speck), reason, season, peanut, teacher, eastern, dealing, speaker, sneaker, treated, eating, leaving, hearing, healed, heated, steaming

ee   bee, creep, see, deer, flee, free, green, keep, wheel, three, jeep, creek, fleet, bleed (bled), beet (bet), peep (pep), weed (wed), beetle, between, canteen, fifteen, sixteen, indeed, needle, freedom, coffee, bleeding, creeped, wheeled, peeping

ue   cue, due, sue, rescue, argue, tissue, value, statue

ew   new, few, flew, chew, slew, stew, drew, grew, curfew, nephew

ey   hockey, money, donkey, turkey, whiskey, valley, alley, monkey, honey

igh   fight, light, right, tight, might, high, sigh

ir   bird, birth, dirt, first, shirt, sir, skirt, stir, third, whirl, bird (bid), first (fist), shirt (short), stir (star), dirty, birthday, stirring, whirled, thirsty, thirty

kn   knock, know, knee, knife, knight, knit, knob, knot, known

<u>oa</u>	boast, coat, cloak, float, road, roast, oak, soap, throat, toast, boat (boot), coal (cool), load (loud), oar (our), oatmeal, toaster, unload, approach, railroad, seacoast, soapy, charcoal, coaster
<u>oi</u>	boil, join, noise, point, spoil, soil, moist, oil, voice, coil (cool), foil (fool), coin (con), boiler, appoint, adjoin, disappoint, poison, avoid, joined, noisy, boiling
<u>ol</u>	bold, bolt, cold, colt, roll, fold, gold, hold, hole, scold, sold, told, toll, volt, control, enroll, folder, golden, holder, holster, roller, swollen, unfold, roller, folding, holding
<u>oo</u>	boot, cool, food, fool, hoop, mood, moon, moose, room, soon, tool, pool, stoop, smooth, tooth, too, spoon, shoot (shot), stoop (stop), soon (son), hoop (hop), cartoon, bedroom, noodle, poodle, shampoo, igloo, bamboo, fooling, moody, shooting, raccoon, teaspoon, harpoon
<u>or</u>	born, lord, porch, torn, stork, shore, fort, sport, torch, storm, north, corn (con), for (far), pork (park), port (part), short (shot), normal, order, organ, ordeal, border, conform, escort, forty, hornet, perform, inform, popcorn, story, morning
<u>ou</u>	cloud, clout, loud, pout, pouch, scout, blouse, count, ground, found, out, round, sound, about, aloud, amount, around, counter, thousand, trousers, outside, cloudy, counting, grounder, bout (boot), mouse (moose), noun (noon), mouth (moth), our (or)
<u>ow</u>	blow, crow, glow, grow, know, low, owe, row, slow, show, throw, shown, thrown, grown, elbow, fellow, below, follow, hollow, pillow, shadow, yellow, window
<u>oy</u>	boy, toy, joy, Troy, annoy, employ, enjoy, cowboy, oyster, royal
<u>ph</u>	phone, graph, photo, phrase, photograph, physics, typhoon, alphabet, elephant, dolphin, orphan, pamphlet, trophy, nephew, paragraph
<u>sh</u>	shed, shin, shut, shun, dish, wish, rush, lash, flash, fresh, crash, brush, trash, shine, chime, shame, shape, share, ship (slip), shot (slot), shop (stop), shell (sell), shack (sack), cash (cast), fish (fist)
<u>th</u>	that, them, this, with, tenth, eleventh, twelfth, thirteenth, fourteenth, fifteenth, sixteenth, seventeenth, eighteenth, then (ten), than (tan)
<u>ur</u>	church, curb, cur, hurt, purr, spurt, surf, turn, burst, curse, curve, purse, nurse, purple, turkey, Thursday, disturb, further, return, turtle, injure, burn (born), fur (far), curl (Carl)
<u>wh</u>	when, whip, which, what, white, while
<u>wr</u>	wrap, wreck, wrench, wring, wrist, write, wrong, wrapper, wreckage, wrestle, wrinkle, writer, wrongful

Suffixes (Chapter 10)

<u>a</u>	panda, comma, Anna, soda, drama, china, zebra, mamma, papa
<u>able</u>	likeable, teachable, touchable, expendable, drinkable, enable, unable, portable, reasonable, returnable

<u>age</u>	luggage, package, village, image, voyage, storage, passage, hostage, cottage, manage, language, wreckage, usage
<u>al</u>	sandal, formal, postal, local, vocal, final, journal, metal, total, legal, criminal
<u>ance</u>	clearance, entrance, performance, distance, instance, annoyance
<u>ed</u>	hugged, killed, missed, ripped, tipped, bumped, helped, jumped, picked, rocked, clapped, dripped, dropped, flipped, grabbed, grinned, gripped, pressed, smelled, spelled, tricked, flipped, dotted, patted, petted, dusted, handed, landed, tested, lasted, hunted, ended, blasted, planted, slanted, trusted, twisted
<u>ence</u>	absence, sentence, audience, patience, silence, influence, evidence, confidence
<u>er</u>	batter, bigger, butter, fatter, hotter, letter, madder, sadder, bumper, faster, helper, hunter, blacker, dresser, slipper, speller, sticker, swinger, swimmer
<u>es</u>	glasses, misses, passes, messes, foxes, mixes, taxes, boxes, wishes, dishes, fishes, mashes
<u>est</u>	biggest, fattest, hottest, maddest, saddest, dampest, fastest, blackest, flattest, stiffest
<u>ful</u>	handful, careful, useful, helpful, cheerful, mouthful, watchful, faithful, fearful
<u>ible</u>	horrible, sensible, possible, flexible, admissible, responsible, permissible, convertible, terrible, invisible
<u>ic</u>	traffic, picnic, arctic, antic, frantic, plastic, magic, tragic, comic, panic, basic, music, critic
<u>ing</u>	batting, betting, cutting, digging, filling, getting, killing, letting, petting, bending, dusting, ending, helping, jumping, picking, testing, clapping, dripping, grabbing, grinning, planning, smelling, spending, swimming
<u>ion</u>	fashion, champion, region, union, companion, opinion, religion, million, billion
<u>ish</u>	snobbish, selfish, sluggish, publish, foolish, furnish, establish, accomplish, astonish, punish, finish, radish
<u>ive</u>	active, captive, attentive, expensive, impressive, attractive, constructive, corrective, defective, destructive, positive
<u>le</u>	battle, cattle, juggle, middle, paddle, riddle, saddle, wiggle, apple, bottle, giggle, little, puddle, handle, ankle, bundle, candle, jungle, uncle, grumble, twinkle, trample
<u>ment</u>	agreement, argument, basement, attachment, development, employment, movement, payment, appointment, shipment
<u>less</u>	endless, groundless, matchless, toothless, speechless, sleepless, helpless, careless, restless, lifeless, nameless, useless
<u>ness</u>	madness, badness, freshness, dullness, witness, dryness, likeness
<u>tion</u>	action, mention, fraction, question, invention, inspection, section, suction, portion, construction, celebration, circulation, congratulation, combination, decoration, education, formation

<u>ture</u>   feature, creature, fracture, lecture, picture, puncture, structure, culture, venture, capture, torture, mixture, adventure, furniture, nature, future

<u>ward</u>   northward, inward, forward, backward, coward, skyward, onward, awkward

<u>y</u>   funny, muddy, penny, bunny, happy, jelly, silly, rocky, jumpy, handy, lucky, rusty, sandy, windy, candy, empty, fifty, sixty, smelly, snappy, sticky, clumsy, drafty, grumpy, plenty, sloppy, twenty

Prefixes (Chapter 10)

<u>a</u>   about, alive, alarm, around, along, amount, among, apart, asleep, atop

<u>ab</u>   absent, absentee, absorb, absurd

<u>ad</u>   address, adjust, admire, admit, adverb, advertise

<u>ap</u>   appear, appeal, appendix, applaud, appoint, approach

<u>at</u>   attack, attempt, attend, attic, attach

<u>be</u>   because, become, before, begin, behave, behind, behold, belong, beneath, besides, between, beware

<u>com</u>   combine, command, commit, compete, complain, complex, compute

<u>con</u>   concrete, conduct, confess, confine, confirm, conflict, conform, confuse, connect, conserve, consist, control, consult, convict, contract

<u>de</u>   decay, declare, decoy, defeat, define, defrost, delay, delight, demand, depart, depend, describe, design, desire, destruct, detail, devote

<u>dis</u>   disappear, disappoint, discount, disconnect, discuss, dismiss, dismount, display, displease, disagree, disbelieve, discharge, dishonest, discolor, distance

<u>ex</u>   explain, expect, expense, expert, explode, expand, expire, export, explosive, extoll, exclaim, excuse, exact, exam, except, exit, examine, example

<u>for</u>   forbid, forever, forget, forgive, forward

<u>fore</u>   forbid, forearm, forecast, forgive, forehead, forest, forget, forty, foremost, foreman, foreclosure, forefront

<u>im</u>   imperfect, impact, impeach, impress

<u>in</u>   inclose, income, index, infect, inflate, inform, inspect, intend

<u>mis</u>   miscount, misdeal, misfit, misjudge, mislead, misplace, mistake, mistreat, misspell, misprint, mistrust, mismatch

<u>non</u>   nonsense, nonstop, nonprofit, nonconform, nonsupport

<u>over</u>   overall, overboard, overcast, overcome, overdue, overhead, overload, overlook, overrun, oversight, overtake, overtime, overturn, overstep, overshoes, overshadow

<u>per</u>   percent, perfect, perfume, perhaps, permanent, persist, person, perplex, perspire, perturb

<u>post</u>   postage, postcard, postman, postpone, postmark, postal

<u>pre</u>   predict, pretend, preheat, prepay, prepare, precook, preside, precede

<u>pro</u>   profile, protest, propose, produce, provoke

<u>re</u>   return, rebake, recall, recount, refill, reflex, reform, refresh, refuse, regain, regard, relay, release, remark, repair, repay, report, replay, reprint, respect, retreat, reverse

<u>sub</u>   subdue, subject, submerge, submit, subnormal, subside, subsist, subtract, suburb, subway

<u>super</u>   superman, supervise, supertanker, supersonic, supermarket, supersede, supernatural

<u>trans</u>   transfer, transform, transit, translate, transmit, transparent, transplant, transport

<u>un</u>   unable, unarm, uncage, unchain, unclean, unhappy, uneven, unlock, unreal, untie, unfair, unseen, unsafe, unlucky, unsure

<u>under</u>   undercharge, underdog, undergo, underline, understand, underground, undertake, understood, underworld, underwear

<u>up</u>   uphill, upkeep, uplift, upright, upsidedown, uptown, upward, uphold, upon, uproar, upstream

CVCe Derivative Words (Chapter 10)

(Not all the words in parentheses are minimally different.)

1. Words with *s* Endings

a		i		o		e-u	
canes	(cans)	bites	(bits)	cones	(cons)	Petes	(pets)
cares	(cars)	files	(fills)	globes	(globs)	cubes	(cubs)
hates	(hats)	fines	(fins)	hopes	(hops)	uses	
mates	(mats)	miles	(mills)	mopes	(mops)		
planes	(plans)	shines	(shins)	robes	(robs)		
shakes	(shacks)	times					
stares	(stars)	wines	(wins)				

2. Words with *er* Endings

a		i		o		e-u	
later	(latter)	filer	(filler)	closer	(hotter)	cuter	(cutter)
shaver	(slammer)	diner	(dinner)	smoker	(robber)	ruder	(rudder)
crater	(batter)	finer	(winner)	homer	(logger)	user	

a		*i*		*o*		*e-u*
braver	(hammer)	riper	(hitter)			
saver	(madder)	timer	(ripper			
biter	(bigger)					

3. Words with *ed* Endings

a		*i*		*o*		*e-u*
hated	(tapped)	filed	(filled)	hoped	(hopped)	used
named	(jammed)	smiled	(ripped)	closed	(robbed)	
waved	(fanned)	timed	(kidded)	smoked	(nodded)	
skated	(rammed)	piled	(fitted)	stoned	(rotted)	
blamed	(batted)	glided	(fibbed)	roped	(logged)	
faded	(matted)					

4. Words with *ing* Endings

a		*i*		*o*		*e-u*
naming	(batting)	filing	(filling)	hoping	(hopping)	using
skating	(tapping)	riding	(hitting)	roping	(robbing)	
waving	(slamming)	timing	(ripping)	closing	(logging)	
hating	(napping)	piling	(kidding)	smoking	(stopping)	
shading	(snapping)	biting	(winning)	roving	(mopping)	

5. Words with *y* Endings

a		*i*		*o*		*e-u*	
gravy	(Tammy)	spicy	(Timmy)	bony	(Tommy)	cuty	(nutty)
shady	(batty)	shiny		smoky	(Dotty)	tummy	
wavy	(fanny)	tiny		stony	(foggy)		
shaky	(Sammy)	wiry					

6. Words with *est* Endings

a	*i*	*u*
bravest	ripest	cutest
latest	wisest	rudest
safest	widest	surest
tamest		

Two-Syllable Words with a Single Consonant or Consonant Blend in the Middle (Chapter 10)

a	e	i	o	u
paper	legal	Bible	frozen	music
satin	fever	visit	holy	bugle
travel	pedal	china	local	punish
cable	meter	prison	profit	human
label	clever	final	moment	super
planet	zebra	limit	copy	pupil
table	seven	finish	motor	humid
chapel	metal	minus	topic	study
rapid	defend	silent	robin	rumor
magic	second	tiger	poker	
crazy	seven	pilot	soda	
favor	devil	spinach	total	
vacant	petal	spider	solid	
taxi	evil	river	robot	
crater		tiny	modern	
panic			proper	
maple			pony	
			comic	
			motel	
			motor	
			promise	
			model	
			robin	
			total	

Appendix B

Oral Language Screening Test and Record Form

circle 1: yellow   circle 2: brown

Directions—Color circle 1 yellow. Color circle 2 brown.

1. (Point to circle 1 and ask) "What color is this?"
2. (Point to circle 2 and ask) "What color is this?"
3. "I'll say sentences. Say them just the way I say them. Listen." (pause) "A big boy sat on a dirty bench." (Repeat the sentence once if the student did not say it verbatim. If the student says it correctly verbatim on the first or second trial, score the item correct.)
4. "Listen." (pause) "Mary was baby-sitting for her little sister last night. Say that." (Repeat the sentence once if the student did not say it verbatim. If the student says it correctly verbatim on the first or second trial, score the item correct.)
5. "I'm going to say a sentence, then ask you some questions. Listen carefully. A little cat slept in the park yesterday. Listen again. A little cat slept in the park yesterday." "Where did the cat sleep?" (In the park.)
6. "When did the cat sleep in the park?" (Yesterday)
7. "How are a mouse and a cow different?" (Accept reasonable answers.)
8. "Listen. Monday, Tuesday, Wednesday, Thursday, Friday. Say that." (Repeat the days once if the student did not say them correctly. If the student says them correctly on the first or second trial, score the item correct.)
9. "What is a person who fixes your teeth called?"
10. "What is a pencil usually made of?"

Record Form for Oral Language Screening Test

Student's Name	1 yellow	2 brown	3 statement (1)	4 statement (2)	5 where	6 when	7 different	8 days	9 dentist	10 wood

Appendix C

Beginning Phonics Assessment

The Beginning Phonics Assessment is a quick screener that teachers can use as a preliminary indicator of student's mastery of letter-sound correspondences, upper-case letters, and reading regular word types.

Who to Test?	Administer this test to beginning students who are still learning letter-sound correspondences.
Materials	• Student copy • Student record form • Class record form
Testing and Scoring Procedure	• Test *each* section. You may discontinue testing in a section if the student misses five items in a row. Go on to the next section. • Class results can be summarized on the class record form. Letter-sound correspondences: • Point to each letter and ask, "What sound does this letter make?" • If the student identifies the sound, write +. • If the student does not produce the sound within 5 seconds, tell the student the answer and write NR for no response. • If the student says the letter name, write LN and ask if he or she knows what sound it makes. If the student says the sound, add + next to LN. • If the student misidentifies the sound, write 0 and record what the student said. Capitals: • Point to each letter and ask, "What sound does this letter make?" • Follow the prior procedure for scoring. Regular words: • Point to each word and say, "Read this word." • If the student reads the word correctly, write +. • If the student misidentifies the word, write what the student said. • If the student sounds out the word first, then says the word, record SO+. • If the student does not identify the word within 5 seconds, tell the student the word and write NR for no response.

Student Copy

Sounds

a	m	t	s	i
f	d	r	o	g
l	h	u	c	b
n	k	e	v	p
y	j	x	w	q
z				

Student Copy

Capitals

D	A	R
N	G	B
E	M	H

Regular Words

it	am	mad	cat
him	tag	must	hand
flag	drop	skin	stamp
strap	split	skunk	

Student Name: _____   Date: _____

Examiner Name: _____   Grade: _____

Beginning Phonics Assessment
Student Record Form

#	Item	Response
Sounds (What sound?)		
1	a	
2	m	
3	t	
4	s	
5	i	
6	f	
7	d	
8	r	
9	o	
10	g	
11	l	
12	h	
13	u	
14	c	
15	b	
16	n	
17	k	
18	e	
19	v	
20	p	
21	y	
22	j	
23	x	
24	w	
25	q	
26	z	

Sounds (What sound?)

#	Item	Response

Capitals (What sound?)

#	Item	Response
27	D	
28	A	
29	R	
30	N	
31	G	
32	B	
33	E	
34	M	
35	H	

Regular Words (What word?)

#	Item	Response
36	it	
37	am	
38	mad	
39	cat	
40	him	
41	tag	
42	must	
43	hand	
44	flag	
45	drop	
46	skin	
47	stamp	
48	strap	
49	split	
50	skunk	

Beginning Phonics Assessment
Class Record Form

Sounds		Students										
1	a											
2	m											
3	t											
4	s											
5	i											
6	f											
7	d											
8	r											
9	o											
10	g											
11	l											
12	h											
13	u											
14	c											
15	b											
16	n											
17	k											
18	e											
19	v											
20	p											
21	y											
22	j											
23	x											
24	w											
25	q											
26	z											

(continued)

Capitals		Students												
27	D													
28	A													
29	R													
30	N													
31	G													
32	B													
33	E													
34	M													
35	H													
Words														
36	it													
37	am													
38	mad													
39	cat													
40	him													
41	tag													
42	must													
43	hand													
44	flag													
45	drop													
46	skin													
47	stamp													
48	strap													
49	split													
50	skunk													

Appendix D

Primary Phonics Assessment

The Primary Phonics Assessment is a quick screener that teachers can use as a preliminary indicator of what phonic and structural elements the student does and does not know. Phonic and structural elements are tested in the context of a word, so caution should be used in interpreting results as a student may recognize a word by sight but may be unable to decode other words with that element.

Who to Test?	Administer this test to students who know most of their letter-sound correspondences and are reading at mid first through third grade.
Materials	• Student record form • Student copy of words • Class record form
Testing Procedure	• Give the student a copy of the words to read. • Begin testing with the first item. Ask the student to read the words across the page. • Record student responses (see next section) on the student record form. • Discontinue testing if the student misses five items in a row. • *Note:* If the student is unable to read at least 5 of the first 10 words correctly, discontinue and administer the Beginning Phonics Assessment. • Class results can be summarized on the class record form.
Scoring	• If the student reads the word correctly, record +. • If the student is unable to decode a word within 3 seconds, record NR for no response (you may tell the student the word). • If the student misidentifies a word, write what the student said. • Leave blank any untested items.

Student Name: _____   Date: _____

Examiner Name: _____   Grade: _____

Primary Phonics Assessment
Student Record Form

#	Item	Response	#	Item	Response
1	th—bath		29	ew—stew	
2	er—hunter		30	ph—graph	
3	ing—testing		31	wr—wrap	
4	sh—shop		32	au—haunt	
5a	ed—handed		33	aw—hawk	
5b	ed—licked		34	con—confuse	
5c	ed—missed		35	ment—payment	
6	wh—when		36	de—demand	
7	qu—quiz		37	al—sandal	
8	ol—fold		38	ful—handful	
9	y—sunny		39	dis—distant	
10	est—fastest		40	able—enjoyable	
11	oa—loan		41	less—useless	
12	ar—cart		42	ness—darkness	
13a	VCe—fine		43	pro—protect	
13b	VCe—hope		44	tion—invention	
13c	VCe—cane		45	ist—artist	
14	ea—neat		46	ible—sensible	
15	oo—hoop		47	age—package	
16	le—candle		48	sion—mission	
17	ee—meet		49	ence—silence	
18	ai—pain		50	ish—selfish	
19	ch—lunch		51	pre—predict	
20	or—port		52	ex—expand	
21	ay—pray		53	over—overtime	
22	ou—proud		54	ion—million	
23	ir—thirst		55	com—compare	··
24	ur—curb		56	ture—venture	
25a	VCe + taped		57	ive—detective	
25b	VCe + hoping		58	ac—accuse	
25c	VCe + timer		59	ous—joyous	
26	kn—knock		60	ic—panic	
27	oi—boil		61	ward—forward	
28	oy—enjoy		62	ize—realize	

Student Copy

1–4	bath	hunter	testing	shop
5–6	handed	licked	missed	when
7–10	quiz	fold	sunny	fastest
11–13	loan	cart	fine	hope
13–16	cane	neat	hoop	candle
17–20	meet	pain	lunch	port
21–24	pray	proud	thirst	curb
25–26	taped	hoping	timer	knock
27–30	boil	enjoy	stew	graph
31–34	wrap	haunt	hawk	confuse
35–38	payment	demand	sandal	handful
39–42	distant	enjoyable	useless	darkness
43–46	protect	invention	artist	sensible
47–50	package	mission	silence	selfish
51–54	predict	expand	overtime	million
55–58	compare	venture	detective	accuse
59–62	joyous	panic	forward	realize

Primary Phonics Assessment
Class Record Form

	Item—word	Students													
1	th—bath														
2	er—hunter														
3	ing—testing														
4	sh—shop														
5a	ed—handed														
5b	ed—licked														
5c	ed—missed														
6	wh—when														
7	qu—quiz														
8	ol—fold														
9	y—sunny														
10	est—fastest														
11	oa—loan														
12	ar—cart														
13a	VCe—fine														
13b	VCe—hope														
13c	VCe—cane														
14	ea—neat														
15	oo—hoop														
16	le—candle														
17	ee—meet														
18	ai—pain														
19	ch—lunch														
20	or—port														
21	ay—pray														
22	ou—proud														
23	ir—thirst														
24	ur—curb														
25a	VCe + taped														
25b	VCe + hoping														
25c	VCe + timer														
26	kn—knock														
27	oi—boil														

(continued)

	Item—word	Students											
28	oy—enjoy												
29	ew—stew												
30	ph—graph												
31	wr—wrap												
32	au—haunt												
33	aw—hawk												
34	con—confuse												
35	ment—payment												
36	de—demand												
37	al—sandal												
38	ful—handful												
39	dis—distant												
40	able—enjoyable												
41	less—useless												
42	ness—darkness												
43	pro—protect												
44	tion—invention												
45	ist—artist												
46	ible—sensible												
47	age—package												
48	sion—mission												
49	ence—silence												
50	ish—selfish												
51	pre—predict												
52	ex—expand												
53	over—overtime												
54	ion—million												
55	com—compare												
56	ture—venture												
57	ive—detective												
58	ac—accuse												
59	ous—joyous												
60	ic—panic												
61	ward—forward												
62	ize—realize												

References

Adams, G. L., & Engelmann, S. (1996). *Research on direct instruction: 25 years beyond DISTAR,* Adams and Engelmann Educational Achievement Systems.

Archer, A., Flood J., Lapp D., & Lungren L. (2002). Phonics for Reading. MA. Curriculum Associates, Inc.

Armbruster B., Lehr, F., & Osborne J. (2001). *Put reading first. The research building blocks for teaching children to read.* Partnership for Reading. Washington D. C.

Beck, I. L., McKeown, M. G., & Kucan, L. (2002). *Bringing words to life: Robust vocabulary instruction.* New York: The Guilford Press.

Beck, I. L., McKeown, M. G., & Omanson, R. C. (1987). The effects and uses of diverse vocabulary instructional techniques. In M. G. McKeown & M. E. Curtis (Eds.), *The nature of vocabulary acquisition* (pp. 147–163). Hillsdale, NJ: Erlbaum.

Berkeley, M. (2002). The importance and difficulty of disciplined adherence to the educational reform model. *Journal of Education for Students Placed at Risk, 7*(2), 221–239.

Bower, B. (1992). Reading the code, reading the whole: Researchers wrangle over the nature and teaching of reading. *Science News, 141*(9), 138–141.

Burmeister, L. E. (1968). Usefulness of phonic generalizations. *Reading Teacher, 21,* 349–356.

Carlson, C. D., & Francis, D. J. (2002) Increasing the reading achievement of at-risk children through direct instruction: Evaluation of the rodeo institute for teacher excellence. *Journal of Education for Students Placed at Risk, 7*(2), 141–166.

Dimino, J. (1988). *The effects of a story grammar comprehension strategy on low-performing students' ability to comprehend short stories.* Unpublished doctoral dissertation, University of Oregon.

Engelmann, S., & Bruner, E. (1988). *Reading Mastery I.* Columbus, OH: Science Research Associates.

Engelmann, S., & Davis, K. L. (2001). *Reasoning and writing—Level A: Direct instruction program.* Columbus, OH: Science Research Associates.

Engelmann, S., & Osborn J. (1999). *Language for learning.* Columbus OH: Science Research Associates.

Engelmann, S., & Osborn J. (2002). *Language for thinking.* Columbus, OH: Science Research Associates.

Engelmann, S., Engelmann, O., & Davis, K. L. (2001). *Funnix.* Eugene, OR: Royal Limited Partnership.

Engelmann, S., Osborn, S., & Hanner, S. (2001). *Corrective reading program: Comprehension skills.* Columbus, OH: Science Research Associates.

Engelmann, S., Haddox P., & Bruner, E. (1983). *Teach your child to read in 100 easy lessons.* New York: Simon and Schuster.

Graves, M. F. (1986). Vocabulary learning and instruction. *Review of Research in Education, 13,* 49–90.

Graves, M. F., Juel, C., & Graves, B. B. (1998). *Teaching reading in the 21st century.* Des Moines, IA: Allyn and Bacon.

Gurney, D. E. (1987, January–February). Teaching mildly handicapped high-school students to understand short stories using a story-grammar-comprehension strategy. *Dissertation Abstracts International, 47*(8), 3047A.

Hanna, G. S. (1976). Effects of total and partial feed-back in multiple-choice testing upon learning. *The Journal of Educational Research, 69,* 202–205.

Hart, B., & Risley, T. R. (1995). *Meaningful differences in the everyday experience of young American children.* Baltimore: Brookes Publishing Co.

Hasbrouck, J. E., & Tindal, G. (1992, Spring). Curriculum-based oral reading fluency norms for students in grades 2–5. *Teaching Exceptional Children, 24*(3), 41–44.

Irvin, J. L. (2001, May). *Strategies to improve reading in the content areas.* Presentation sponsored by Staff Development Resources, Portland, OR.

Jitendra, A., & Kameenui, E. J. (1994). A review of concept learning models: Implications for special education practitioners. *Intervention in School and Clinic, 30*(2), 91–98.

Jitendra, A., & Kame'enui, E. J. (1988). A design of instruction analysis of concept teaching in five basal language programs: Violations from the bottom up. *The Journal of Special Education, 22,* 199–219.

Kame'enui, E. J. (1996). Shakespeare and beginning reading: "The readiness is all." *Teaching Exceptional Children, 28*(2), 77–81.

Nagy, W. E., Herman, I. A., & Anderson, R. C. (1985). Learning words from context. *Reading Research Quarterly, 29*(2), 233–253.

National Institute of Child Health and Human Development. (2000). Report of the National Reading Panel. Teaching children to read: An evidence-based assessment of the scientific research literature on reading and its implications for reading instruction: Reports of the subgroups (NIH Publication No. 00-4754). Washington, DC: U.S. Government Printing Office.

RAND Reading Study Group (2002). *Reading for understanding. Toward an R&D program in reading comprehension.* A report prepared for the Office of Education Research and Improvement (OERI).

Smith, R. W. L. (1966). *Dictionary of English word-roots.* Totowa, NJ: Littlefield, Adams & Co.

Smith, S. B., Simmons, D. C., & Kame'enui, E. J. (1995). *Synthesis of research on phonological awareness: Principles and implications for reading acquisition* (Tech. Rep. No. 21). Eugene, OR: University.

Stahl, S. A., & Shiel, T. G. (1999). Teaching meaning vocabulary: Productive approaches for poor readers. *Read all about it! Readings to inform the profession.* Sacramento: California State Board of Education, 291–321.

Torgesen, J. K. (2004). Lessons Learned from the Last 20 Years of Research on Interventions for Students Who Experience Difficulty Learning to Read. In P. McCardle, & V. Chhabra, (Eds.), *The voice of evidence in reading research.* Baltimore: Brookes Publishing.

Index